POPULAR IMAGES OF THE PRESIDENCY

Engrav'd by E. Prud'homme, for the Percy Anecdotes, 1832.

F. Miller, Printer

POPULAR IMAGES OF
THE PRESIDENCY

From Washington to Lincoln

Noble E. Cunningham, Jr.

University of Missouri Press ★ Columbia and London

Copyright © 1991 by
The Curators of the University of Missouri
University of Missouri Press, Columbia, Missouri
65201
Printed and bound in Japan

5   4   3   2   1   95   94   93   92   91

Cunningham, Noble E., 1926–
    Popular images of the presidency : from Washing-
ton to Lincoln /
Noble E. Cunningham, Jr.
        p.   cm.
    Includes bibliographical references and index.
    ISBN 0-8262-0782-0
    1. Presidents—United States—History. 2. United
States—Popular culture—History. I. Title.
E176.1.C97   1991
973'.0992—dc20   91-9124
                                    CIP

Designer: Kristie Lee
Typesetter: Graphic Composition, Inc.
Printer: Dai Nippon
Binder: Dai Nippon
Typefaces: Novarese Medium, Vivaldi, and Galliard

Frontispiece: Presidents Washington through Jackson. Engraving by John Francis Eugene
Prud'homme, published as frontispiece in *The Percy
Anecdotes* (revised edition, New York, 1832), volume 2.

*For
Jane and Frank Rodgers*

CONTENTS

PREFACE

TWENTY years after the inauguration of the first president, the United States had a roster of presidents long enough to be published in historical registers along with lists of the kings of Europe. During the administration of James Madison, the fourth president, a Baltimore publisher issued a volume entitled *Mnemonika: or, Chronological Tablets, Exhibiting in a Methodical Manner the Most Remarkable Occurrences, from the Creation of the World to the Present Time*. A roster of presidents of the United States appeared on a page opposite lists of the kings of Denmark from 1523 and the kings of Prussia from 1701. Only a few years would pass until the register of American presidents conveyed as much of an impression of historical continuity as did those of most of the established states of Europe. In less than half a century under the Constitution, the United States had a roster of past presidents as long as the list of English monarchs since the Glorious Revolution of 1688. For a young nation searching for a past to compete in a world of nations with long histories, the rapid institutionalization of the presidency served it well.

More impressive than lists of presidents' names were prints with all their portraits and various popular series of individual presidential prints. Even the time and expense of engraving in the early years of the republic did not discourage the making of presidential prints, and their popularity increased as the historical record of the presidency grew. By the 1840s the successful application of the technology of lithography, encouraged by the profits to be made from popular prints, had led to a nationwide proliferation of presidential images. In separate prints and collective posters, artists and publishers honored and popularized, exalted and exploited, celebrated and satirized the presidency.

In 1825 when President John Quincy Adams sat for Gilbert Stuart to take his likeness, he became the last president of the United States to have his portrait painted by the early republic's most famous portraitist, who had painted life portraits of all the presidents since George Washington sat for him in 1795. In the 1840s when the aging Adams posed for several daguerreotypes, he gained the distinction of being the earliest president to have his portrait recorded by the newly emerging technology of photography. By the time Abraham Lincoln became president in 1861, the techniques of photography were sufficiently developed to enable Mathew Brady to record a gallery of portraits of the sixteenth president. Since Lincoln's day the advance of technology has permitted the taking of likenesses of American presidents with increasing frequency, projecting before the American public an ever-expanding array of presidential images, culminating with television in the second half of the twentieth century. These images have displayed and reinforced the centrality of the presidency in American culture.

The widening recognition of the importance of visual images in society today has aroused increasing historical interest in the images seen by earlier generations. Before the age of photography, visual horizons were limited, but those earlier representations are nonetheless revealing of the past. In this book I have employed visual materials as historical documentation, seeking to throw new light on the place of the presidency in American culture by examining the popular images of the presidency between the inauguration of President Washington and that of President Lincoln.

Considerable research for this study has been directed toward assembling from widely scattered sources—in libraries, museums, art galleries, and other depositories—a visual record relating to the presidency before the Civil War. Many little-known images are reproduced here for the first time, supplementing the familiar portraits of early presidents painted by such prominent artists as Gilbert Stuart, Rembrandt Peale, and Thomas Sully.

The focus of the work is on images widely seen by the public. Contemporaries did not often view the oil portraits painted from life by accomplished artists. Most Americans gained their impressions of the presidents from engraved prints and later—and more widely—from popular lithographs. Presidential images also appeared on ceramics and on medals, in books and in magazines, and on other material items. Because portraits were the basic source for the presentation of presidential images, these works have been given particular attention in this book, not as works of art but as cultural icons. The engravings and lithographs that derived from original portraits are more central to this study than the life paintings themselves, only a limited number of which have been reproduced here. I have sought not to offer a study of the art of portraiture of presidents, nor to assemble a record of all the portraits of each individual president, but to examine presidential portraiture in the broader context of American culture.

Many Americans besides presidents, of course, had their portraits painted. Some of the more prominent among them saw their likenesses appear as engravings in magazines or

in books such as [Joseph] *Delaplaine's Repository of the Lives and Portraits of Distinguished American Characters* (2 vols., Philadelphia, 1815–1818), or James Barton Longacre and James Herring's *The National Portrait Gallery of Distinguished Americans* (4 vols., Philadelphia, 1834–1839). There were also separate prints of prominent public figures; and military heroes, such as Generals Andrew Jackson and Zachary Taylor, were popular subjects. But as a group, the presidents of the United States were the most common subjects of portrait prints circulating in America before the Civil War. In his catalogue of popular lithographs for sale in 1851, Nathaniel Currier listed few portraits except those of presidents, for each of whom he offered an individual portrait print. In addition, he advertised a print containing the portraits of all thirteen presidents on a single sheet.

Presidents did not receive equal treatment from artists and publishers. Washington's unique place as both *pater patriae* and first president brought him more attention than that received by any of his successors before the Civil War. For that reason he has been given special consideration in the opening chapter of this book. No other president prior to Lincoln offers a comparable subject for iconographic study, and the scholarship relating to Washington is rich. My attention to Washington, however, is not intended to be exhaustive but is centered on those presidential images that reached a wide audience and became incorporated into American popular culture. The same focus is directed to Washington's successors in the first office. A few prints published after 1861 portraying images of Lincoln have been reproduced, because of special content or a relationship to earlier prints, but the image of Lincoln as president—already extensively treated in other works—has not been included here.

From the numerous engravings, lithographs, and other popular images of the presidents examined, I have selected for publication those that display patterns and traditions in the popular portrayal of presidents and the presidency as an institution. From these can be derived a sense of American political culture to be gained only by looking at the visual images themselves—seeing their repetitiveness, the popularity of eagles, flags, and other symbols of the new nation. These are not works of art that lend themselves to elaborate iconographic readings but rather popular images that provide revealing glimpses into an earlier age.

Readers will recognize that some images reproduced to illustrate the subject of a particular chapter also illustrate themes elsewhere in the book. The aim has been not to classify images but to group them in ways helpful in seeing common patterns and traditions. At the same time, additional themes may be noted throughout the work. Examples illustrating the association of the presidents of the United States with the Constitution will be found in a number of chapters.

Excluding no medium in which presidential images were depicted, I have included caricatures and advertising. The chapter on the presidency in caricature is closely focused on prints that portray a president while in office or reflect on the office of the president. Cartoons of presidential candidates have been excluded except for incumbent presidents seeking reelection. Throughout I have been careful to distinguish between presidents and presidential candidates. Although some representations of presidents seeking reelection have been included, campaign images in presidential elections are beyond the scope of this study.

The images assembled here display the limitations of the visual horizons of Americans in the early republic. They also reveal the dramatic broadening of visual boundaries during the 1840s and 1850s made possible by the application of new technologies for the mass reproduction of prints and magazines. Popular images both reflected and molded ideas about the presidency. They enable us to understand better how the American people perceived the presidency and how the institution shaped American culture.

POPULAR IMAGES OF THE PRESIDENCY

CHAPTER I
The First President Enshrined

THE NAME of George Washington, the most celebrated hero of the American Revolution, had already been enrolled in the pantheon of the new nation long before the former commanding general took the oath of office as the first president of the United States on April 30, 1789. Eight years later, when Washington left that office, the image of statesman had superseded that of military hero, reconfirming his unrivaled claim to the title *pater patriae*. Unique as was Washington's place as the father of the country, the presidency was the pinnacle of his public life. Even before retiring from the presidency, Washington's enshrinement as the first president of the Republic had begun.

In 1795 the Philadelphia artist Walter Robertson published a print of Washington containing all the symbolic embellishments needed to elevate the president's image to national symbol (fig. 1–1). Based on Robertson's miniature portrait of President Washington made in 1794, the plate represented the combined efforts of Robert Field, who engraved the portrait, and John James Barralet, who conceived the symbolic design that framed the portrait. Barralet's first effort in presenting the image of Washington, the design early revealed a skill in the use of symbolic embellishments that would bring fame to Barralet's later *Apotheosis of Washington*. Framed with a border of oak leaves, Washington's portrait is cradled

in the spread wings of the federal eagle, shown grasping the banner "E Pluribus Unum" in its beak while carrying a military baton and the scales of justice upon its back. Above Washington's portrait a laurel wreath inscribed "Libertas" encircles a sword capped by a liberty cap. Banners and palm branches adorn the print, the whole image being suspended in clouds with the rays of a sunburst radiating from the crowning motif.[1] Among the numerous prints of President Washington published in his lifetime, few displayed with such effective symbolism Washington's honored place in the minds and hearts of his countrymen.

Similar themes appeared in designs on pieces of Liverpool pottery produced for the American market. One striking example (fig. 1–2), despite the poor likeness, shows Washington being crowned with laurels by Liberty beneath towering pines—a commonly used symbol of immortality.[2] The scene, together with the national emblem, is encompassed by a linked chain of the fifteen states then forming the Union, indicating that the design was made after the admission of Vermont and Kentucky during Washington's first term. English pottery makers—motivated by commercial interest rather than respect for American presidents—copied designs from American prints and other models, and they included portraits often with little knowledge of, or regard for, the accuracy of the images employed. Never-

1

Figure 1–1. *George Washington, President of the United States*. Engraving, 13½ x 9¹³⁄₁₆ inches, by Robert Field after Walter Robertson and John James Barralet. Published by Walter Robertson, Philadelphia and New York, August 1, 1795. Historical Society of Pennsylvania.

Figure 1–2. *Washington crowned with Laurels by Liberty.* Liverpool pitcher, 9¼ inches high, circa 1795. National Museum of American History, Smithsonian Institution.

Figure 1–3. *Long Live the president of the United States.* Liverpool mug, 4¾ inches high, circa 1790–1796. Henry Francis du Pont Winterthur Museum.

Figure 1–4. Washington memorial locket. Gold memorial medal set in locket, 2⅞ inches diameter, designed and executed by Joseph Perkins, Newburyport, Massachusetts, 1800. National Museum of American History, Smithsonian Institution.

theless, the pieces were popular in America. Another earthenware piece (fig. 1–3), proclaiming "Long Live the president of the United States," depicts the goddess of Liberty pointing to Washington's portrait as "My Favorite Son," while the goddess of Justice intones: "Deafness to the Ear that will patiently hear and Dumbness to the Tongue that will utter a Calumny against the immortal Washington."[3]

Despite such rhetorical admonitions, Washington as president did not escape criticism and political opposition. Republican principles and lingering fears of monarchy restrained hero worship and veneration even of Washington.[4] Among the milder criticisms of President Washington, a poem by Philip Freneau, published in his *National Gazette* in 1793, protested:

George, on thy virtues often have I dwelt,
And still the theme is grateful to mine ear:
Thy gold let chemists ten times over melt,
From dross and base alloy they'll find it clear.

Yet thou'rt a man—although, perhaps, the first;
But man, at best, is but a being frail;
And since with error human nature's curst,
I marvel not that thou should'st sometimes fail.

That thou hast *long* and *nobly* serv'd the state,
The nation *owns*, and *freely* gives thee thanks:
But, sir!—whatever speculators prate,
She gave thee not the power t'establish BANKS.[5]

More strongly, another critic of Washington averred, "The stern, tho unerring voice of posterity, will not fail to render the just sentence of condemnation on the man who has entailed upon his country deep and incurable public evils."[6] In a similar vein Thomas Paine pronounced the first president "a hypocrite in public life" and said that "the world will be puzzled to decide whether you are an apostate or an imposter, whether you have abandoned good principles, or whether you ever had any?"[7] Such attacks, however, did nothing to dislodge Washington from the special place accorded him by most Americans. Later presi-

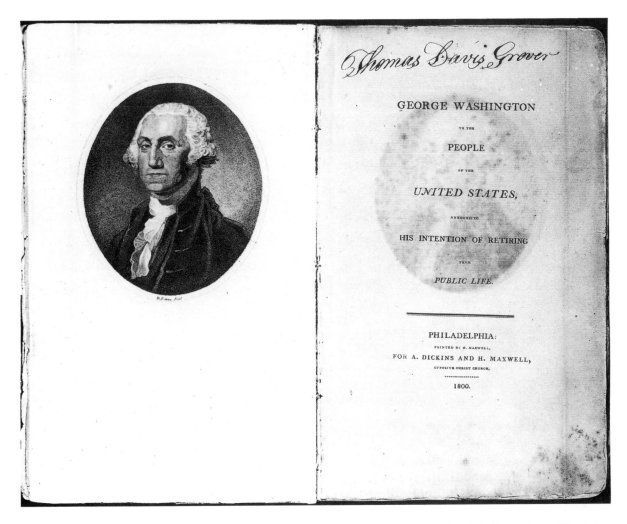

Figure 1–5. *George Washington to the People of the United States, Announcing His Intention of Retiring from Public Life* (Philadelphia, 1800), frontispiece and title page. Published by Asbury Dickens and Hugh Maxwell. Frontispiece engraved by David Edwin after Gilbert Stuart. American Antiquarian Society.

dents would be subjected to far more stinging political attacks than was Washington, yet the presidential office would continue to raise its occupants to an unrivaled status in the American pantheon.

Washington's death on December 14, 1799, less than three years after he left the presidency, produced an outpouring of public mourning unprecedented in America and rarely, if ever, equaled again in the nation's history. Across the land memorial services, solemn processions, and lengthy eulogies—spoken and written—focused the nation's attention on the loss of its most celebrated leader, first president, and *pater patriae*. Remembrance cards were printed with Washington's portrait and his life

dates.[8] Theaters in New York and Philadelphia, their stages draped in black and decorated with symbolic ornaments and allegorical figures, gave memorial performances.[9] In Boston, Joseph Perkins, a leading engraver and goldsmith, designed a funeral medal with Washington's likeness, struck in gold, silver, and white metal. The medal was inscribed "He in Glory, The World in Tears." Perkins also mounted the gold medal in lockets, decorating the other side of the locket with a miniature mourning picture painted on ivory (fig. 1–4).[10]

Philadelphia printer Hugh Maxwell rushed through the press a new and "superb edition" (according to a newspaper advertisement) of Washington's farewell address "ornamented

Figure 1–6. *Dead March and Monody*. Sheet of music performed at memorial service for George Washington in Philadelphia, December 26, 1799. Published by Benjamin Carr, Philadelphia, 1799. Engraving of Washington by unidentified artist after Gilbert Stuart. National Portrait Gallery, Smithsonian Institution.

with a capital Portrait by one of the first artists" (fig. 1–5).[11] Before the end of December, Philadelphia music publisher Benjamin Carr advertised the forthcoming publication of the *Dead March and Monody* of his own composition, performed at the Lutheran Church of Philadelphia as part of a memorial service for the late president.[12] One of the first American publishers to add illustrations and ornaments to his musical publications,[13] Carr included a small engraving of Washington on the sheet of music (fig. 1–6).

It was probably early in 1800 when Philadelphia publishers Pember and Luzarder issued a hand-colored etching depicting Washington on his deathbed attended by Drs. James Craik and Gustavus Brown (fig. 1–7). A prototype for the popular deathbed scenes of Washington appearing later in nineteenth-century lithographs, the print is less elaborate in design than

those later prints.[14] Although the 1800 print gives the impression of immediate reportage, no artist had been at Mount Vernon to record the scene. All the images are imaginary, and the grieving Martha Washington, seated at the foot of the bed, has much the same profile as the attending Doctors Craik and Brown. The print depicts a scene recorded by Tobias Lear, Washington's private secretary, in a letter to President John Adams dated December 15, 1799, and published in numerous newspapers. Lear had written: "His last scene corresponded with the whole tenor of his life, not a groan nor a complaint escaped him in extreme distress. With perfect resignation and in full possession of his reason, he closed his well spent life."[15] None of the classical symbols so common in mourning pictures adorns the print, and the only emblem of the importance of the man is the shield of the Union, encircled by the

Figure 1—7. *G. Washington in his last Illness attended by Docrs. Craik and Brown.* Etching, 9⅞ x 9⅜ inches, by unidentified artist. Published by Pember and Luzander, Philadelphia, 1800. National Portrait Gallery, Smithsonian Institution. Inscribed: "Americans behold and shed a grateful Tear / For a man who has gained your freedom most dear / And now is departing unto the realms above / Where he may ever rest in lasting peace and love."

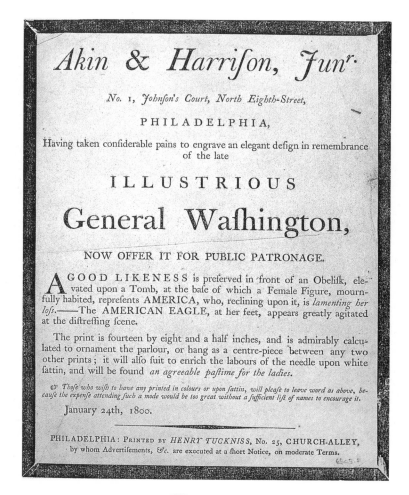

Figure 1–8. Broadside, 9⅞ x 7 inches, by James Akin and William Harrison, Jr., January 24, 1800. Printed by Henry Tuckniss, Philadelphia, 1800. Library Company of Philadelphia.

Figure 1–9. *America lamenting her Loss at the Tomb of General Washington.* Print, 14 x 8³/₁₆ inches, designed, engraved, and published by James Akin and William Harrison, Jr., Philadelphia, January 20, 1800. Historical Society of Pennsylvania.

Figure 1–10. *Washington in Glory, America in Tears.* Transfer design of figure 1–9 on Liverpool pitcher, 13¼ inches high, circa 1800. Henry Francis du Pont Winterthur Museum.

America lamenting her Loss at the Tomb of
GENERAL WASHINGTON
Intended as a tribute of respect paid to departed Merit & Virtue, in
the remembrance of that illustrious Hero & most Amiable man who died Dec.r 14 1799.

stars of the sixteen states, on the drapery above the bed. By July 1800 the print had appeared with slight variations on pocket handkerchiefs printed in Scotland. The *Mercantile Advertiser* of New York reported on July 24, 1800: "In the stores of some of our dry-goods merchants, we observe a neat tribute to the memory of the illustrious Washington.—It is a pocket handkerchief, lately imported from Glasgow . . . on which is wrought a scene representing the Death of the General. . . . To this print is a companion, representing the Genius of Liberty weeping over the urn of her Hero."[16]

In a black-bordered broadside, issued January 24, 1800 (fig. 1–8), James Akin and William Harrison, Jr., Philadelphia artists and publishers, announced the completion of one of the most important prints to memorialize Washington's death (fig. 1–9). Its designers publicized the work as elegant, carefully engraved, and "admirably calculated to ornament the parlour, or hang as a centre-piece between any two other prints." Dated January 20, 1800, the engraving itself is inscribed, "America lamenting her Loss at the Tomb of General Washington, Intended as a tribute of respect paid to departed Merit and Virtue, in the remembrance of that illustrious Hero and most amiable man who died Decr. 14, 1799." Akin and Harrison described their design as presenting a good likeness of Washington and identified the mourning female figure leaning upon the tomb as representing America. At her feet the American eagle appears greatly agitated at the distressing scene.[17] In addition, the artists employed other classical symbols of mourning adapted from Europe, including the urn—the central symbol of mourning, reaching back in origin to the Etruscans. Willow trees and evergreens—prominent in all mourning art and complex in religious symbolism but broadly representative of mortality and immortality—fill their expected places.[18] A laurel wreath crowns the portrait of Washington dominating the obelisk, and the major accomplishments of his life are listed on the plaque beneath his image. Along with his command of the Continental Army and his presidency of the United States, the plaque gives equal recognition to Washington's having served as the president of the Constitutional Convention of 1787.

The likeness of Washington followed the profile drawn by James Sharples, picturing him in uniform, but that portrait was replaced in a later state of the plate by a classical bust more appropriate to the departed president.[19] The Akin and Harrison print had a widespread influence. English pottery makers transferred copies onto numerous pieces of Liverpool ware, commonly with borders or ribbons proclaiming "Washington in Glory, America in Tears" (fig. 1–10).[20] The print's influence on later mourning art also was significant. One authority has called it "a prototype for the American mourning art that was to flourish in the decades after the death of Washington."[21]

Akin and Harrison promoted their design in advertisements as well suited for needlework, promising to print it on white satin if demand warranted. Whether or not that was done has not been determined, but the glorification of Washington's death inspired the proliferation of mourning art in America. In the early decades of the nineteenth century such needlework rapidly became a distinctive art form, attracting the interest and participation of numerous American women.[22] The scene most widely reproduced in Washington mourning pictures was a work by Samuel Folwell of Philadelphia. One well-executed example depicts the grieving figure of Liberty at Washington's tomb (fig. 1–11). Inscribed "Thy Loss Ever Shall We Mourn" and "Sacred to the Memory of the Illustrious Washington," the tomb is topped by an urn bearing Washington's portrait and draped by branches of weeping willow trees. Nearby, a wounded Revolutionary War soldier mourns, while in the clouds a cherub carrying a laurel crown sounds the trumpet of glory.

The imagery of apotheosis, present in some prints of Washington even before he left the presidential office (fig. 1–1), found its most elaborate expression after his death in a print by John James Barralet (fig. 1–14). Before that work appeared, William Woolley—an English engraver then in New York—expressed the theme in an engraving published by David Longsworth at the Shakespeare Gallery, where Woolley's original painting was on display. Visitors to the gallery could subscribe for the engraving as early as January 23, 1800, with the promise of the print in six weeks, though it was four months before the plate was completed.

Figure 1–11. *Sacred to the Memory of the Illustrious Washington.* **Mourning picture after drawing by Samuel Folwell. Needlework and watercolor on silk, 20 x 23 inches, circa 1805. Abby Aldrich Rockefeller Folk Art Center, Williamsburg.**

The large print, 24 x 19 inches (fig. 1–12), sold for four dollars. Washington's portrait—a poor copy after Gilbert Stuart—prominently displayed on a pedestal in the center of the work is the focal point of apotheosis imagery, which includes a beam of light from above with heavenly clouds breaking through the dark clouds of grief. The figures of Liberty on the left and Justice on the right are joined by Virtue in the center. In an advertisement for the print, Longsworth described "Virtue holding over the Portrait her Crown, and pointing to Heaven as the reward of her Hero." He also identified the two figures seated in the foreground on the left as Poetry and History, "who, with dulcet verse and noble sentiment,

applaud the merit of the great and good." On the right, as explained by the publisher, "America is personified in the figure of a female Aboriginal, whose grief evinces the deep regret impressed on the minds of all real Americans—Also that those unfortunate people have lost a Just Friend." The publisher admitted that a general gloom pervaded the work, but reasoned that it proved "the universal sensibility" produced by Washington's death.[23]

Symbols and imagery of the new nation and of Washington's place in history filled most of the memorial prints, but the *Apotheosis of Washington* engraved by David Edwin (fig. 1–13), after a portrait by Rembrandt Peale, contains no such symbolism. Instead, a highly ethereal

Figure 1–12. *Dedicated to the Memory of His Excellency Geo. Washington, Esq.* Memorial print, 24 x 19 inches, drawn and engraved by William Woolley after Gilbert Stuart. Published by David Longsworth, New York, 1800. Historical Society of Pennsylvania.

Figure 1–13. *Apotheosis of Washington*. Engraving, 24 x 14½ inches, by David Edwin after Rembrandt Peale. Published by Samuel Kennedy, Philadelphia, 1800. National Portrait Gallery, Smithsonian Institution.

interpretation depicts Washington rising through the clouds from Mount Vernon to receive a crown of immortality and be welcomed by Gen. Joseph Warren, felled at Bunker's Hill, and Gen. Richard Montgomery, killed during the 1775 assault on Quebec. The battlefield deaths of both generals had been memorialized in celebrated paintings by John Trumbull, but their heavenly likenesses are unclear, and it is fortunate that a newspaper notice announcing the publication of the print by Samuel Kennedy of Philadelphia provided their identifica-

tion. The notice praised the "elegant engraving" for revealing in one view "all that can be said of the Soldier, the Statesman, the Husband and the Friend."[24]

Publishers Simon Chaudron and John James Barralet announced in December 1800 that a proof print of their *Apotheosis of Washington* was on display for subscribers to view at their shops in Philadelphia, but the engraving (fig. 1–14) did not appear until February 1802.[25] Combining imagery of classical and Christian traditions with symbols of the new American

Figure 1–14. *Apotheosis of Washington*. Engraving, 25¾ x 19⅞ inches, designed and engraved by John James Barralet. Published by Barralet and Simon Chaudron, Philadelphia, 1802. Metropolitan Museum of Art. Gift of William H. Huntington, 1883.

Figure 1–15. *Apotheosis*. Transfer design of figure 1–14 on Liverpool pitcher, 10½ inches high, circa 1800. National Museum of American History, Smithsonian Institution.

Figure 1–16. *In Memory of Abraham Lincoln. The Reward of the Just*. Lincoln's head replacing Washington's in copy of Barralet's *Apotheosis*. Lithograph, 24 x 18¾ inches, by D. T. Wiest. Published by William Smith, Philadelphia, 1865. Library of Congress.

nation, Barralet produced an elaborate and complex plate that would enjoy a long popularity.[26] The initial advertisement of the work described the allegory as depicting "Washington raised from the tomb, by the spiritual and temporal Genius—assisted by Immortality. At his feet America weeping over his Armour, holding the staff surmounted by the cap of Liberty, emblematical of his mild administration, on the opposite side, an Indian crouched in surly sorrow. In the third ground the mental virtues, Faith, Hope, and Charity."[27] The figure of Father Time, identified here as the "spiritual and temporal Genius," was called the "Poetical and Historical Genius" in a later advertisement. Contemporary descriptions of allegorical figures allowed viewers considerable latitude in interpretation.[28]

In addition to the allegory described by the publishers, the engraving also includes impor-

tant symbols linking Washington to the new nation. By Liberty's side, the national eagle with shield, olive branch, and "E Pluribus Unum" ribbon adds a vigorous presence. Two rattlesnakes remind Americans of that symbol of colonial resistance,[29] while the mourning Indian gives a New World presence to the classical scene. Draped on ribbons over the edge of the open tomb, medals of the order of Freemasons and the Society of the Cincinnati display emblems from Washington's personal life. Through the shadows the inscription "Sacred to the Memory of Washington" can be read on the tomb, and the Stuart head of Washington is easily recognized.[30] Published without a title, the print was a glorification not only of Washington but also of the nation that chose him as its first president.

The work's contribution to the enshrinement of the presidency would be long lasting.

Three transfer-printed variations of Barralet's design appeared on ceramics—some with additional embellishments and the word *Apotheosis* (fig. 1–15).[31] The design was also copied by Chinese artists and appeared in reverse painting on glass plaques made for the American market.[32] Republished three times in the nineteenth century, the engraving would be transformed after the death of the sixteenth president in 1865 into the apotheosis of Abraham Lincoln (fig. 1–16), the head of the martyred president replacing that of the first president.[33]

The public mourning for Washington produced some of the most important contributions to the iconographic record of the young republic, but it also revealed an early manifestation of what Samuel Miller, a New York Presbyterian minister and social commentator, called the commercial spirit of Americans. There was some justice to the charge, Miller wrote in his *A Brief Retrospect of the Eighteenth Century*, published in 1803, that "the *love of gain* peculiarly characterizes the inhabitants of the United States."[34] That Washington was first in the hearts of his countrymen is unquestionable, but it is also true that there were many Americans anxious to make money out of the affection of their fellow citizens for their first president. Mason Locke Weems rushed his short biographical sketch of Washington into print soon after Washington's death and kept reprinting and embellishing it with myths in order to capitalize on the widespread popular interest in everything relating to Washington. He once told Mathew Carey, his Philadelphia publisher: "You have a great deal of money lying in the bones of old George if you will but exert yourself to extract it."[35]

Weems was not alone in Washingtonian entrepreneurship. Gilbert Stuart continued to make steady money painting Washington portraits, and other artists joined in the competition to fill the public demand for portraits. Six years after Washington's death William Dunlap would say of painting heads of Washington, "these I look on as Cash."[36] Nothing, however, equaled the flood of Washington mementos produced in 1800. Memorial prints, medals, rings, and lockets were widely offered for sale.[37] In February 1800, a New York confectioner informed the public that he had for sale at his store on Broadway "a Monument in

Sugar to the memory of the late illustrious, General Washington." The design included a portrait of Washington, two figures of a weeping Columbia, and other memorial decorations, "the elegance and ingenuity" of which, the proprietor insisted, "will scarcely fail to excite the admiration of the curious."[38] Later in the year, a merchant on New York's Greenwich Street announced the arrival of twelve dozen Washington medals ordered from England.[39] The marketing of Washington mementos prompted one wit to write in the *New York Commercial Advertiser*:

> To all Immigrants who have at least one shirt to their back, and want another—to all Scribblers and Poetasters, great and small, foreign or native, who intend to become famous and rich, by making ballads on Gen. Washington's death, or by writing his life—It is humbly recommended, that instead of *daubing* the memory and character of that illustrious man, they set themselves to solve the following question—"Whether a person can grin when he has no teeth?"[40]

This bit of irreverence indicates that as much as Americans honored their presidents and enshrined the office, excesses of glorification, in whatever guise, might be expected to provoke derision in a republican society. But popular interest in Washington never waned. More than two decades later the American Academy of Fine Arts in New York complained, "We are cursed as a nation with the common, miserable representations of our Great Hero, and with the shocking counterfeits of his likeness by every pitiful bungler that lifts a tool or brush, working solely from imagination without authority for their representations and deceptions, and bolstered by every kind of imposture."[41] This protest, however, was directed as much against a fellow artist as against "pitiful bunglers," for the object of rebuke was Rembrandt Peale, who had just completed a controversial composite portrait of Washington, which soon appeared in a popular lithograph (fig. 1–17).

As a young artist who had joined his father, Charles Willson Peale, for portrait sittings by Washington, Rembrandt Peale had drawn the president in 1795. In the 1820s, claiming distinction as the youngest living artist to have painted Washington from life, he professed

Figure 1–17. *Washington: Patriae Pater*. Lithograph, 24 x 17¾ inches, by Rembrandt Peale from his painting (circa 1824). Published by Pendleton lithography company, Boston, 1827. National Portrait Gallery, Smithsonian Institution.

himself dissatisfied with all the life portraits of Washington. "Each possesses something good which the others do not, and each has its own peculiar faults," he wrote to Thomas Jefferson in 1824. Describing his project to employ the images by Gilbert Stuart and Jean-Antoine Houdon together with those by his father and himself to produce "a National Portrait and standard likeness," he explained, "The Portrait I am now painting has a grand and imposing aspect and is calculated for public buildings."[42] Peale's portrait of Washington drew sharp resentment from members of the American Academy of Fine Arts, several of whom had painted Washington from life. Among them

was the society's president, John Trumbull, whose portrait of General Washington in full military regalia hung in New York City Hall.[43] But Peale's portrait is less important as a work of portraiture than as a representation of Washington for the new nation.

When Peale sought to paint a composite portrait of Washington to represent the man for posterity, he shunned military symbolism and produced the image of the statesman. Around the portrait he painted a stone tablet of classical design carved with "Patriae Pater" and an oak leaf garland to honor his patriotism. Peale told a congressional committee considering the purchase of his painting, "There

Figure 1–18. *Washington*.
Lithograph, 14⁵/₁₆ x 10¹³/₁₆
inches. Published by E. B.
and E. C. Kellogg, Hartford,
Connecticut, 1844. National
Portrait Gallery, Smithsonian Institution.

never was a Portrait painted with feelings of higher excitement. No human being could have felt more devoted admiration of the character of Washington, and no Artist ever found his pride more strongly excited by the magnitude and interest of his purpose than mine to rescue from oblivion the aspect of a Man who would forever be venerated as the 'Father of his Country.'"[44]

Despite its rebuff by the American Academy of Fine Arts, Peale's *Patriae Pater* attracted considerable favorable attention and was sold to Congress for two thousand dollars.[45] The artist also made numerous smaller replicas of the painting and in 1827 drew the portrait on stone for publication by the Pendleton lithography establishment of Boston (fig. 1–17). In recognition of this early example of that new art in America, the Franklin Institute of Philadelphia awarded Peale a silver medal "for the best specimen of lithography, to be executed in the United States."[46] As lithography rapidly proliferated, so also did Washington's image as the father of his country. A popular lithograph by an unknown artist, published by the Kellogg Company of Hartford in 1844, shows Washington as the rock upon which the country was built, the national eagle displaying his framed profile upon a gigantic rock inscribed "Washington" (fig. 1–18).[47]

Along with his unique place as the father of his country, Washington's image as president continued to be celebrated. His inaugural addresses (published both separately and in collections with those of later presidents) and his farewell address were reprinted for many years.

Sometimes his words appeared in pamphlets with his portrait, such as the publication of his farewell address sponsored by the Worcester Washington Benevolent Society in 1812 (fig. 1–19). In other instances, his addresses appeared inscribed and embellished on prints designed for framing and display on the walls of homes, schools, and other buildings. An engraved text of Washington's farewell address published in Philadelphia in 1821, embellished with a portrait of Washington at the top and a vignette drawn by Thomas Sully at the bottom, measures 40 x 26⅞ inches (fig. 1–20). A smaller engraved text of Washington's first inaugural address, decorated with a portrait and a floral border, offers also a tribute in verse (fig. 1–21):

Tho' shrin'd in dust, great Washington now lies,
The memory of his deeds shall ever bloom:
Twin'd with proud Laurels shall the Olive rise,
And wave unfading o'er his honoured Tomb.

To him ye Nations yield eternal Fame,
First on th' Heroic list enroll his name:
High on th' ensculptur'd marble let him stand
The undaunted Hero of his native land.

The attention directed to honoring Washington set precedents that would contribute to the enshrining of his successors in the memory of the nation, but the image of no later president gained the place of icon that Washington's likeness attained. Despite Rembrandt Peale's opinion that Gilbert Stuart's interpretation of the first president was inadequate, the popularity of Stuart's portraits was unmatched. Peale thought Stuart's drawing was inaccurate, exaggerated, and "particularly defective about the mouth, which looks as if it was full of water," but he admitted that "Stuarts portrait is full of dignity and character."[48] Stuart's productivity in painting replicas of his Washington portrait contributed to Washington's widespread presence. The artist painted about seventy variations of the "Athenaeum" head of Washington (plate 1), drawn from life in 1796—the final year of Washington's presidency. Stuart kept the life portrait, with the background unfinished, in his possession for the rest of his life.

Stuart made every effort to prevent others from copying his portrait of Washington, but with only limited success. When he sold a Washington portrait to John E. Sword of Philadelphia in 1801, he required the purchaser to "promise and assure . . . that no copies thereof should be taken." Nonetheless, a year later Stuart appeared in court claiming that Sword "did shortly afterwards take the same with him to China and there procured above one hundred copies thereof to be taken by Chinese artists and hath brought the same copies to the United States, and proposes to vend the same to your orator's great injury." In this case Stuart succeeded in securing a United States Circuit Court injunction ordering Sword to desist from selling or otherwise disposing of the copies of the portrait.[49] How many of these reverse paintings on glass were disposed of either before or after the court injunction is unknown. But copies survive in the United States today, as does the painting of Washington that Stuart sold to Sword.[50] Despite his efforts to keep his portraits of Washington from being copied, Stuart ultimately failed. In the end his image of Washington became the nation's and the world's.

Hundreds of engravings were made of the Washington likeness recorded by Stuart in his "Athenaeum" portrait, and it became almost literally "the household Washington."[51] A Russian visitor traveling in America from 1811 to 1813 observed that the country was "glutted with bust portraits of Washington" from the brush of Gilbert Stuart. "Every American considers it his sacred duty to have a likeness of Washington in his home, just as we have images of God's saints," he noted, adding, "Washington's portrait is the finest and sometimes the sole decoration of American homes."[52] A quarter-century later the editor of the *American Magazine*, published in Boston, introducing a series of vignettes of the presidents of the United States, observed that "in some of its innumerable representations" the face of Washington "must have met every eye." The surest evidence of the universal respect for Washington's memory, he thought, was "that prints of Washington dark with smoke are pasted over the hearths of so many American homes."[53] Still later, Ralph Waldo Emerson would confide in his journal: "The head of Washington hangs in my diningroom . . . I cannot keep my eyes off of it. It has a certain Apalachian

Figure 1–19. *Washington's Farewell Address to the People of the United States* (Boston: Worcester Washington Benevolent Society, 1812), title page and frontispiece. Portrait engraved by William Leney, New York. Ellis Library, University of Missouri–Columbia.

strength, as if it were truly the first-fruits of America, and expressed the country."[54]

There is striking artistic evidence to confirm the ubiquitous presence of Washington's portrait in the homes of ordinary Americans. On his canvas of the *Quilting Frolic* (fig. 1–22), completed in 1813, John Lewis Krimmel captured a common scene in an ordinary house. In the place of honor above the mantel, he painted a framed portrait of Washington, flanked by two prints of naval battles.[55] Even in the crowded painting, Washington's portrait has the lighting and central location to catch the eye. When the painting was displayed in Philadelphia in 1813 at the third annual exhibition of the Columbian Society of Artists and the Pennsylvania Academy of Fine Arts, a reviewer pronounced it "an original and very excellent picture." The presence of the portrait of Washington above the mantel was unremarkable enough to attract no notice from the reviewer, who concluded: "Throughout the whole of this charming and very interesting subject we can perceive strong marks of the ge-

Figure 1–20. *Washington's Farewell Address to the People of the United States*. Engraving, 40 x 26⅞ inches, by Charles H. Parker and Charles Toppan. Portrait by Gilbert Stuart and vignette by Thomas Sully engraved by Gideon Fairman. Published by Gideon Fairman, Benjamin H. Rand, and Charles Toppan, Philadelphia, 1821. Henry E. Huntington Library and Art Gallery.

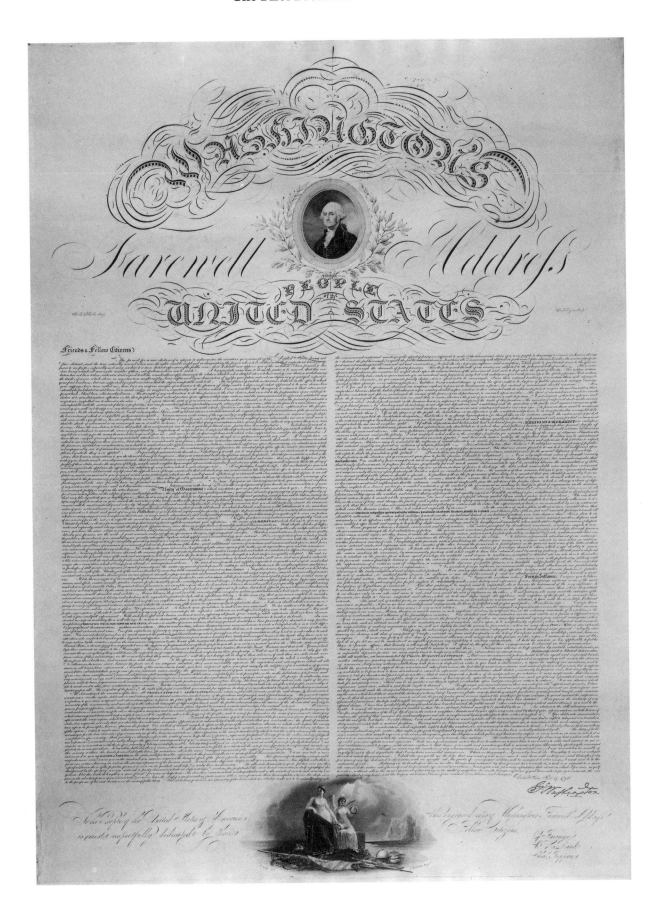

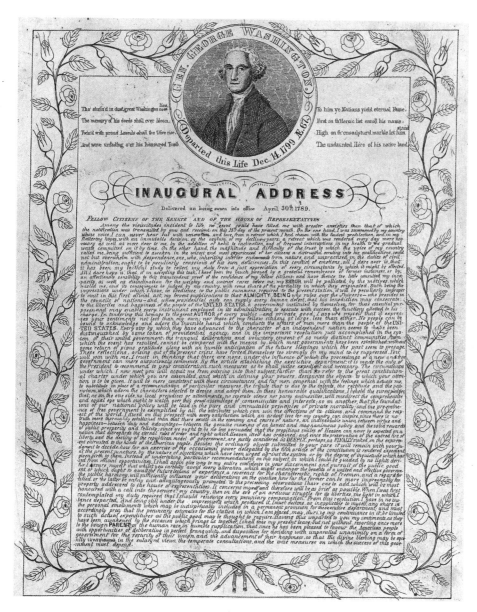

Figure 1–21. George Washington, *Inaugural Address Delivered on being sworn into office April 30th 1789*. Engraved broadside, 6 x 4½ inches, undated. Boston Public Library.

nius of the painter."[56] Four decades later, when Francis William Edmonds painted the interior of another ordinary dwelling in his *Taking the Census* (1854), he placed a similar portrait of the first president above the mantel (fig. 1–23). Washington was still in his accustomed place in *Home Again*, a painting by Trevor McClurg showing a Union officer returning from the war, published as a lithograph in 1866 by Endicott and Company of New York (fig. 1–24).[57]

Despite the many memorial tributes to Washington and the pervasiveness of his image throughout the country, Americans were ambivalent about an official, national memorial to him. A bill introduced in the House of Repre-

sentatives to erect "a mausoleum of American granite and marble, in a pyramidal form, one hundred feet square at the base, and of a proportionate height," touched off a public debate on the appropriate monument for a president of a republic.[58] "Congress is not agreed whether it is best to erect Pyramids, or Tombs, to the memory of the immortal Washington!" exclaimed one New York paper, offering as an alternative an obelisk of American marble, and concluding: "Expence would be avoided and the end answered—This is Washington's Pillar!"[59] After the House of Representatives proposed to appropriate two hundred thousand dollars to build a mausoleum for Washington

Figure 1–22. *Quilting Frolic*. Oil on canvas, 16⅞ x 22⅜ inches, by John Lewis Krimmel, Philadelphia, 1813. Henry Francis du Pont Winterthur Museum.

Figure 1–23. *Taking the Census*. Oil on canvas, 28 x 38 inches, by Francis William Edmonds, 1854. Private collection.

Figure 1–24. *Home Again.* Lithograph, 26½ x 34 inches, by Dominique C. Fabronius of a painting by Trevor McClurg. Published by Endicott and Company, New York, 1866. Library of Congress.

in the nation's capital, the Senate amended the bill to substitute *monument* for *mausoleum* and to reduce the appropriation to fifty thousand dollars.[60] The bill, as one member reported, was passed back and forth between the two houses and "caused such a variety of emotions and discussions" that it was ultimately postponed to the next session.[61] "In the infancy of our empire, an elegant but simple marble tomb or statue would be more honorable to the United States than a Mausoleum of a hundred or a thousand feet base," declared the *Spectator* of New York. "Could the illustrious hero rise from the grave, he would weep over the distractions of our Councils and our public follies."[62] With no agreement reached, Washington was allowed to rest in peace in the simple tomb at Mount Vernon. Not until 1848 was the Washington Monument begun, and not until 1885 would it be completed.[63]

CHAPTER II
The Presidency Celebrated and Enshrined

*A*FTER George Washington's death, a quarter of a century passed before another man who had held the presidential office died. Death, however, was no prerequisite for the enshrinement that enveloped the presidency. Just as Washington's elevation began before his death, so, too, did that of many of his successors. Because for two decades after Washington left office the men who gained the presidency were leaders who had played important roles in the founding of the Republic, they formed a group particularly appropriate for honoring as the builders of a new nation. Washington's successors were more directly involved in partisan politics than the first president had been, but they still received the respect and the attention accorded to none others; and the presidency, as an institution, continued to serve as a unifying and nationalizing symbol. Presidents did not endear themselves to all of their countrymen while in power, but they generally were rewarded with an honored place when they left office.

When John Adams succeeded Washington as president in 1797, he wrapped himself in the mantle of the first president. Retaining all the members of Washington's cabinet and continuing the social and ceremonial practices initiated by his predecessor, Adams sought to demonstrate continuity in the presidency. So successful had Washington been in beginning the institutionalization of the presidency and

establishing respect for the new government that the public was ready to accord to his successor the same honors given to the first president. While not abandoning their fascination with Washington, engravers and printmakers turned their attention also to President Adams (figs. 5–2 and 5–3).[1] At least one publisher offered prints of Washington and Adams as a set, advertising: "Striking Likenesses of John Adams and George Washington, Esquires. . . . engraved by two eminent English artists from pictures painted from the life; to be had elegantly framed in best burnish gold frames, with enamel glasses, &c. at six dollars a pair; Printed in colours on white Sattin, at Eight Dollars."[2] Adams, however, never shared the same public admiration Washington enjoyed, and the controversial policies of his administration kept him from becoming a popular president. Yet even after being denied reelection in 1800, Adams retained an honored place in the annals of the Republic, and his image joined that of Washington in celebration of the presidency.

When Vice-President Jefferson ran against President Adams in the election of 1800, printmakers rushed to get Jefferson's likeness before the public. After Jefferson's victory the popular new president, already heralded as the author of the Declaration of Independence, was increasingly the subject of the painter's brush and the engraver's stylus.[3] To mark Jefferson's

Figure 2–1. *Thomas Jefferson. President of the United States*. Engraving, 11 x 8¾ inches, by Cornelius Tiebout after painting by Rembrandt Peale. Published by Mathew Carey, Philadelphia, 1801. National Portrait Gallery, Smithsonian Institution.

Figure 2–2. *Thomas Jefferson*. Oil on canvas, 23⅛ x 19¼ inches, by Rembrandt Peale. Painted from life in 1800 and the source of numerous engravings of President Jefferson. The White House.

inauguration on March 4, 1801, Philadelphia publisher Mathew Carey offered a portrait of the new president engraved by Cornelius Tiebout from Rembrandt Peale's recent portrait of Jefferson painted in 1800. Tiebout's engraving (fig. 2–1), copied directly from Peale's canvas, was the best made from it, though it still did not fully capture Peale's image (fig. 2–2). After seeing an early proof of the engraving, Congressman Mathew Lyon told the publisher, "The likeness is not thought to be a good one. The face is a little too broad, the countenance too grave and there is a defect in the nose."[4] Whether any alterations were made in the plate after Lyon's criticism is not known, but in response to another early critic's suggestion to put some lines of poetry under the portrait, Carey added some lines from the Declaration of Independence, reminding viewers of Jefferson's past contributions.[5] Whatever the

alterations before publication, the new print sold briskly. During the three months following Jefferson's inaugural, Carey printed eight hundred copies of this engraving. The unframed prints sold for two dollars apiece, but one out of three patrons purchased a framed portrait at five dollars.[6] Tiebout copied the same head for a full-length engraving of Jefferson, which competed for public favor in the months following the president's inauguration (fig. 5–9). Many engravers who did not have access to a life portrait of the president commonly copied and recopied images from other engravings. Jefferson himself called such prints "miserable caracatures,"[7] and must have had in mind such examples as that appearing in an 1800 edition of his *Notes on the State of Virginia* (fig. 2–3).

Considerable progress was made in the art of engraving in America during the period of Jef-

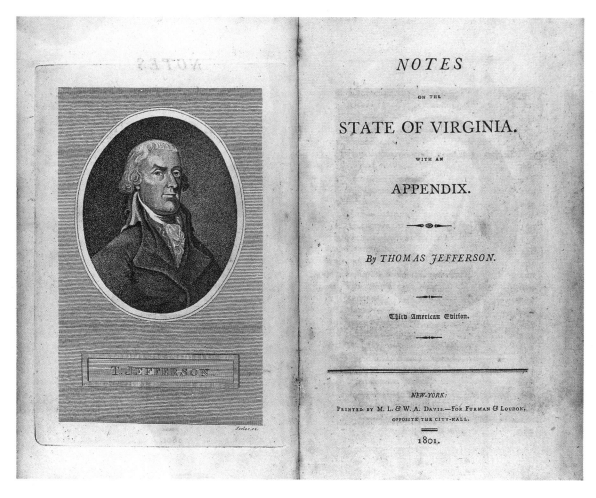

Figure 2–3. *Notes on the State of Virginia*, by Thomas Jefferson (New York, 1801), frontispiece and title page. Engraving by John Scoles. Private collection.

Figure 2–4. *Thomas Jefferson*. Engraving, 5⅞ x 5⅛ inches, by Robert Field after Gilbert Stuart. Published by Robert Field, Boston, March 14, 1807. Metropolitan Museum of Art, Bequest of Charles Allen Munn, 1924.

EXPLANATION.

In the Center is the Goddess of Liberty sitting on the Globe supporting on her knee with one Hand, the Portrait of THOMAS JEFFERSON, President of the United States, with the other she is pointing him out as the Favorite of the People. Round her head are the six-teen Stars to represent the different States. On the Monument is the Portrait of the late General GEORGE WASHINGTON. The eyes of the Goddess are fixed thereon in remembrance of past services. The rays of glory from the sixteen Stars strike their splendid beams on each Por-trait. The emblems of Monarchy are under the foot of the Goddess. At the foot of the Monument is the Genius of Peace, presenting the Olive Branch to the Portrait of Gen. Washington. The Genius of Gratitude is crowning him with Laurels. The Back Ground is distinguished by the Rays of Glory, shining on a Vessel at a distance, to denote the protection of Commerce. The Supporters to the Work are:

Nᵒ1 *Brittania*   Nᵒ2 *Neptune*   Nᵒ3 *Fame*   Nᵒ4 *Abundance*

Pubᵈ Salem Janᵞ 15ᵗʰ 1807. Price two Dollars.

Figure 2–5. Goddess of Liberty holding portrait of Thomas Jefferson. Engraving, 14⅝ x 17⅜ inches, by John Norman. Published in Salem, Massachusetts, January 15, 1807. Yale University Art Gallery, Mabel Brady Garvan Collection.

ferson's presidency. Before the end of his second term, his admirers could buy for one dollar an excellent engraving by Robert Field (fig. 2–4) of the portrait painted from life by Gilbert Stuart in 1805 (plate 6).[8] Stuart's likeness soon replaced in popularity that by Rembrandt Peale, and it became the predominant icon of Jefferson throughout the nineteenth century.[9]

In harmony with Jefferson's own emphasis on simplicity and equality, many of the engravings of Jefferson published during his presidency contained little in the way of embellishment. Inscriptions commonly were limited to

his name and title—sometimes only his name.[10] But midway through his second term an allegorical print appeared full of symbolism enshrining Jefferson along with Washington in the nation's pantheon (fig. 2–5). Engraved by John Norman, the print was published in Salem, Massachusetts, January 15, 1807, and sold for two dollars. In the center of the design the goddess of Liberty holds Jefferson's portrait on her knee, while with her other hand pointing him out as "the Favorite of the People"—according to the explanation provided on the print. The portrait of Jefferson—based on a widely copied engraving of Rem-

Figure 2–6. *Thos. Jefferson the Pride of America, Retired March 4, 1809.* Engraving, 7⅝ x 5¾ inches, by Thomas Gimbrede, New York, 1809. American Philosophical Society.

brandt Peale's 1800 portrait by David Edwin—was one that would have been familiar to viewers. Liberty, seated before a monument displaying Washington's portrait, fixes her eyes upon it "in remembrance of past service." The genius of Peace is shown presenting an olive branch to Washington's portrait, while Gratitude crowns him with laurels. Stars representing the sixteen states glow around the head of Liberty, casting "rays of glory" on both portraits. The overturned crown of monarchy lies under the foot of Liberty, and an American

eagle is close by her side. Rays of glory also reach a ship in the distance "to denote the protection of Commerce." Supporting figures representing Britannia, Neptune, Fame, and Abundance reflect New England's interest in maintaining friendly commerce with England at a time of growing strain between the two nations.

Before the end of his second term, Jefferson's popularity reflected in this print was seriously eroded by the effects of the embargo enacted near the end of 1807. Nonetheless, his

TH: JEFFERSON

St. Mémin del. & sc.

Figure 2–7. *Th: Jefferson.* Engraving, 2¹⁵⁄₁₆ x 2⁷⁄₁₆ inches, by Charles-Balthazar-Julien Févret de Saint-Mémin, Washington, D.C., 1805. From drawing taken from life by Saint-Mémin, 1804. Princeton University Libraries.

retirement in March 1809 provided the occasion for the publication of a print that would confirm for posterity his enshrinement in the memory of the nation (fig. 2–6). Entitled *Thos. Jefferson the Pride of America, Retired March 4, 1809,* the print was designed and engraved by Thomas Gimbrede in apotheosis imagery. The bust of Jefferson, after a profile by Charles-Balthazar-Julien Févret de Saint-Mémin (fig. 2–7), appears in the clouds accompanied by the goddess of Wisdom with the figure of Fame below. Minerva, personifying reason, was particularly appropriate when applied to Jefferson.[11] In sending Jefferson a copy of the print, the artist referred to it as "a Little Sketch in Cameo," but Jefferson would not have failed to recognize the imagery that testified to his enshrinement.[12] By dispensing with many of the ceremonies that Washington had initiated and Adams had continued, Jefferson sought to keep the presidency close to the people and to assure its republican character. Whatever the artist's precise intent, Jefferson would not have favored such celebration of those who held the presidential office. When he wrote the epitaph for his own simple tombstone, he would not list the presidency among the major accom-

plishments for which he wished to be remembered. But he voiced no protest against Gimbrede's imagery when he thanked the artist for "the very elegant Cameo" and the "flattering mark of the indulgence with which Mr. Gimbrede has been so good as to contemplate his public conduct."[13]

Like Washington's inaugural speeches and farewell address, Jefferson's inaugural addresses were printed in forms appropriate for framing and public display. Among numerous printings of Jefferson's first inaugural address, Mathew Carey of Philadelphia published a print with a miniature likeness of the president at the top (fig. 2–8). Both Jefferson's first and second inaugural addresses were printed on satin suitable for framing, which appears to have been done frequently.[14] The daybook of John Doggett, a Roxbury, Massachusetts, glass and mirror importer and talented picture framer, contains a number of entries recording the sale of frames and glass for President Jefferson's inaugural speech of March 4, 1805.[15] The continuance of the custom can be seen in a satin print of James Madison's inaugural address in 1809 (fig. 2–9) and in prints of Andrew Jackson's farewell address (fig. 2–10)—the first

Figure 2–8. *Speech of Thomas Jefferson, President of the United States, Delivered at His Instalment, March 4, 1801, at the City of Washington.* Silk broadside, 19½ x 15⁵⁄₁₆ inches. Published by Mathew Carey, Philadelphia, 1801. Massachusetts Historical Society.

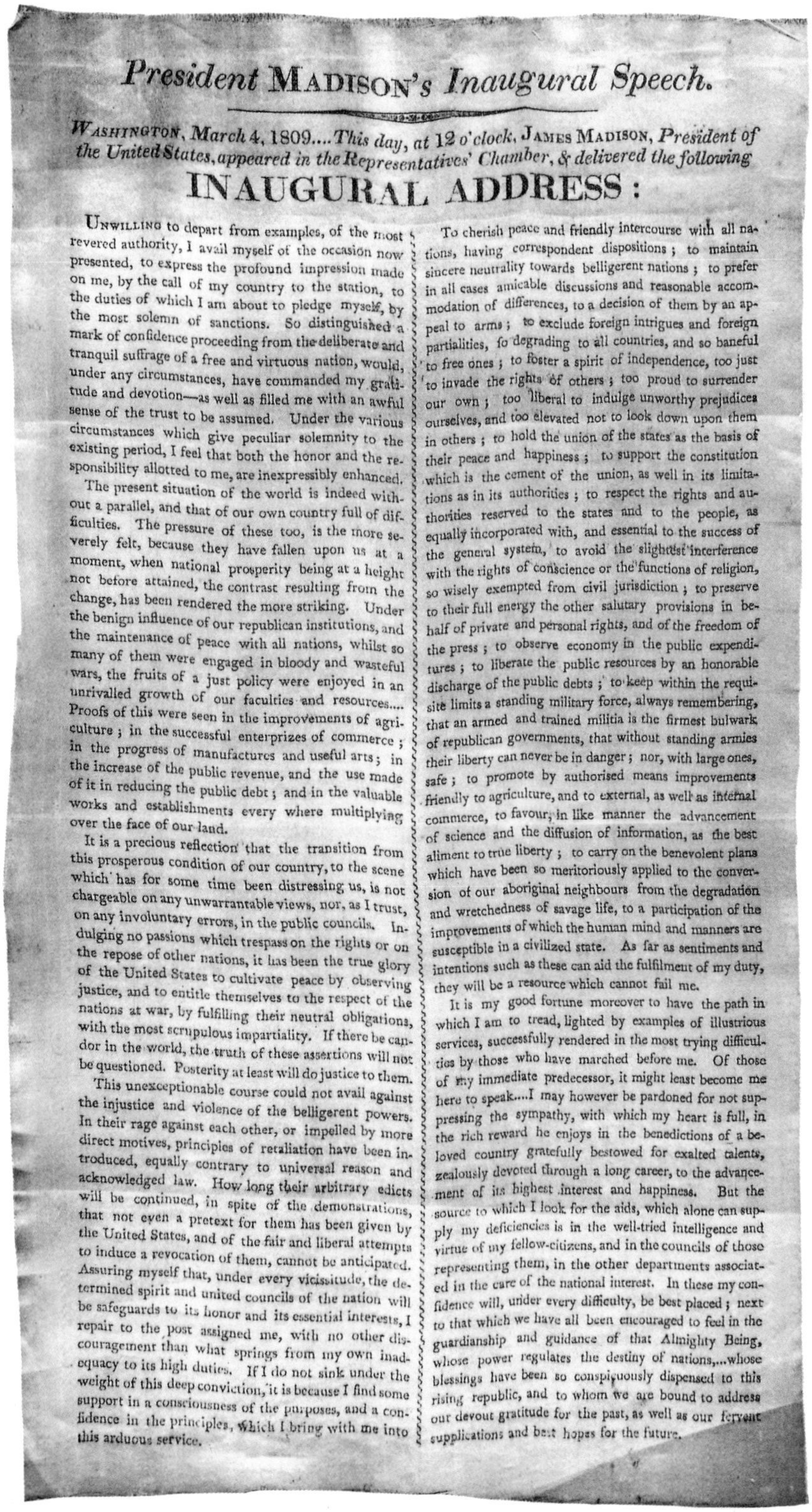

President MADISON'S *Inaugural Speech.*

WASHINGTON, *March* 4, 1809....*This day, at* 12 *o'clock,* JAMES MADISON, *President of the United States, appeared in the Representatives' Chamber, & delivered the following*

INAUGURAL ADDRESS:

UNWILLING to depart from examples, of the most revered authority, I avail myself of the occasion now presented, to express the profound impression made on me, by the call of my country to the station, to the duties of which I am about to pledge myself, by the most solemn of sanctions. So distinguished a mark of confidence proceeding from the deliberate and tranquil suffrage of a free and virtuous nation, would, under any circumstances, have commanded my gratitude and devotion—as well as filled me with an awful sense of the trust to be assumed. Under the various circumstances which give peculiar solemnity to the existing period, I feel that both the honor and the responsibility allotted to me, are inexpressibly enhanced.

The present situation of the world is indeed without a parallel, and that of our own country full of difficulties. The pressure of these too, is the more severely felt, because they have fallen upon us at a moment, when national prosperity being at a height not before attained, the contrast resulting from the change, has been rendered the more striking. Under the benign influence of our republican institutions, and the maintenance of peace with all nations, whilst so many of them were engaged in bloody and wasteful wars, the fruits of a just policy were enjoyed in an unrivalled growth of our faculties and resources.... Proofs of this were seen in the improvements of agriculture; in the successful enterprizes of commerce; in the progress of manufactures and useful arts; in the increase of the public revenue, and the use made of it in reducing the public debt; and in the valuable works and establishments every where multiplying over the face of our land.

It is a precious reflection that the transition from this prosperous condition of our country, to the scene which has for some time been distressing us, is not chargeable on any unwarrantable views, nor, as I trust, on any involuntary errors, in the public councils. Indulging no passions which trespass on the rights or on the repose of other nations, it has been the true glory of the United States to cultivate peace by observing justice, and to entitle themselves to the respect of the nations at war, by fulfilling their neutral obligations, with the most scrupulous impartiality. If there be candor in the world, the truth of these assertions will not be questioned. Posterity at least will do justice to them.

This unexceptionable course could not avail against the injustice and violence of the belligerent powers. In their rage against each other, or impelled by more direct motives, principles of retaliation have been introduced, equally contrary to universal reason and acknowledged law. How long their arbitrary edicts will be continued, in spite of the demonstrations, that not even a pretext for them has been given by the United States, and of the fair and liberal attempts to induce a revocation of them, cannot be anticipated. Assuring myself that, under every vicissitude, the determined spirit and united councils of the nation will be safeguards to its honor and its essential interests, I repair to the post assigned me, with no other discouragement than what springs from my own inadequacy to its high duties. If I do not sink under the weight of this deep conviction, it is because I find some support in a consciousness of the purposes, and a confidence in the principles, which I bring with me into this arduous service.

To cherish peace and friendly intercourse with all nations, having correspondent dispositions; to maintain sincere neutrality towards belligerent nations; to prefer in all cases amicable discussions and reasonable accommodation of differences, to a decision of them by an appeal to arms; to exclude foreign intrigues and foreign partialities, ſo degrading to all countries, and so baneful to free ones; to foster a spirit of independence, too just to invade the rights of others; too proud to surrender our own; too liberal to indulge unworthy prejudices ourselves, and too elevated not to look down upon them in others; to hold the union of the states as the basis of their peace and happiness; to support the constitution which is the cement of the union, as well in its limitations as in its authorities; to respect the rights and authorities reserved to the states and to the people, as equally incorporated with, and essential to the success of the general system, to avoid the slightest interference with the rights of conscience or the functions of religion, so wisely exempted from civil jurisdiction; to preserve to their full energy the other salutary provisions in behalf of private and personal rights, and of the freedom of the press; to observe economy in the public expenditures; to liberate the public resources by an honorable discharge of the public debts; to keep within the requisite limits a standing military force, always remembering, that an armed and trained militia is the firmest bulwark of republican governments, that without standing armies their liberty can never be in danger; nor, with large ones, safe; to promote by authorised means improvements friendly to agriculture, and to external, as well as internal commerce, to favour, in like manner the advancement of science and the diffusion of information, as the best aliment to true liberty; to carry on the benevolent plans which have been so meritoriously applied to the conversion of our aboriginal neighbours from the degradation and wretchedness of savage life, to a participation of the improvements of which the human mind and manners are susceptible in a civilized state. As far as sentiments and intentions such as these can aid the fulfilment of my duty, they will be a resource which cannot fail me.

It is my good fortune moreover to have the path in which I am to tread, lighted by examples of illustrious services, successfully rendered in the most trying difficulties by those who have marched before me. Of those of my immediate predecessor, it might least become me here to speak....I may however be pardoned for not suppressing the sympathy, with which my heart is full, in the rich reward he enjoys in the benedictions of a beloved country gratefully bestowed for exalted talents, zealously devoted through a long career, to the advancement of its highest interest and happiness. But the source to which I look for the aids, which alone can supply my deficiencies is in the well-tried intelligence and virtue of my fellow-citizens, and in the councils of those representing them, in the other departments associated in the care of the national interest. In these my confidence will, under every difficulty, be best placed; next to that which we have all been encouraged to feel in the guardianship and guidance of that Almighty Being, whose power regulates the destiny of nations,...whose blessings have been so conspicuously dispensed to this rising republic, and to whom we are bound to address our devout gratitude for the past, as well as our fervent supplications and best hopes for the future.

Figure 2–9. *President Madison's Inaugural Speech*, Washington, March 4, 1809. Silk broadside, 17 x 9 inches. American Antiquarian Society.

Figure 2–10. *Farewell Address of Andrew Jackson*. Silk broadside, 27 x 19½ inches. Published at *New York Times* office, 1837. National Museum of American History, Smithsonian Institution.

such presidential farewell after Washington's. Such practices reflected the special attention accorded the first office and added to the aura of the presidency.

The idea of publishing a series of presidential portraits found expression as soon as their number was sufficient to form a sequence. In July 1804 the editor of *The Literary Magazine, and American Register*, published in Philadelphia, initiated a series of portraits of "all eminent and illustrious men among his countrymen" by publishing the portrait of Washington (fig. 2–11). In the next two issues of the magazine, portraits of John Adams (fig. 2–12) and Jefferson (fig. 2–13) appeared, accompanied by biographical sketches. As later publishers followed this example, presidential portrait series became a popular tradition.[16]

By the time of Madison's presidency, enough men had served in the high office to compose an impressive group of four presidents who were also founders of the nation. The first artists to give artistic recognition to this memorable historical record were David Edwin and George Murray, who produced a plate containing the portraits of Washington, Adams, Jefferson, and Madison for the frontispiece of the third volume of a new edition of Robert Bisset's *The History of the Reign of George III to the Termination of the Late War* (fig. 2–14). Published in Philadelphia in 1811, the print is the earliest example located pre-

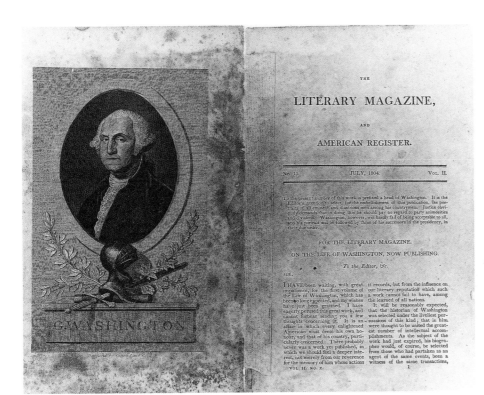

Figure 2–11. *The Literary Magazine, and American Register*, Philadelphia, July 1804. Plate of Washington designed by John James Barralet, engraved by Alexander Lawson after Gilbert Stuart. Published by Conrad and Co. Virginia State Library.

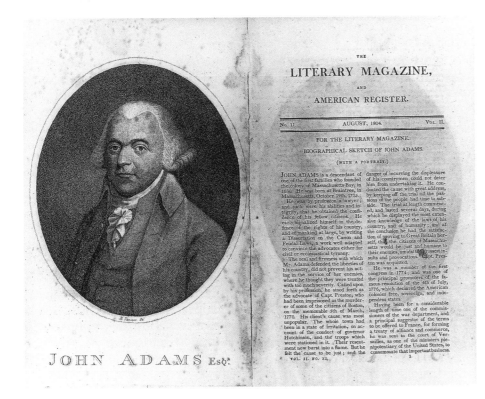

Figure 2–12. *The Literary Magazine, and American Register*, Philadelphia, August 1804. Engraving of John Adams by Benjamin Tanner after William Joseph Williams. Virginia State Library.

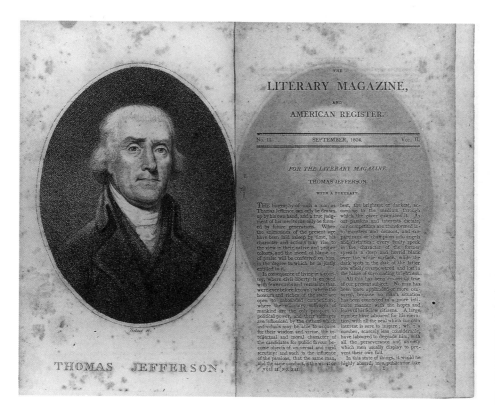

Figure 2–13. *The Literary Magazine, and American Register*, Philadelphia, September 1804. Engraving of Jefferson by Cornelius Tiebout after Rembrandt Peale. Virginia State Library.

senting the images of all the presidents of the United States on a single sheet. Edwin, one of the most prolific engravers of presidential portraits, engraved the likenesses, while Murray contributed the design. Except for Adams, the portraits were all copied from Gilbert Stuart's popular likenesses. Although Stuart also had painted President Adams, he had not completed the portrait begun in 1798 and had withheld it from engravers. For Adams's portrait, Edwin employed a likeness by Edward Savage that he himself may have engraved in 1800 while he worked for Savage soon after coming to America.[17] The ornamental design was of a style common in England, where Murray had worked before emigrating. He presented the portraits against a decorated entablature displaying books, inkwell, pen, paper, and a rattlesnake, the symbol of colonial resistance in America. Offering appropriate presidential likenesses, equal in size and dress, with the placement of Washington's portrait at the top as the only special mark of honor, the print had a long life.

During James Monroe's presidency, the plate was redesigned to include the current president and appeared as the frontispiece of the first volume of Frederick Butler's *A Complete History of the United States of America*, published in Hartford in 1821 (fig. 2–15). Later, John Quincy Adams was added to the original design, along with an improved likeness of Monroe, and the revised plate decorated an 1825 edition of the addresses and messages of all the presidents (fig. 2–16).[18] When Andrew Jackson was added to the plate, it filled a crowded page with the likenesses of the first seven presidents (fig. 2–17). This record illustrates how rapidly the tradition of printing the portraits of all the presidents on a single sheet became established. A similar plate, offering superior likenesses and more elaborate embellishments, engraved by John Francis Eugene Prud'homme, appeared as the frontispiece of volume 2 of *The Percy Anecdotes*, published in New York in 1832 (frontispiece).[19] The portraits of the first five presidents derived from Stuart's images; John Quincy Adams's likeness was taken from Thomas Sully, and Jackson's portrait followed James Barton Longacre.

Several artists, in fact, implemented similar ideas of collective presidential portraits about the same time. Portraits of all the presidents appeared in the complex print *The First Great*

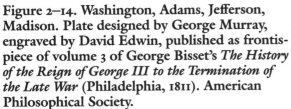

Figure 2–14. Washington, Adams, Jefferson, Madison. Plate designed by George Murray, engraved by David Edwin, published as frontispiece of volume 3 of George Bisset's *The History of the Reign of George III to the Termination of the Late War* (Philadelphia, 1811). American Philosophical Society.

Figure 2–15. Washington, Adams, Jefferson, Madison, Monroe. Engraving published as frontispiece of Frederick Butler's *A Complete History of the United States of America* (Hartford, 1821). Library of Congress.

Western Empire, published by Jonathan Clark in 1812 (plate 5).[20] Another example is a print designed and engraved by Thomas Gimbrede, who had earlier memorialized Jefferson's retirement (fig. 2–18). Published in New York on January 30, 1812, the engraving presents presidential portraits in separate ovals placed within a drapery, the folds of which form a kind of canopy over the pictures and create a shrinelike motif. Washington appears in uniform beneath the "American Star," containing thirteen smaller stars. Crossed flags with the national emblem and a laurel wreath add to the patri-

otic imagery. The portrait of James Madison, then in the presidential chair, is directly below that of the first president and is flanked by pictures of the second and third presidents. Except for Adams, the likenesses were derived from portraits by Gilbert Stuart. Washington's likeness taken in 1796 and Jefferson's, painted in 1805, present images from their presidential years. Madison had aged somewhat since Stuart had painted his portrait in 1804, but only Adams's portrait was inappropriate for his presidential image. Derived from a portrait painted by John Singleton Copley in 1783, it depicts Adams as much younger than he was during his presidential tenure.[21] Printed on pa-

Figure 2–16. Frontispiece of *The Speeches, Addresses and Messages, of the Several Presidents of the United States* (Philadelphia, 1825). McAlpin Collection, New York Public Library, Astor, Lenox and Tilden Foundations.

Figure 2–17. Engraving of Presidents Washington through Jackson; page from unidentified book. American Philosophical Society.

per measuring 11½ x 18 inches, the engraving was designed for framing and display.[22] The imagery of a presidential shrine in which Washington occupied the place of honor set a style frequently to be imitated in the years ahead.

This early example of commemoration of the presidency also set the pattern for blurring or ignoring the partisanship that enveloped the office while presidents held power. In the political environments of their administrations, the first four presidents were sharply divided. Federalists Washington and John Adams and Republicans Jefferson and Madison were aligned on opposite sides of the first party divisions in

the United States. Indeed, at the time Thomas Gimbrede was designing his plate of the first four presidents, late in 1811, Adams and Jefferson had not communicated with one another since the end of the bitterly contested election of 1800. The defeated Adams had even displayed his bitterness on the morning of Jefferson's inaugural by leaving the capital before daylight to avoid being present at his successor's inauguration. Gimbrede's celebratory print conveyed an image of national political unity more idealized than real. It was only a coincidence that in the same month in which Gimbrede's engraving was published, January 1812, Jefferson and Adams finally became reconciled and reopened their long-lapsed correspondence.[23]

Gilbert Stuart, the most famous portrait

Figure 2–18. The first four presidents. Engraving, 9 x 10¾ inches. Designed, engraved, and published by Thomas Gimbrede; printed by Andrew Maverick, New York, January 30, 1812. Historical Society of Pennsylvania.

painter in the early republic and the foremost portraitist of early presidents, had an unmatched role in contributing to the emerging tradition of series of presidential portraits. In the 1820s Stuart completed two series of replicas of his portraits of the first five presidents of the United States. One set (fig. 2–19), painted for Col. George Gibbs of Newport, Rhode Island, finished in 1825, survives complete and hangs today in the National Gallery of Art in Washington, D.C., celebrated as the most important existing set of presidential portraits by a single artist.

Contemporaneously more influential than the Gibbs set was the series that Stuart had pre-

viously painted for John Doggett, who earlier had framed portraits and speeches of presidents in his store in Roxbury. From this series of the first five presidents, only the portraits of Madison (fig. 2–20) and Monroe (fig. 2–21) survived a fire in the Library of Congress in 1851, which destroyed the canvases of Washington, Adams, and Jefferson.[24] But Stuart's replicas for Doggett had early been put on public exhibition, and they quickly gained widespread familiarity through lithographs copied from the portraits—prints that were among the earliest lithographs circulated in America. More than any other work, this series of presidential portraits, which came to be referred to

(1) *George Washington*, replica of the "Athen-aeum" head (plate 1).

(2) *John Adams*, replica of portrait taken in 1798 and 1815.

(3) *Thomas Jefferson*, replica of portrait taken in 1805.

(4) *James Madison*, replica of portrait taken in 1804.

(5) *James Monroe*, replica of portrait taken in 1817.

Figure 2–19. Portraits of the first five presidents. Oil on wood panels, about 26 x 21 inches each, by Gilbert Stuart. Painted for George Gibbs, circa 1825. National Gallery of Art.

as the "American Kings," influenced the popular presentation of presidential portraits for the next two decades.

An entry made by John Quincy Adams in his diary in September 1821 shows that Stuart was at work on the series for Doggett by that date. Reporting that Stuart had visited his father and brought his portrait of the elder Adams completed in 1815, the younger Adams noted that his aged father had sat two or three hours for the artist. "Stewart paints this picture for a Mr. Doggett, as one of the five Presidents of the United States," he recorded. "He is to paint them all for him."[25] A piece in the *Boston Daily Advertiser* for June 20, 1822, reporting the exhibition of the Doggett set of presidential portraits, fixes the date by which Stuart had completed the series. The reviewer of the exhibition lavishly praised the series, declaring, "Had Mr. Stuart never painted any thing else, these alone would be sufficient to 'make his fame' with posterity. No one . . . has ever surpassed him in fixing the *very soul* on canvas; but in the present instance he has done more; he has invested the individual of nature with the ideal of art."[26]

At the time he painted the Doggett set, Stuart had access to his own portraits of the first five presidents taken during or near the period of their presidencies. The artist still had in his possession the unfinished head of Washington taken in 1796, the final year of Washington's presidency.[27] Not yet referred to as the "Athenaeum" head, that portrait, already much copied, had become the preeminent likeness of the first president (plate 1). The portrait of John Adams that Stuart carried with him on his visit to the second president in 1821 had been finished in 1815, but it was originally taken in 1798, while Adams was president. During the early months of 1821, Stuart also still retained in his studio the portrait that he had taken of Jefferson in 1805, midway through his presidency (plate 6), though in late May 1821 the painting was finally shipped to Jefferson and arrived safely at Monticello in August.[28] The artist had no portrait of Madison readily available, and he traveled to Brunswick, Maine, to copy the replica he had painted for James Bowdoin III of his portrait of Madison taken in 1804, five years before the subject became president. Had he not copied Jefferson's portrait before sending it to Monticello, Stuart's replica for Bowdoin of Jefferson's 1805 sitting was also available in Brunswick.[29] For Monroe's likeness, Stuart could copy the portrait he painted when Monroe visited Boston in July 1817 soon after becoming president. That Monroe had taken time from a very busy schedule in Boston to arrange three early-morning sittings with the artist before leaving the city was recognition of the status that Stuart had attained as the portraitist of presidents.[30]

Stuart himself had replicated some of these portraits—especially Washington's—and many of the artist's images had been copied by others, but his work for Doggett was Stuart's first effort to paint a set of presidential portraits. When he painted another set for Gibbs, Stuart did not have available all of the sources he could draw on for the Doggett series. But his replicas for Doggett were available in Boston, and it is not unlikely that he drew on some of them in painting the set for Gibbs.

Figure 2–20. *James Madison*. **Oil on canvas, 40 x 32 inches, by Gilbert Stuart, replicating portrait taken in 1804. Painted for John Doggett, circa 1821. Mead Art Museum, Amherst College, Bequest of Herbert L. Pratt, class of 1895.**

Figure 2–21. *James Monroe*. **Oil on canvas, 40¼ x 32 inches, by Gilbert Stuart, replicating portrait taken in 1817. Painted for John Doggett, circa 1821. Metropolitan Museum of Art, Bequest of Seth Low, 1929.**

It is unfortunate that all of the series for Doggett did not survive. As the portraits of Madison and Monroe show, Stuart painted half-length portraits with backgrounds more elaborate than the ones he customarily employed. Doggett's son John Doggett, Jr., believed that Stuart had endeavored to make the backgrounds emblematic of the character of the administration of each president and said that the sheathed sword and rainbow in the portrait of Washington signified "that the war and strife had ceased, and the storms of the Revolution passed away."[31] The inclusion of Houdon's bust of Franklin in Jefferson's portrait may symbolize the enlightened views that Jefferson and Franklin shared. The depiction of papers and books is a common feature of all the portraits.[32] The younger Doggett said that Stuart introduced tassels to represent the number of terms that each president had served, but if this was true in the original paintings, it was not consistently reproduced in the lithographs made from them.

Despite the high opinion of John Doggett, Jr., respecting the portraits, the series has rarely been regarded as among Stuart's best work. Furthermore, the lithographic reproductions (figs. 2–22 through 2–26) taken from the portraits present considerably altered images, creating impressions little in harmony with the original paintings or with the Gibbs series, which was not reproduced in popular prints. President John Quincy Adams, one of the earliest commentators to record his reaction upon seeing the lithographs made from the Doggett portraits, was blunt in indicating his disapproval. "I did not like them," he said.

The art itself, though superior to that of engraving upon wood, is essentially inferior to that of engraving upon copper-plate. But of these portraits, the originals painted for Doggett were not in Stuart's best manner; the engravings were made after copies taken by I know not whom, made in France, with a gloss of the mannerism of inferior French artists; and they have metamorphosed the five grave Presidents of the

GEORGE WASHINGTON,
FIRST PRESIDENT OF THE UNITED STATES.
*From the Original Series painted by Stuart,
for the Mess.ʳˢ Doggett of Boston.*

Figure 2–22. *George Washington, First President of the United States.* Lithograph, 16½ x 13 inches, attributed to Nicholas Maurin. "From Original Series painted by Stuart, for the Messrs. Doggett of Boston." Published by Pendleton lithography company, Boston, [1828]. National Portrait Gallery, Smithsonian Institution.

JOHN ADAMS,
SECOND PRESIDENT OF THE UNITED STATES.

*From the Original Series painted by Stuart.
for the Mess.rs Doggett of Boston.*

Figure 2–23. *John Adams, Second President of the United States.* Lithograph, 16¾ x 13 inches, attributed to Nicholas Maurin. "From the Original Series painted by Stuart for the Messrs. Doggett of Boston." Published by Pendleton lithography company, Boston, [1828]. Library of Congress.

THOMAS JEFFERSON,

THIRD PRESIDENT OF THE UNITED STATES.

From the Original Series painted by Stuart.
for the Mess.ʳˢ Doggett of Boston.

Figure 2–24. *Thomas Jefferson, Third President of the United States*. Lithograph, 16½ x 13¼ inches, attributed to Nicholas Maurin. "From the Original Series painted by Stuart for the Messrs. Doggett of Boston." Published by Pendleton lithography company, Boston, [1828]. Library of Congress.

JAMES MADISON,

FOURTH PRESIDENT OF THE UNITED STATES.

*From the Original Series painted by Stuart
for the Messrs. Doggett of Boston*

Entered according to the Act of Congress.

Figure 2–25. *James Madison, Fourth President of the United States.* Lithograph, 16½ x 13 inches, attributed to Nicholas Maurin. "From the Original Series painted by Stuart for the Messrs. Doggett of Boston" (fig. 2–20). Published by Pendleton lithography company, Boston, [1828]. National Portrait Gallery, Smithsonian Institution.

JAMES MONROE,

FIFTH PRESIDENT OF THE UNITED STATES.

From the Original Series painted by Stuart for the Mess.rs Doggett of Boston

Entered according to the Act of Congress.

Figure 2–26. *James Monroe, Fifth President of the United States.* Lithograph, 16½ x 13 inches, attributed to Nicholas Maurin. "From the Original Series painted by Stuart for Messrs. Doggett of Boston" (fig. 2–21). Published by Pendleton lithography company, Boston, [1828]. National Portrait Gallery, Smithsonian Institution.

United States into five petits-maitres, courtiers of the old Court. All likeness and character and truth of nature have vanished in the process.[33]

Although Adams dismissed the prints, the public was more receptive. Few Americans outside Boston had seen the original portraits, and the opportunity to acquire a set of the "American Kings" was inviting. Details concerning the making and distribution of the prints are sparse, but enough is known to offer a suggestive glimpse into the beginnings of mass circulation of popular presidential portraits.

On November 16, 1825, the *Columbian Centinel* of Boston published the following notice:

> *Portraits of the Presidents.* Messrs. Doggetts of this city, have received from France *Lithographic Plates* of the fine Portraits of the five Presidents of the United States, from the pencil of Stuart; and which adorned the residence of the Nation's Guest during his visit to this city. We learn that the plates are most excellent samples of the skill of the first of the French Artists; and that with the plates, Messrs. Doggetts have received a press to strike off the impressions, and a French pressman to conduct the work.

Every reader of this announcement would have known that the reference to "the Nation's Guest" was to the Marquis de Lafayette and his famous visit to America in 1824. During that unprecedented reception, Boston rivaled other cities in the warmth of its welcome and—according to a report in the *Boston Evening Gazette*—housed the Revolutionary hero in a "large and splendid mansion which had been fitted up in a very rich style for his residence," at the corner of Park and Beacon streets.[34] Here Lafayette could gaze upon the portraits of the first five presidents of the new nation for which in its infancy he had fought.

In implying an early availability of lithographic prints of the paintings, the press notice was premature. The prints would not be ready until 1828. The reasons for the delay can be only partially reconstructed from the surviving evidence. The most revealing record is a diary of John Doggett's son-in-law Jonathan Cobb, who in late 1825 was actively engaged in obtaining subscriptions for the presidential lithographs. Cobb recorded that the prints were to be produced by John Pendleton of Boston, but after three months he learned that Pendleton could not perform the work; Cobb then canceled his contract to market the lithographs and disgustedly withdrew from the venture.[35]

Doggett, however, did not sever relations with Pendleton, who had acquired his knowledge of lithography on a trip to Paris as a purchasing agent for Doggett in 1825.[36] In the summer of 1826 Pendleton again sailed to Europe to purchase plate glass and looking-glass plates for Doggett.[37] Whether he also made arrangements regarding lithographic plates or presses can only be surmised. But by early 1828 prints were available in Boston, and John Quincy Adams saw copies in Washington in early March.[38] In May, John Doggett sent "a bundle of Prints containing two setts of the 'American Kings'" to Messrs. Charles Humberston and Company of Liverpool in care of the captain of a ship bound for that English port.[39]

The prints that Doggett thus early dubbed the "American Kings" had been produced by the Pendleton lithography company of Boston from stones prepared by Nicholas Maurin, a prominent French engraver and lithographer, the stones and presses having been imported from France. Each portrait is identified by name and presidential title and inscribed "From the Original Series painted by Stuart for the Messrs. Doggett of Boston" (figs. 2–22 through 2–26). The prints (unframed) sold for two dollars each on standard paper, two dollars and a half on India paper.[40]

Information regarding the marketing of such mass-produced prints has only rarely survived, but a letterbook of John Doggett and Company provides an unusual glimpse of how Stuart's presidential portraits reached the people. A letter from John Doggett and Company of Boston, dated May 8, 1829, advised Salmon Brown in Mobile, Alabama:

> Agreeable to the directions of Messrs. Pendletons we have forwarded to the care of Mr. William G. Hewes, New Orleans (there being no vessell here bound to Mobile) 20 Boxes each containing a sett of the Presidents nicely framed and packed and shall in the course of a few weeks send the other 30 sett ordered by you—the bill

lading of the present shipment goes to Mr. Hewes. We have made insurance on the same including the value of the prints and as the Gen. Stark by which they were shipped is an old vessell, were obliged to pay 2% per ct. premium—no other vessell at this time being up for N. Orleans. The total amount of $311.50 is to your debit in Account and as they are put up at cash prices and the boxes given in, we trust you will remit us for the same as soon as practicable.[41]

The market for the prints must have been strong, for six weeks later, instead of the thirty additional sets promised in the above letter, Doggett shipped seventy boxes, each containing "a sett of Presidents," at a cost of $1,078.[42]

Increased public attention was directed to the Doggett-Pendleton set of presidential portraits upon the death of Gilbert Stuart in Boston in July 1828, just as the distribution of the lithographs from his paintings was gaining momentum. In August 1828 the Boston Athenaeum held a major retrospective exhibition of Stuart's portraits. Over two hundred portraits painted by the artist were on display. Among the major attractions was the series of portraits of Washington, John Adams, Jefferson, Madison, and Monroe, described in the catalogue of the exhibition as "painted expressly for the Messrs. Doggett" and composing "the only uniform series of the Presidents in existence."[43] This indicates that the Gibbs series was unknown to the organizers of the exhibition and that Gibbs, unlike the numerous individuals who loaned portraits for the exhibition, did not offer his series for public display. The exhibition also included a portrait of John Quincy Adams by Stuart, the catalogue noting, "This makes the sixth President he has painted, himself standing unrivalled during the whole space of time, in his particular branch of Art."[44]

What most attracted attention at the exhibition—assembled to raise money for Stuart's family—was the "Athenaeum" head of Washington that Stuart had kept unfinished and in his possession since he had drawn it from life in 1796 (plate 1). The reviewer of the exhibition for the *Boston Evening Gazette* wrote: "Were there no other attractions to this Gallery but the head of Washington, no person of taste can be excused from visiting it. This single portrait, from which all that we now correctly see of Washington has been taken, and which transmits his Godlike countenance to posterity, ought to be, and perhaps in some future time, may be, a fortune to his surviving family."[45] It was this head that Stuart had copied for his presidential sets for Doggett and Gibbs.

Although Stuart's earlier portraits of individual presidents were well known through engravings, the influence of his uniform series for Doggett was particularly important. The availability of the images from the Doggett set led to their employment in a notable memorial tribute to two former presidents, John Adams and Thomas Jefferson, who died on the same day in 1826. The coincidence of their deaths was the more startling because the date was July 4, 1826, the fiftieth anniversary of the adoption of the Declaration of Independence, of which Jefferson had been the principal author and Adams a fellow member of the drafting committee. In France, where both Adams and Jefferson had served as diplomats, the National Manufactory of Sèvres, that nation's most famous maker of exquisite porcelain, produced a pair of ornate memorial urns with portraits of Adams and Jefferson (plates 7 and 8). The portraits adorning the tall, gold-finished, matching urns are unmistakably derived from Stuart's portraits for John Doggett. The images may have come from the Pendleton lithographs (figs. 2–23 and 2–24) or from the copies from which those prints were made.

In America, remembrances of Adams and Jefferson were less elaborate. When he learned of the deaths of his father and of Jefferson, President John Quincy Adams, who had presided over the celebration of the fiftieth anniversary of independence in Washington unaware that either man had died, joined many Americans in seeing evidence of Divine favor.[46] But no depictions of apotheosis, such as glorified Washington's death, memorialized the deaths of the second and third presidents. Their portraits appeared in simpler and more modest displays of mourning. One small, round engraving offers miniature portraits of Jefferson and Adams with their birth dates and common date of death (fig. 2–27). A similar design appeared on memorial ribbons (fig. 2–28). One elaborate memorial ribbon presents busts of Adams and Jefferson on pedestals below which were a pen and inkwell, the Decla-

Figure 2–27. Jefferson–Adams memorial engraving, 2¼ inches diameter, [1826]. Henry Francis du Pont Winterthur Museum.

Figure 2–29. John Adams–Thomas Jefferson memorial ribbon, 6¾ x 2⅝ inches, [1826]. American Philosophical Society.

Figure 2–28. Adams–Jefferson memorial ribbon, 1½ x 8 inches, [1826]. DeWitt Collection, University of Hartford.

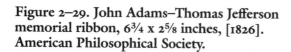

Figure 2–30. *James Madison: 4th President of the United States*. Lithograph, 16½ x 13 inches, by W. Ball after figure 2–25. Published by George Endicott, New York, circa 1834. Library of Congress.

Figure 2–31. *James Monroe: 5th President of the United States*. Lithograph, 16½ x 13 inches, by W. Ball after figure 2–26. Published by George Endicott, New York, circa 1834. Library of Congress.

Figure 2–32. *John Quincy Adams: 6th President of the United States*. Lithograph, 16 x 12⅝ inches, by W. Ball. Published by George Endicott, New York, circa 1834. Library of Congress.

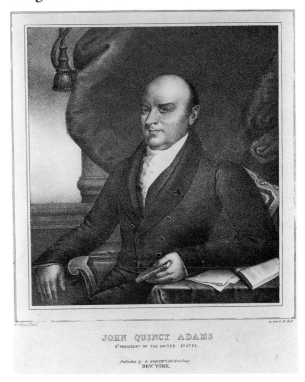

ration of Independence, and the inscription "Together they laboured for our Country, together they have gone to meet their reward" (fig. 2–29). Above their heads willow branches drape the scene, and the national eagle spreads its wings and supports the flags of the young nation.

Nothing so elegant as the Sèvres urns was produced from the Doggett series in America, but the Pendleton prints, as the first popular set of lithographs of all the presidents, provided a model widely imitated. The lithographs carried a notice of copyright, but no record of their registration has been located, and more than one artist copied from the set.

Figure 2–33. *Les Présidents des Etats Unis: Dédié à leur ami le Général Lafayette.* Lithograph, 22¾ x 18¾ inches, drawn by Antoine Maurin, lithographed by Langlumé, Paris, circa 1827–1828. Library of Congress.

Figure 2–34. Washington, John Adams, Jefferson, Madison, Monroe, and John Quincy Adams. Lithograph, 10¼ x 6⅞ inches, by Langlumé, Paris, circa 1827–1828. American Philosophical Society.

Lithographer W. Ball added John Quincy Adams to the series for a presidential set published by George Endicott in New York, but otherwise he obviously copied from the Doggett set, as the examples of the prints of Madison (fig. 2–30) and Monroe (fig. 2–31) show. Stuart's portrait of John Quincy Adams painted in 1818 and a widely available engraving of it by James Barton Longacre provided Ball's source for the sixth president (fig. 2–32), which he adapted to the style of the portraits of the earlier presidents in the Pendleton-Doggett prints.[47] Less carefully executed, more popularized versions by other publishers soon followed.

Stuart's likenesses of the first six presidents were employed in group portraits of the presidents as well as in separate prints. French artists and lithographers, still ahead of their American counterparts in the new techniques of lithography, contributed an impressive poster of *Les Présidents des Etats-Unis* (fig. 2–33). Dedicated to the presidents' friend General Lafayette, the print pictures the first six presidents in the clouds above an imposing depiction of the American eagle. The images, drawn by Antoine Maurin, follow Stuart's portraits, with Washington in a place of honor at the forefront. A German edition of the print was published in Leipzig.[48] Either before or after Maurin's print appeared, his Paris lithographer issued a smaller lithograph with the portraits sketched in the same arrangement in the clouds, each portrait numbered and identified by a list of names below (fig. 2–34). The print also served as the source for two designs on textile. The earliest pattern, on French toile, reproduces the six presidential portraits at intervals in the clouds with the eagle and "Les Présidents des Etats-Unis" separating the repeat of the presidential images (fig. 2–35).[49] A cotton fabric printed while Andrew Jackson was pres-

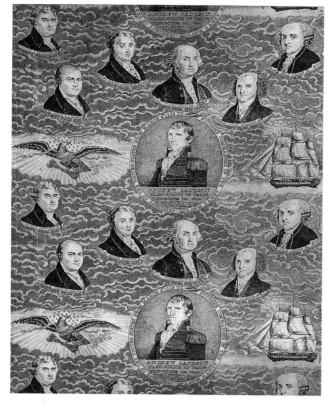

Figure 2–35. Les Presidents des Etats-Unis. Roller-printed French toile, based on figure 2–33, circa 1827–1828. Smithsonian Institution.

Figure 2–36. President Andrew Jackson and previous presidents. Roller-printed cotton textile, based on figure 2–33, circa 1830. New-York Historical Society.

Figure 2–37. *The Presidents of the United States.* **Lithograph, 14 x 12 inches, by W. Blanchard, Sonefelder Lithography Company. Published by Charles Ellms, Boston, 1830. Smithsonian Institution.**

ident and suitable for draperies in American buildings and homes of Jacksonian supporters presents a framed portrait of President Jackson at the center of the design and adds the frigate *Constitution* to the eagle flanking Jackson's portrait (fig. 2–36). The name and the administration dates of each president are printed below each portrait.[50]

After Jackson became president, the lithograph by Maurin with its cloud motif (fig. 2–33) was copied by W. Blanchard for a print of *The Presidents of the United States* published in Boston in 1830 (fig. 2–37). Blanchard added a portrait of Jackson to the grouping, but otherwise he must have copied directly from the Maurin print, as shown by the reverse images of all the portraits. A modification of the cloud

motif appears in a lithograph published by Prentiss Whitney while Van Buren was president (fig. 2–38). The print presents bust portraits grouped in a circle around a wreath inscribed "Presidents of the U. States." Identifications at the bottom of the print include birth or life dates and dates of presidential inaugurations.

In August 1834 the *New-York Mirror, A Weekly Journal, Devoted to Literature and the Fine Arts* published one of the most important prints to celebrate the early presidency. Rejecting the indifferent portraits often found in popular prints, George P. Morris, the editor of the *New-York Mirror*, sought to produce a work that would present accurate likenesses by lead-

Figure 2–38. *Presidents of the U. States.* Lithograph, 20 x 16½ inches, by Jenkins Lithography. Published by Prentiss Whitney, circa 1837–1840. American Antiquarian Society.

ing artists and faithfully represent the art of portraiture in the United States. The print that Morris envisioned was in the tradition of the engraving by Thomas Gimbrede of the portraits of the first four presidents on a single sheet (fig. 2–18). With seven presidents to portray, the task was greater, and Morris employed a wealth of talent to undertake the project. He engaged Asher Brown Durand to make copies of two original portraits and to paint one from life. Robert W. Weir designed the plate, and John W. Casilear executed the engraving. Having gained a considerable reputation as the engraver of Trumbull's *The Declaration of Independence* and Thomas Sully's portrait of John Quincy Adams (fig. 5–15), Durand was the best-known artist employed by Morris and was charged with the overall supervision of the engraving.[51]

In publishing the finished plate (fig. 2–39), accompanied by biographical sketches of each of the presidents, in the issue of the *Mirror* for August 9, 1834, Morris introduced the offering by writing:

> The amount of time, labour and expense that have been devoted to the production of the engraving with which the Mirror of this week is adorned, has been hitherto without precedent, as we believe we may say without hazard of contradiction, in the whole progress of art in the United States. Nearly two years have elapsed since the first step of its preparation was taken, and yet there has been not a week, we might almost affirm not a day, of all that time, in which some measure requisite for its completion in the highest attainable state of finish and beauty, was not in active performance. The subject was deemed one of such universal and permanent interest as to justify every exertion; and it was our determination from the first, that nothing on our part should be wanting for the production of such a work as should not fail to become an honour to all the artists employed and to the journal, as well as acceptable to our patrons.[52]

Publishers are rarely modest in praising their productions, but in this case surviving historical records—more numerous than usual relating to such publications—lend support to Morris's claim. William Dunlap, who published his *History of the Rise and Progress of the Arts and Design in the United States* in the same year that Morris's print appeared, praised Morris as a friend of artists and the arts of design and noted, "In the very expensive plate of 'The Presidents,' portrait painters and the first engravers were employed at liberal prices."[53] Morris's private correspondence also provides a rare opportunity to follow the making of a major engraving of presidential portraiture.

Morris went to extraordinary lengths to arrange for engravings of portraits that were highly regarded as superior likenesses of each president. He sent Durand to Boston to copy what was widely accepted as Stuart's best portrait of Washington, the "Athenaeum" head taken in 1796. Durand sent five days copying the portrait at the Boston Athenaeum, where he received, he wrote at the time, "the flattering assurance that it is the best copy ever made from Stuart's original."[54] Durand also went to West Point to copy Jefferson's likeness from the portrait that Sully had painted of Jefferson for the Military Academy. Sully had drawn Jefferson's likeness from life at Monticello in 1821, the last portrait painted of the third president. His full-length portrait of Jefferson was hanging in the library at West Point in 1823, when James Fenimore Cooper viewed it and sensed "a dignity, a repose, . . . a loveliness, about this painting, that I have never seen in any other portrait" of Jefferson.[55]

Morris appealed directly to John Quincy Adams for portraits of him and his father to copy for the engravings, stressing his aim to reproduce likenesses "striking and undeniable" in a print "creditable to the arts of the country."[56] Adams replied unequivocally, "There is but one portrait of my father painted when he was President of the United States and worth engraving. It is by Stuart . . . . the only one which as a work of art and as a likeness at the time of my father's presidency can give a correct idea of his countenance and person then and the only one I should ever take pleasure in seeing as a representation of him at that period." The portrait was in his possession, and he was willing to permit its engraving but unwilling to commit the painting to the hazards of transportation. As for his own portrait, he wrote to Morris, "I have no portrait of myself fit to be engraved and bearing any likeness to me when I was President." He recommended the portrait belonging to Harvard University, the head of which had been painted by Stuart,

Figure 2–39. "The Presidents of the United States. From Original and Accurate Portraits, Printed & Engraved expressly for the New York Mirror." Engraving, 18 x 14½ inches, designed by Robert W. Weir; engraved by John W. Casilear; printed by Casilear, Durand, and Company, New York. Published in the *New-York Mirror*, August 9, 1834. Historical Society of Pennsylvania.

although the rest of the painting had been completed after Stuart's death by Sully (fig. 5–19).[57] Adams insisted, "No engraving from any other Pictures will as a *likeness* be worth a five cent piece."[58]

Morris, who shared Adams's desire to present accurate likenesses, accepted his judgment. Perhaps because Durand was not available to make a return trip to Boston, or because of the pressures of time, or for other reasons, Morris engaged David Claypoole Johnston, a Boston painter, engraver, and caricaturist, to copy both John Adams's portrait at Quincy and John Quincy Adams's portrait at Cambridge.[59] For the portrait of Monroe, Morris borrowed the original portrait painted by John Wesley Jarvis, a well-regarded New York portraitist, in the possession of Silas E. Burrows of New York. Casilear made the engraving directly from the painting, which Morris described as "the last for which Mr. Monroe ever sat; the original is esteemed faultless in point of resemblance."[60]

In making the arrangements for the copying and the engraving of each portrait, Morris insisted that "*the likeness must be correct*, and any sacrifice *must* be made to have them so." He said, "It will not answer to engrave from portraits already issued in engravings."[61] Unable to obtain a suitable portrait of Madison to copy after learning that Mrs. Madison would not consent to shipping Stuart's portrait to New York for engraving,[62] Morris appealed to Durand to go to Montpelier and take Madison's portrait from life. "You might take a likeness of the man *as he is*, which would be just the thing we want," he wrote to the artist. "No other portrait will answer. If you will go, I will cheerfully defray all charges, etc." Elaborating on his determination to make "the plate of *the first order of merit*," he confessed, "This presidential cluster is a load of responsibility upon my mind, and you will not wonder, if I feel very anxious about it."[63] Durand accepted the assignment, found the Madisons most hospitable, and after two sittings wrote from Montpelier: "Even in its present state Mrs. Madison pronounces it perfect and is almost afraid to have me touch it again. I think I shall satisfy myself as far as regards likeness with one more sitting."[64]

Although Madison's portrait was the only

new likeness that Morris commissioned, he worried especially about offering a good likeness of President Jackson, then in the White House. "No head in the whole cluster will be more closely scrutinized than that of Genl. Jackson," he told Durand.[65] When he saw the portrait of Jackson painted by Ralph E. W. Earl hanging in the office of New York Governor William L. Marcy, he decided "it is just the thing we want for our engraving" and promptly obtained permission from Vice-President Martin Van Buren, who owned the painting, to allow him to have it engraved.[66] Governor Marcy's military secretary, Thomas W. Harman, who handled the details of shipping the portrait to New York, pronounced the likeness "as nearly perfect as can be drawn except for the hand," but that defect was of no concern in making the bust portrait required for Morris's plate.[67] "There must be 'no mistake' about this likeness," Morris instructed Durand. "Nothing but an *exact copy* of the picture will answer." Earl himself had made a number of copies of the portrait but never succeeded in equaling the original, Van Buren warned. Claiming that his portrait of Jackson was "the only likeness of the president extant," Van Buren feared that the engraving would not be so good as the original. These concerns Morris passed on to Durand, pleading: "Please be careful—and let Mr. Casilear exert his utmost skill upon the general."[68]

If there were comparable problems in designing the plate, no record of them has been found. Editor Morris proudly explained the design in the *Mirror*:

> The whole picture is intended to represent one end of a room in the capitol of the United States. In the centre is a large mirror, reflecting a statue of the Goddess of Liberty from the opposite side, and surmounted by the American Eagle with banners. Immediately under the mirror is a pier-table, of classic and beautiful form, and on each side of this a large vase, standing upon the floor of tesselated marble. The portraits, seven in number, are disposed, each in a chaste but elegant frame, around the mirror, three at each side, and that of Washington at the top. The background is a tapestried wall, indistinctly figured with leaves and flowers.
>
> The details are simple, yet the general effect is not only rich, but magnificent; and, while care has been taken by the skilful arrangement of

light and shadow, not only to keep the portraits distinct, but also to make them the most striking and prominent objects, the accessaries have been wrought up to a high point of loveliness by the grace of their disposition and form, and the exquisite style in which they are finished. The whole picture exhibits at one view the lineaments of a succession of eminent men, whose lives, and actions, and characters, are identified with the history of our country.[69]

This description, like Morris's letters, shows that the print was designed as a celebration not only of the presidency but also of the arts in America. The pantheon of presidential portraits, the goddess of Liberty, and the American eagle are complemented by the elegant frames, the tessellated marble floor, and the delicately flowered, tapestried wall. Morris told Madison that he intended to publish "a Splendid National Engraving . . . executed in the best manner, and by the most eminent Artists" and "a specimen of the fine arts highly creditable to the country."[70] That the likenesses of the presidents are the dominant theme of the print reflects the place of the presidency in American culture as the United States approached a half-century since the inauguration of its first president.

The influence of the engraving published by Morris in the *Mirror* can be seen in the lithograph *The Presidents of the U. States*, which appeared in Philadelphia a few years later, while Martin Van Buren was president (fig. 2–40). Published by J. Middleton, Jr., the revised design replaced the bust portrait of Washington with a larger, featured reproduction of the popular engraving of Washington derived from the portrait Gilbert Stuart had painted for the Marquis of Lansdowne in 1796 (plate 2). Aside from this change and the addition of Van Buren's portrait, the other portraits are the same as in the *Mirror* print. The flags and eagle are more prominent in the Middleton print, which also includes a drawing of the Capitol at Washington, overall giving the lithograph a more popularized character than the artistically subdued engraving in the *Mirror*. The Middleton print, unlike its predecessor, identifies the portraits by names keyed to numbers.

While the care that Morris demonstrated in the making of the presidential print for the

Mirror was rarely matched, an engraving by Denison Kimberly, published in Boston in 1842 (fig. 2–41), followed Morris's example. Kimberly identified the artist from whom each of his careful engravings was derived. The likenesses of the first five presidents were all taken from portraits by Gilbert Stuart. John Quincy Adams's portrait came from Asher Brown Durand, Jackson's from James Barton Longacre, Van Buren's from Henry Inman, Harrison's from Albert Gallatin Hoit, and Tyler's from Charles Fenderich. The standing portrait of Washington in the center was from Stuart.

Morris's *The Presidents of the United States*—like the two presidential series that Stuart painted for John Doggett and George Gibbs—was indicative of the interest in collective presidential portraiture. Within a few months after the print's publication in the *Mirror*, Luman Reed, a wealthy New York merchant, engaged Durand, who had played such a major role in Morris's production, to paint another series of portraits of the seven presidents of the United States. As a patron of the arts, Reed wished to encourage Durand's transition from engraver to painter, and he also planned to present the portraits to a public institution for display.[71] He instructed Durand to paint two sets of the portraits in order to keep one set for himself.

Commissioned to copy Stuart's portraits of the first five presidents and to paint John Quincy Adams and Andrew Jackson from life, Durand would go again to Boston to copy Stuart's "Athenaeum" head of Washington, as he had done for the *New-York Mirror*. While there he also copied the Stuart portrait of John Adams that David Claypoole Johnston had earlier copied for the *Mirror*.[72] For the third president, Durand borrowed a copy of Stuart's 1805 portrait of President Jefferson from James Barton Longacre.[73] Although Durand had painted Madison from life two years earlier for the *Mirror*, Reed wanted portraits that were more contemporaneous with the periods during which the presidents served in office, and he sent Durand to Brunswick, Maine, to copy Stuart's portrait painted for James Bowdoin III from Madison's 1804 sitting.[74] Stuart himself had replicated that image for Doggett's set (fig. 2–20). Because of its older image, Reed also regarded the portrait of Monroe that had been

Figure 2–40. *The Presidents of the U. States.* Lithograph, 11½ x 8 inches, printed by Wild and Chevalier, Philadelphia. Published by J. Middleton, Jr., circa 1837–1839. Metropolitan Museum of Art. Gift of William H. Huntington, 1883.

Figure 2–41. *The Presidents of the United States.* Engraving, 19 x 14 inches, by Denison Kimberly; designed by C. H. H. Billings; printed by W. V. and A. W. Coles. Published by Charles A. Wakefield, Boston, 1842. Historical Society of Pennsylvania.

Figure 2–42. *Andrew Jackson*. Oil on canvas, 30 x 25 inches, by Asher Brown Durand. Taken from life, March 1835. New-York Historical Society.

Figure 2–43. *John Quincy Adams*. Oil on canvas, 30¼ x 25¼ inches, by Asher Brown Durand. Taken from life, June 1835. New-York Historical Society.

used for the *Mirror* plate as unacceptable. For Durand to copy, he located Stuart's 1817 portrait of Monroe in the possession of Monroe's granddaughter in Baltimore.[75] Although it was frequently difficult, and not always possible, to locate life portraits, Reed's search for Stuart's original portraits reflected a growing American interest in the artistic values of original portraiture.

Durand enthusiastically directed his energies to copying Stuart's portraits and to obtaining the creditable likenesses of John Quincy Adams and Jackson that Luman Reed desired. Reed was delighted when both Adams and Jackson agreed to sit for new portraits. "I am anxious that these two portraits should be the standard portraits of the Nation," he wrote to Durand in Washington, "and I wish you to take every possible pains to give a perfect identity without regard to time or expence." To encourage the busy statesmen to allow sufficient time for the sittings, Reed instructed Durand to inform both men confidentially that "their portraits will occupy a conspicuous place in the public institution that I intend to present them

to, and where they will be seen by all distinguished men of the nation as well as foreigners."[76]

Having arrived in Washington in late February 1835 near the end of the congressional session, Durand found that President Jackson had no time to sit for him until after Congress adjourned.[77] Even then, it was not easy to get Jackson to sit. "I have a great deal of difficulty in painting the President he has been so pressed with business," Durand wrote his son. "The General has been part of the time in a pretty good humour, but some times he gets his 'dander up' and smokes his pipe prodigiously."[78] After four sittings, Durand still needed another to finish the portrait (fig. 2–42), and Reed urged him to persist and "spare no pains nor expense towards producing the best likenesses" of Jackson and Adams. Meanwhile, Durand had been more fortunate in painting the portrait of former President John Quincy Adams, now a member of Congress. As the work neared completion, the artist told his wife, "My picture of him is said to be the best ever taken."[79] Pleased as he was, when he

Figure 2–44. *National Galaxy, or, Portraits and Biographies of All the Presidents of the United States.* Engraving, 21½ x 28¾ inches, by Nathaniel Dearborn; printed by J. Howe. Published by J. Greenleaf, Boston, 1840. American Antiquarian Society.

went to Boston in June to copy Stuart's head of Washington at the Athenaeum, he got Adams to sit again.[80] "I have painted an entire new head of Mr. Adams," he reported, "and I flatter myself far better in every respect than the first."[81] It was this likeness of John Quincy Adams that was included in the series for Reed (fig. 2–43).

In adding the two most recent presidents to Stuart's series of the first five presidents, Durand continued and reinforced the tradition of celebrating the presidency in sets of portraits. The portraits went on public display almost immediately and remain so today. In December 1835 Reed presented one set to the Brooklyn Naval Lyceum. After the Lyceum closed in 1892, the portraits were transferred to the United States Naval Academy at Annapolis, where they still hang. Reed's own set of the

portraits is now in the portrait gallery of the New-York Historical Society.[82]

The cloud motif popular in several prints enshrining the presidency (figs. 2–33, 2–34, 2–37) gave way to a "National Galaxy." In 1840 J. Greenleaf of Boston published *National Galaxy, or, Portraits and Biographies of All the Presidents of the United States*, a poster containing portraits of the presidents through Van Buren, "engraved on steel, in the highest style of the art" by Nathaniel Dearborn (fig. 2–44). Brief biographies were included under each of the framed portraits, the whole enclosed within a decorative border. Four years later Greenleaf updated the work, adding the portraits of Harrison and Tyler, also engraved by Dearborn, along with their biographical sketches and the text of the Constitution at the bottom of the

Figure 2–45. *National Galaxy.* Engraving, 20⅜ x 34 inches, by Nathaniel Dearborn; printed by Samuel N. Dickinson. Published by J. Greenleaf, Boston, 1844. Rare Book Division, Library of Congress.

print (fig. 2–45). On the print itself the publisher insisted, "This splendid and useful work should be in the possession of every gentleman of taste and lover of his country—it is a subject to which every American of whatever party or opinion may turn with partial and patriotic pride." The print must have been popular, for Greenleaf published a similar work in 1849. The new *National Galaxy*, a lithograph smaller in its overall dimensions than the earlier versions, offers portraits of the twelve presidents with identifications but includes no biographies or other textual matter (fig. 2–46). Reflecting increasing sectional tensions, Greenleaf labeled the new print a "splendid National work," but, otherwise, the publisher's laudatory description remained the same.

Using the plates of the presidents from Washington through Van Buren that he had engraved for Greenleaf, Nathaniel Dearborn published a presidential print with the portrait of Martha Washington in the center (fig. 2–47). The print bears no title or explanation,

and the circumstances that explain the unusual arrangement have not been discovered. When Dearborn later expanded the print by adding the portraits of Harrison, Tyler, and Polk in a fourth row across the bottom, Mrs. Washington's portrait was replaced by a list of vice-presidents and secretaries of state.[83] The explanation for Mrs. Washington being omitted is as elusive as the reason for her initial inclusion. Whatever the explanation, Dearborn produced an unusual and intriguing print that may have reminded viewers that presidential wives were also a part of the national galaxy.

In the same style of presenting a gallery of presidential portraits was the lithograph published by E. B. and E. C. Kellogg of Hartford while John Tyler was president (fig. 2–48). In addition to the individually framed portraits, pictures of the Capitol and the White House add interest to the print. Most of the likenesses in the mass-produced lithograph are crudely drawn—John Tyler is hardly recognizable—but the overall impression of the inexpensive

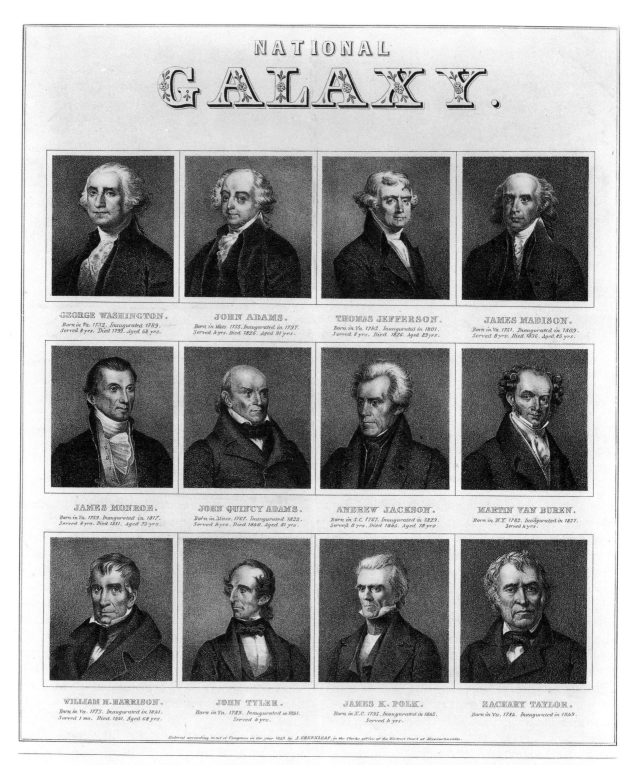

Figure 2–46. *National Galaxy.* Lithograph, 16½ x 13 inches. Published by J. Greenleaf, [Boston], 1849. Library of Congress.

Figure 2–47. Presidents of the United States with Martha Washington. Engraving, 12 x 9½ inches, by Nathaniel Dearborn. Published by N. Dearborn and Son, Boston, circa 1840. New-York Historical Society.

Figure 2–48. *Presidents of the United States.* Lithograph, 16 x 22 inches. Published by E. B. and E. C. Kellogg, Hartford, Connecticut, circa 1842. New-York Historical Society.

print is pleasing, and it may have hung on many a schoolroom wall and in the homes of many Americans.

With the death of Madison in 1836, the nation bade farewell to the last of the first five presidents, whose likenesses Gilbert Stuart and his many imitators had long since enshrined for posterity. Monroe had died five years before Madison, and upon the latter's death the *National Intelligencer* reminded Americans that now "the last of the great lights of the Revolution . . . has sunk below the horizon."[84] Accustomed to mourning former presidents who died in the twilight of long lives, Americans were unprepared for the sudden death of William Henry Harrison on April 4, 1841, one month after he took the oath of office as the ninth president of the United States.

Because Harrison was the first president to die in office, his death produced the greatest display of public mourning since Washington's demise four decades earlier. The mourning, though, was as much out of respect for the presidency as for the man. Not in office long enough to establish an image as president, candidate Harrison of the Log Cabin campaign of 1840 had not been revered by all Americans. But the mantle of the presidency had quickly enveloped the man, and mourning for the departed president swept through the land. At age sixty-eight Harrison had been the oldest president to take office, but he had conducted a vigorous campaign for election, and his death so soon after his inauguration shocked the nation. It was the more unsettling because the country had never faced such a test of presidential succession.

More iconographic evidence of the mourning for Harrison survives than for the death of any president since Washington. The extent of the public mourning can be seen in the numer-

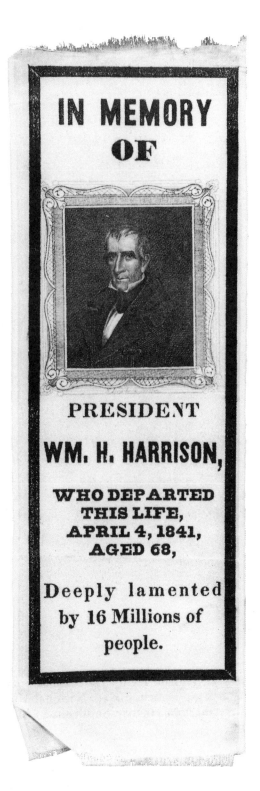

Figure 2–49. William Henry Harrison memorial ribbon, 8 x 3 inches, with eagle pin. National Museum of American History, Smithsonian Institution.

Figure 2–50. William Henry Harrison memorial ribbon, 8⁹/₁₆ x 2⁷/₈ inches, 1841. National Museum of American History, Smithsonian Institution.

Figure 2–51. William Henry Harrison campaign ribbon, 6³⁄₈ x 3¹⁄₁₆ inches, 1840. National Museum of American History, Smithsonian Institution.

Figure 2–52. William Henry Harrison memorial ribbon, 6³⁄₄ x 3 inches, 1841. National Museum of American History, Smithsonian Institution.

ous memorial ribbons that survive today. Small satin ribbons to be pinned to coat lapels at times of celebration, mourning, and political campaigning had become increasingly popular in the United States after their introduction to celebrate the visit of Lafayette to the United States in 1824.[85] Ribbons were printed to mourn the deaths of Jefferson and Adams in

1826 (figs. 2–28 and 2–29) and to celebrate the centennial anniversary of Washington's birth in 1832. Ribbons also proliferated in political activities and were never before so ubiquitous as in the presidential election of 1840, which brought William Henry Harrison into the White House. With Harrison's sudden death, ribbons mourning the late president replaced ribbons that a few months earlier had pro-

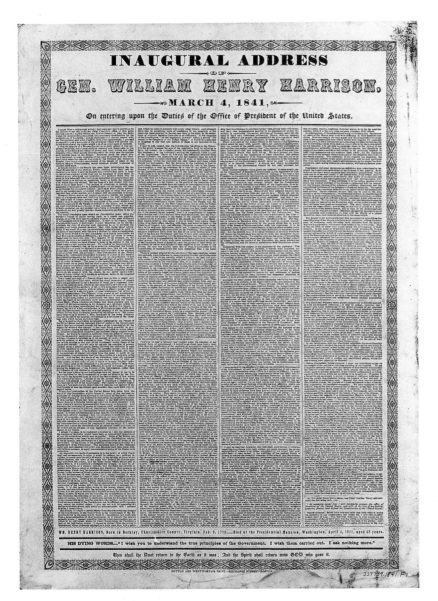

Figure 2–53. *Inaugural Address of Gen. William Henry Harrison, March 4, 1841.* Broadside, 24 x 19¼ inches, printed on silk by Dutton and Wentworth, Boston, 1841. National Museum of American History, Smithsonian Institution.

moted his election. One ribbon, with black bow and eagle pin still attached, shows the modern viewer how such badges of mourning were worn (fig. 2–49). Many such ribbons contain Harrison's portrait. One adds: "Deeply lamented by 16 Millions of people" (fig. 2–50). A campaign ribbon that had earlier heralded Harrison and Tyler as the people's choice (fig. 2–51) was transformed into a mourning ribbon proclaiming, "In Memory of Departed Worth" (fig. 2–52). Harrison's portrait, elaborately embellished with flags, arms, and the national eagle holding a laurel wreath above his head, is unaltered. Several ribbons record Harrison's reported dying words:

"*Sir,*—I wish you to understand the true principles of the Government. I wish them carried out. I ask nothing more."

Other memorial tributes also included Harrison's last words. A silk broadside of his inaugural address, printed in Boston, displays the words in heavy type at the bottom of the print (fig. 2–53). The *Boston Evening Transcript* of May 22, 1841, carried a notice advertising: "General Harrison's Inaugural Address. A New Edition, splendidly printed in crimson gold on a fine card, and on satin, is this day published by Dutton and Wentworth. Persons desirous of preserving a copy of this splendid production for framing can procure them at

Figure 2–54. *William Henry Harrison*. Engraving, 19 x 15 inches, by Oliver Pelton and Denison Kimberly, from a portrait by Albert Gallatin Hoit. Published by Charles A. Wakefield, Boston, 1841. Virginia Historical Society.

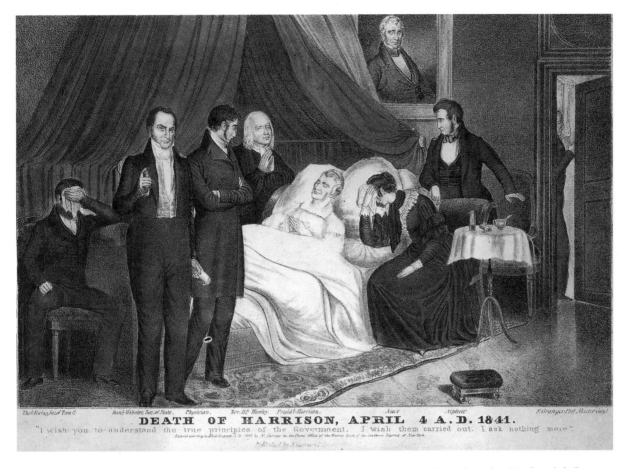

DEATH OF HARRISON, APRIL 4 A.D. 1841.

"I wish you to understand the true principles of the Government. I wish them carried out. I ask nothing more".

Figure 2–55. *Death of Harrison, April 4 A.D. 1841*. Lithograph, 8⁷⁄₁₆ x 12⁷⁄₈ inches, by Nathaniel Currier, New York, 1841. National Portrait Gallery, Smithsonian Institution. *Left to right:* Thomas Ewing, Daniel Webster, physician, the Rev. Dr. Hawley, a niece, a nephew, Francis Granger.

the Transcript Counting Room."

Harrison's dying words can also be found on an impressive portrait print engraved by Oliver Pelton and Denison Kimberly, published in Boston (fig. 2–54). The engraving, taken from a portrait by Albert Gallatin Hoit painted in 1840, is framed by a border more representative of Harrison's military career than the presidential office, except for the Capitol and the White House pictured in the lower corners.[86] Under his portrait a picture of Harrison's home in North Bend, Ohio, more accurately depicts the environs in which he had lived than the log cabin that had adorned so much recent campaign literature. A notice of the publication of the print in the *Boston Evening Transcript* praised the portrait as the best taken of Harrison, reporting, "The likeness is pronounced by those who have seen him often, in various aspects and positions, faultless, and is

the only portrait where the true lineaments of the likeness and figure are true to life." Noting that the steel engraving was being sold for "the moderate price of one dollar," the announcement concluded that the print "should adorn the parlor of every true man, who mourns the loss of a sage, a statesman, and a Father to the great American family."[87]

At least two popular prints portrayed the scene at President Harrison's deathbed. Nathaniel Currier, who three months before Harrison's unexpected death had published a popular lithograph of an imaginary drawing of Washington's deathbed, offered a similar depiction of Harrison's death. Currier's *Death of Harrison, April 4 A.D. 1841* (fig. 2–55) appeared five weeks after the president's death.[88] In Harrison's bedroom, where his portrait hangs above his bed, Currier pictured more cabinet officers than members of his family. At Harri-

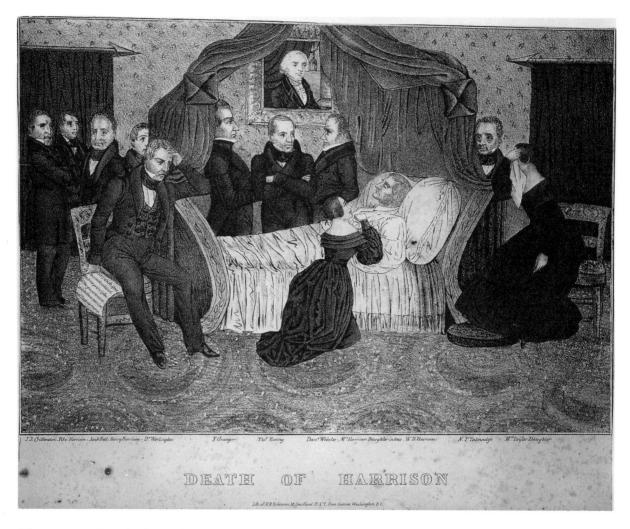

Figure 2–56. *Death of Harrison*. Lithograph, 9 x 13³⁄₁₆ inches, by Henry R. Robinson, New York, 1841. National Portrait Gallery, Smithsonian Institution. *Left to right:* John J. Crittenden, Pike Harrison, John Bell, Henry Harrison, Dr. N. W. Worthington, Francis Granger, Thomas Ewing, Daniel Webster, Mrs. Harrison (daughter-in-law), Nathaniel P. Tallmadge, Mrs. Anne Harrison Taylor (daughter).

son's bedside, Currier identified Treasury Secretary Thomas Ewing and Secretary of State Daniel Webster, while Postmaster General Francis Granger is shown at the door. Only a niece and a nephew represent the president's family in a scene transformed into an official event. Henry R. Robinson published a similar deathbed scene, though he imagined a room more crowded with both political figures and family members (fig. 2–56). Ewing, Webster, and Granger are the only figures who appear in both of the prints. Instead of Harrison's portrait as displayed in Currier's print, Robinson depicted a portrait of Washington above Har-

rison's bed. Currier's *Death of Harrison* exhibits many similarities to *Mort du Général Lafayette* (published in France at the time of Lafayette's death in 1834), a print in which Lafayette's deathbed is surrounded by military officers in full-dress uniform and the general's picture hangs prominently on the wall.[89]

So stylized had the presidential deathbed print become by 1850 that Nathaniel Currier published a lithograph of Zachary Taylor's deathbed only nine days after President Taylor's sudden death on July 9, 1850 (fig. 2–57).[90] The room is crowded with members of his cabinet—far outnumbering family members—

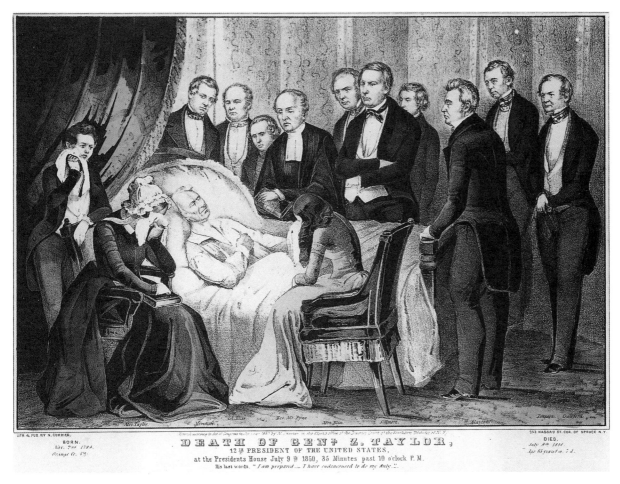

Figure 2–57. *Death of Genl. Z. Taylor, 12th President of the United States.* Lithograph, 8¼ x 12¹⁄₁₆ inches, by Nathaniel Currier, New York, 1850. National Portrait Gallery, Smithsonian Institution. *Left to right:* son, Mrs. Taylor, William M. Meredith, William Bliss, unidentified, the Rev. Mr. Smith Pyne, Mrs. William Bliss (daughter), Jacob Collamer, Millard Fillmore, William B. Preston, John M. Clayton, Reverdy Johnson, George W. Crawford.

and Vice-President Millard Fillmore is positioned prominently in the center of the picture. The print reports Taylor's last words as "I am prepared. I have endeavoured to do my duty." A somewhat different version of the same sentiment appears on a decorated ribbon mourning Taylor's death (fig. 2–58).[91]

Between the deaths of Presidents Harrison and Taylor, three former presidents also died: Andrew Jackson in 1845, John Quincy Adams in 1848, and James K. Polk in 1849. After Jackson's death Nathaniel Currier added a Jackson deathbed print to his list of popular lithographs, and Edward Whaites offered a mourning ribbon (fig. 2–59).[92] Jackson's likeness on the ribbon was taken from an engraving in 1843 by Moseley J. Danforth (fig. 2–60). Although

Danforth's engraving, from a painting by John W. Dodge, was presented as the last likeness of Jackson, the last portrait taken from life was painted by George P. A. Healy shortly before Jackson's death in June 1845.[93]

An unusual Jackson memorial print was published by Charles Phillips in New York in 1845 (fig. 2–61). The lithograph offers small portraits showing Jackson at the ages of forty-nine and seventy-eight years. The younger Napoleonic image—from a portrait painted by John Wesley Jarvis in 1819 and engraved by Phillips in 1842—presents Jackson in military uniform with military embellishments and a view of the battle of New Orleans.[94] The older likeness—based on the portrait by Dodge engraved by Danforth—pictures Jackson in re-

Figure 2–58. Zachary Taylor memorial ribbon, 8⅛ x 3¹⁵⁄₁₆ inches, 1850. National Museum of American History, Smithsonian Institution.

Figure 2–59. **Andrew Jackson memorial ribbon, 8¹⁄₁₆ x 3 inches, 1845. National Museum of American History, Smithsonian Institution.**

Figure 2–60. *Andrew Jackson.* **Engraving, 10³⁄₈ x 8⅛ inches, by Moseley J. Danforth after John W. Dodge, New York, 1843. National Portrait Gallery, Smithsonian Institution.**

tirement supported by the plenty of the land. Connecting the two portraits, the national eagle holds the banner "The Union Must and Shall Be Preserved," symbolizing Jackson's presidency. According to the notable events of his life listed on the print, Jackson was to be remembered also for his veto of the bank bill and his issuance of the proclamation against nullification.

The death of John Quincy Adams—who was felled by a stroke on the floor of the House of Representatives—attracted unsurpassed attention. Writing after attending the service for his father in the chamber of the House, Charles Francis Adams declared that the ceremonies were "as great a pageant as was ever conducted in the United States."[95] Lithographs of the scene of Adams's collapse in the House and of his deathbed soon appeared. A memorial rib-

Figure 2–61. Andrew Jackson memorial print. Lithograph, 13⅛ x 10 inches. Published by Charles Phillips, New York, 1845. Library of Congress.

bon (fig. 2–62) published by Edward Whaites of New York presents Adams's likeness derived from a daguerreotype by Philip Hass, made about 1843 or 1844.[96]

Following a half-century during which only eight men served as president, five men took the oath of office within a ten-year period from 1841 through 1850. The deaths of two presidents and the competitive state of the political parties resulted in no president serving a second term in either the 1840s or the 1850s. One consequence of the rapid succession of presidents was that the enshrinement of individual presidents was less pronounced than it had been earlier. As the 1850s unfolded, the nation's concern was greater for the future preservation of the Union than for the preservation of its past. Still, even amid the growing, threatening sectional tensions and the faltering leadership of Millard Fillmore, Franklin Pierce, and James

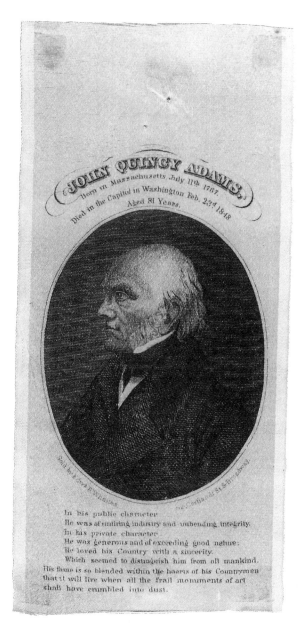

Figure 2–62. John Quincy Adams memorial ribbon, 5³⁄₁₆ x 2⅞ inches, 1848. National Museum of American History, Smithsonian Institution.

Buchanan, popular interest in the presidency seemed undiminished.

The "Group of Portraits of the Presidents of the United States," which appeared in *Gleason's Pictorial Drawing-Room Companion*, June 11, 1853, early in Pierce's presidency, provides striking evidence of the persistence of the tradition of the collective glorification of the presidency (fig. 2–63). The portrait of Washington—in-

GROUP OF PORTRAITS OF THE PRESIDENTS OF THE UNITED STATES

Figure 2–63. "Group of Portraits of the Presidents of the United States." *Gleason's Pictorial Drawing-Room Companion*, June 11, 1853. Ellis Library, University of Missouri–Columbia.

FAMILY MONUMENT

Figure 2–64. *Family Monument from the History of Our Country.* **Engraving, 25½ x 33⅜ inches, by J. M. Enzing-Miller, New York, 1858. New-York Historical Society.**

creasingly employed as sectional divisions intensified—shares the presidential honors with his successors, the responsibilities of the office now falling on Frank Pierce in the foreground of the print. Stars for each of the states arch over the portraits, reaffirming the identification of the presidency with the Union and reminding viewers of that heritage.

Iconographically, the most interesting example of the enshrinement of the presidency is a little-known work by J. M. Enzing-Miller published in New York in 1858 (fig. 2–64). Entitled *Family Monument from the History of Our Country,* the scene was both painted and engraved by Enzing-Miller, a German immigrant who had exhibited work in the American Art-Union Exhibition of 1848.[97] The large engrav-

ing—more than twenty-five inches high and over thirty-three inches wide—was deposited for copyright April 15, 1858, in the Southern District Court of New York.[98]

A complex and symbolically elaborate work, the historical record of America begins with the Norsemen in Vinland shown in the lower right corner, where the date 1000 is inscribed on a rock. The landing of Columbus is prominently displayed on the left. In the center Capt. John Smith strikes a commanding pose, the date 1607 scratched in the ground beside him. Nearby, a settler's family is highlighted. In the foreground, from a boat near Columbus a black slave in chains is about to be brought ashore, while just above in another scene the Pilgrims are landing at Plymouth, the date 1620 etched above them. Battle scenes of the

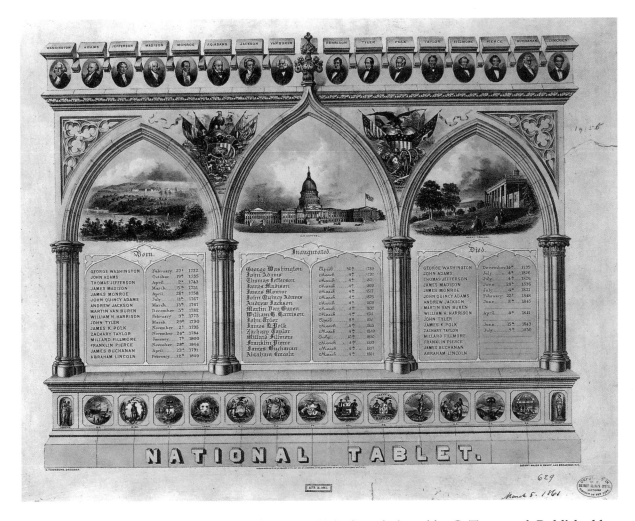

Figure 2–65. *National Tablet.* Lithograph, 24 x 29¾ inches, designed by C. Townsend. Published by Sarony, Major, and Knapp, New York, 1861. Library of Congress.

Revolutionary War fill the background on the right. On the left, the artist depicted the progress of the United States by the mid-nineteenth century with telegraph poles, trains, ships, and an imposing bridge offering a peaceful contrast to the destruction of war. A giant American flag with thirty-one stars waves above the scene, which also includes a public speaker addressing a large crowd of people (not discernible in a reduced reproduction).

A theme of progress pervades the painting. There are weapons of conquest and war, but signs of peaceful activity prevail. An ax, a shovel, and other implements, boats and trains, and also books define an active people. Dominating the center of the picture, a huge rock—the arms of the states carved in its sides—provides a firm foundation supporting

the presidents of the United States. At the base of the monument the artist depicted the national eagle slaying a unicorn that had already killed a lion. The theme of the lion and the unicorn in conflict had been a pattern in art for twenty-five hundred years.[99] In picturing the American eagle as triumphant over both these powerful symbols, the artist assigned to the American republic a mighty presence, more visionary than established, but nonetheless powerful.

On the top of the rock, the artist drew the image of each president carefully enough to present recognizable figures from Washington through Fillmore, indicating that the painting was completed between 1850 and 1853, although the engraving was not published until 1858. With the Capitol behind them, the presidents are pictured standing in a line behind Washington, who with one hand on his heart and the other on the Constitution affirms his oath to defend and support that document. A flag with thirteen stars waves above the altarlike lectern upon which the Constitution rests. Below, a goddess holds the Declaration of Independence, while Liberty and Justice guard the scene from above. The most cherished icons of the Republic thus surround the presidents of the United States at the pinnacle of the national monument.

No more graphic celebration of the institution of the presidency has been found than this remarkable work by a recent immigrant to America. Enzing-Miller sensed the strong presence of the presidency in the American society and in a sweeping visual history of the country recorded a reflection of the enshrinement of the presidency. At the same time, the artist's depiction of the long line of presidents behind Washington, trailing off into the future and implying a steady procession of successors to follow in Washington's footsteps, was an overly optimistic representation of reality in the context of the 1850s. That artistic vision suggested a national cohesiveness that the political climate of the times did not substantiate.

One of the last presidential prints to appear before the Civil War pictures a monumentlike shrine entitled *National Tablet* (fig. 2–65). De-signed by C. Townsend and published by Sarony, Major, and Knapp, leading New York lithographers, the large poster was deposited for copyright on March 5, 1861, the day after Lincoln's inauguration, and stamped as received by the Department of State on April 15, 1861, the day on which Lincoln issued his call to arms and three days after the firing on Fort Sumter. The design presents a triple-arched stone monument built on a foundation of the thirteen original states with cornerstones of Liberty and Justice. The cornice above the arches displays the portraits of all the presidents from Washington through Lincoln. Within the arches, scenes of West Point, the United States Capitol, and Washington's home at Mount Vernon adorn tablets inscribed with the names of the presidents, their birth dates, inauguration dates, and, for deceased presidents, dates of death. Between the arches, two contrasting representations of the national eagle present "Emblems of Peace" and "Emblems of War."

The *National Tablet* reminded Americans that the heritage of the presidency—now threatened as never before—was an edifice worthy of preservation. Presidents from both North and South were enshrined in the monument built over a period of seventy-two years. Four years of civil war would gravely imperil, but fail to destroy, the shrine.

Plate 3. *George Washington*. Oil on canvas, 92 x 62 inches, by John Vanderlyn. Commissioned by Congress in 1832 and now in the chamber of the House of Representatives. Architect of the Capitol.

Plate 4. The Declaration of Independence, with portraits of George Washington, John Adams, and Thomas Jefferson. Printed cotton textile, 32 x 27 inches, circa 1820–1825. The Boston Tea Party is depicted at the lower left and the surrender of Burgoyne at Saratoga at the lower right. American Antiquarian Society.

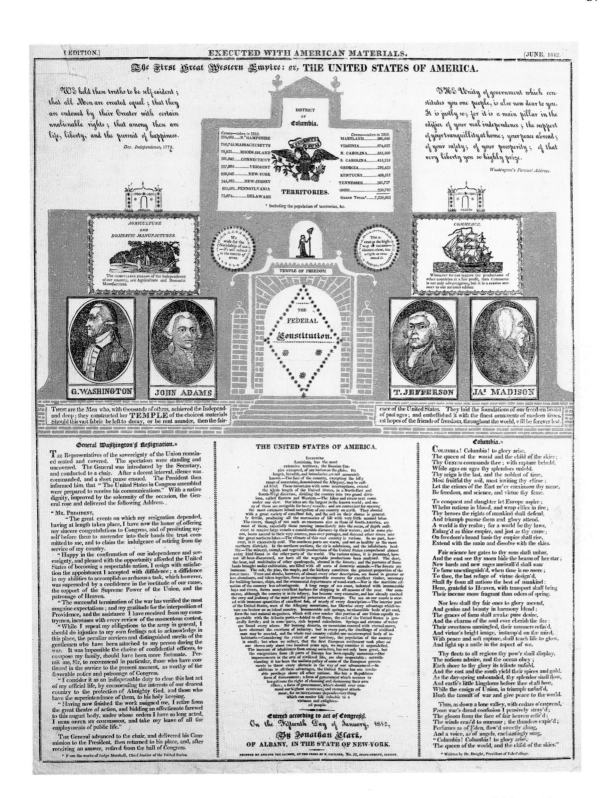

Plate 5. *The First Great Western Empire: or, The United States of America*. Broadside, 20½ x 16½ inches. Published by Jonathan Clark; printed by R. Packard, Albany, New York, 1812. Block print in red and black ink. Henry Francis du Pont Winterthur Museum.

88

Plate 6. *Thomas Jefferson*. Oil on panel, 26⅛ x 21 inches, by Gilbert Stuart, 1805. Owned jointly by the National Portrait Gallery, Smithsonian Institution, and the Thomas Jefferson Memorial Foundation, Monticello. Gift of Regents of the Smithsonian Institution, Thomas Jefferson Memorial Foundation, and Enid and Crosby Kemper Foundation.

Figure 3–2. *Declaration of Independence*. Engraving, 33½ x 14 inches, by George Murray and James Barton Longacre. Published by John Binns, Philadelphia, November 1819. Portraits of Washington, Jefferson, and John Hancock. National Portrait Gallery, Smithsonian Institution.

Figure 3–3. *The Old House of Representatives*. Oil on canvas, 86½ x 130¾ inches, by Samuel F. B. Morse, 1822. The Corcoran Gallery of Art, Museum Purchase.

portraits. He did promise to provide exact facsimiles of the signatures of the signers taken from the original document in the Department of State. Tyler's unadorned print appeared in April 1818.[7]

Before Binns completed his more elaborate print, he also faced competition from William Woodruff, a Philadelphia engraver, who on February 20, 1819, published a folio sheet containing the Declaration of Independence with engraved (but not facsimile) signatures of the signers, encircled by sixteen medallions containing the arms of the thirteen original states and portraits of Washington, Jefferson, and Adams (fig. 3–1). Inferior in execution to Binns's later print (fig. 3–2), which finally appeared in November 1819,[8] Woodruff's engraving was smaller but very similar in design. The resemblance was so striking, in fact, as to give credence to the charge that the print was clandestinely copied by a workman in the school of one of the artists working on Binns's print.[9] The superior artistic merits of Binns's print

were evident when it appeared. George Murray had put considerable effort into engraving the arms of the thirteen original states from drawings by Thomas Sully, and James Barton Longacre had been engaged to engrave the portraits of Washington (after Gilbert Stuart), Hancock (after John Singleton Copley), and Jefferson (after Bass Otis).[10] In contrast, the work on Woodruff's plate was undistinguished in the engraving of both the arms of the states and the portraits.

Binns's print was well received, and he took pleasure in reprinting reviews of the work from other newspapers in his *Democratic Press*. The *Baltimore Federal Gazette* pronounced it "incomparably, the most gratifying evidence of the rapid progress of our countrymen in the fine arts, which we have ever seen." The *New York National Advocate* extolled the design and execution as "the most truly splendid thing ever produced in America."[11] Without the access to the press attention that Binns directed to his own print, Woodruff's engraving was

Plate 7. Porcelain urn, 17½ inches high, with portrait of John Adams after figure 2–23. Produced by the National Manufactory of Sèvres, circa 1828. Private collection.

Plate 8. Porcelain urn, 17½ inches high, with portrait of Thomas Jefferson after figure 2–24. Produced by the National Manufactory of Sèvres, circa 1828. Private collection.

Plate 9. *Andrew Jackson*. Oil on canvas, 126 x 93 inches, by Ralph E. W. Earl, 1837. National Museum of American Art, Smithsonian Institution.

CHAPTER III

The Presidency and the Declaration of Independence

O N FEBRUARY 1813 William P. Gardner, whom President Jefferson had once named to a consulship in the Dutch colony of Demerara, wrote the retired president about his plan to publish a print of the Declaration of Independence. "I have often thought that it should occupy a conspicuous place in the Parlour of every man who feels an attachment to the Liberty, Independence and Rights of America," he explained in enclosing a sketch by John James Barralet of the ornamental features that were to adorn and frame a facsimile of the text. The engraving was to be prepared by George Murray, a skilled Philadelphia engraver, who had agreed to publish the print in partnership with Gardner.[1]

Responding to Gardner's request for comments on the design, Jefferson suggested that John Hancock, as president of the Congress, should "occupy the middle and principal place" and that John Adams ought to "hold a most conspicuous place in the design."[2] Because Barralet's sketch has not survived, it is not known what portraits he proposed to employ to adorn the print, though it may be conjectured that Washington and Jefferson were among them. Jefferson's extended arguments for including Adams suggest that Barralet may not have projected a portrait of that member of the drafting committee.

Gardner sent Barralet's design along with a copy of Jefferson's letter to George Murray to

prepare the engraving. But Gardner heard nothing of Murray's plans until 1816, when he saw a proposal by John Binns, editor of the *Democratic Press* in Philadelphia, to publish a "Splendid Edition" of the Declaration of Independence to be engraved by Murray.[3] Binns projected a "truly national publication." All materials were to be manufactured in the United States, and all designs and engraving were to be the work of American artists, providing a specimen of the state of the fine arts in the United States. As embellishments on the print, he promised medallion portraits of Washington, Hancock, and Jefferson and medallions containing the arms of the thirteen original states.[4] In reporting Binns's announcement, the *Port Folio* of Philadelphia took special note of the promise that the print was to be "ornamented with medallion portraits, engraved in the best style, by American artists."[5]

Although three and a half years passed before Binns published the promised print (fig. 3–2), he claimed to be the first to propose such a publication and sought to discredit all competition.[6] That included Benjamin Owen Tyler, who in February 1818 announced plans to publish the text of the Declaration of Independence to be engraved by Peter Maverick. Having discussed his project with Gardner, Tyler gave Gardner credit for the first proposal and did not plan to ornament his own print with

ed in the press. Yet, a superior print was me to have greater design between the uff employed a por-e of John Hancock. nown and may have reater availability of ould have been be-n publicly criticized n his projected work. ishing his unorna-Declaration of Inde-mbellishments to the nnecessary, but at the ns for not including miniature likenesses rtisan politics.[12] For ck lost out to Adams he had earlier lost out to become Washing-hen Adams's image ton and Jefferson at ion of Independence, emerged. These men t in the drafting and instrument, but they e presidents of the

esentatives displayed ive work in handsome r the fireplaces at the When Samuel F. B. -famous scene of the s in 1822 (fig. 3–3), he the print prominently –4). Copies of Binns's ver the preserved fire-f the House of Repre-o doubt members of Hancock, president of ss, an appropriate fig-; with Washington, Jef-tion of Independence; r the choice of all those uality of the engraving. placed Washington, s the progenitors, ration of Independence st widely adopted for s. The cost of Binns's

Figure 3–4. Detail of *The Old House of Representatives* (fig. 3–3). The Corcoran Gallery of Art, Museum Purchase.

print at ten dollars may have played some part in limiting its circulation. The *New York Columbian*, indeed, offered the opinion that "this truly beautiful engraving will meet the patronage of our wealthy citizens."[13] For whatever reasons, the prints of the Declaration of Independence that most widely appeared before the public bore the images of the first three presidents and claimed for the presidency an identification with that cherished document never to be relinquished. It is not known which of the several reproductions of the Declaration of Independence Garrett Sickles, a master shoemaker in New York City, had on the wall of his home, but when he died in 1822 he left in his estate a gilt-edged framed print of the Declaration of Independence.[14]

Copies of the Declaration of Independence ornamented with images of Washington, Adams, and Jefferson appeared not only on prints to be hung on parlor walls and in public buildings but also on brightly colored silk and cotton scarves. A variation of Woodruff's plate was printed on silk (fig. 3–6), and similar designs appeared on a number of popular textile

Figure 3–5. John Binns's print of the *Declaration of Independence* in the old House of Representatives, United States Capitol. United States Senate Historical Office.

pieces (fig. 3–7 and plate 4). These prints popularized the design of the Declaration of Independence encircled by the arms of the thirteen states and the portraits of Washington, Adams, and Jefferson. With the national eagle hovering over the head of Washington, Jefferson on his right and Adams on his left, the images of the three statesmen catch the viewer's eye and dominate the prints. In the style of Binns's design, Woodruff's print and its derivatives employ banners and cornucopias supporting Washington's portrait, but the sword beneath Washington's portrait in Binns's print is not

found in Woodruff's or its popular derivatives. Although Washington's portrait is slightly larger than the other two, the omission of any special symbol of military command leaves the image of the statesman prevailing. Washington, Adams, and Jefferson could be seen as claimants to a common fame as presidents of the new nation that the Declaration of Independence had proclaimed.

Once the first three presidents were enshrined with the Declaration of Independence, that place of honor and the association with that sacrosanct instrument were not to be de-

1. *Declaration of Independence.* Engraving, 26⅞ x 18¹³⁄₁₆ inches, by William Woodruff. d in Philadelphia, dated February 20, 1819. Portraits of Washington, John Adams, and McAlpin Collection, New York Public Library, Astor, Lenox and Tilden Foundations.

Figure 3–6. Declaration of Independence. Silk textile, 28¼ x 21⅛ inches, from engraving by William Woodruff. Printed by H. Brunet and Company, Lyon, France, circa 1820. New-York Historical Society.

Figure 3–7. Declaration of Independence. Silk textile, 28 x 27½ inches, circa 1820. Portraits of Washington, John Adams, and Jefferson. New-York Historical Society.

nied to later presidents. Each new president joined the ranks that tied him to the founding of the nation. As time passed, the identification of the presidency with the Declaration of Independence grew until it came to be one of the preeminent symbols with which that high office was popularly portrayed.

By the late 1830s, prints of the Declaration of Independence were adorned with Washington's portrait and those of each of his successors in the presidential office. George G.

Smith, of Boston, engraved and published a print with Martin Van Buren, then in office, and Andrew Jackson, the most recent former president, anchoring a gallery of eight presidential portraits (fig. 3–8). In the style of earlier prints, the presidential likenesses are joined with the arms of the original states in a chain framing the text of the Declaration. When additional presidents joined the ranks, Smith updated his plate. By the end of the 1840s, the portraits of twelve presidents crowded the

Figure 3–8. *Declaration of Independence*. Print, 12 x 9½ inches, engraved and published by George G. Smith, Boston, circa 1837–1840. Portraits of Presidents Washington through Van Buren. New-York Historical Society.

Figure 3–9. *Declaration of Independence.* Later state of figure 3–8, circa 1849–1850. Portraits of Presidents Washington through Taylor. American Philosophical Society.

Figure 3–8. *Declaration of Independence*. Print, 12 x 9½ inches, engraved and published by George G. Smith, Boston, circa 1837–1840. Portraits of Presidents Washington through Van Buren. New-York Historical Society.

Figure 3–9. *Declaration of Independence.* Later state of figure 3–8, circa 1849–1850. Portraits of Presidents Washington through Taylor. American Philosophical Society.

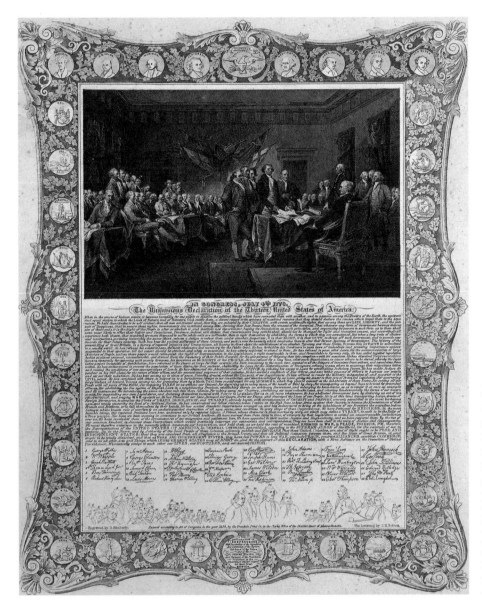

Figure 3–10. *The Declaration of Independence.* Engraving, 12 x 10¼ inches, with etching of John Trumbull's depiction of the signing, engraved by Denison Kimberly. Published by Franklin Print Company, Boston, 1838. Harvey D. Parker Collection, Museum of Fine Arts, Boston.

print (fig. 3–9).[15] The portraits in Smith's engravings are of better quality than those in Woodruff's early print or its popular derivatives.

As designs expanded, another icon joined the text of the Declaration of Independence and the portraits of the presidents: a reproduction of John Trumbull's painting of the signing of the famous document. A large replica painted for the rotunda of the United States Capitol in 1818 and an engraving of the original painting completed by Asher Brown Durand in 1823 brought increasing public attention to the painting in whose design Jefferson himself years earlier had assisted the artist.[16] An etch-ing of Trumbull's work shares equal space with the text of the Declaration of Independence in a print published by the Franklin Print Company of Boston in 1838 (fig. 3–10). Although Trumbull's scene dominates the print, medallion images of all the presidents claim places in the top border, and the arms of the states fill the other borders. The interesting print, which follows a popular scheme of identifying the persons in the painting, appears to have been widely available. It could be purchased in Washington at Farnham's Bookstore on Pennsylvania Avenue a few blocks from the White House.[17] If Trumbull's painting overshadows the presidents in this print, a second state,

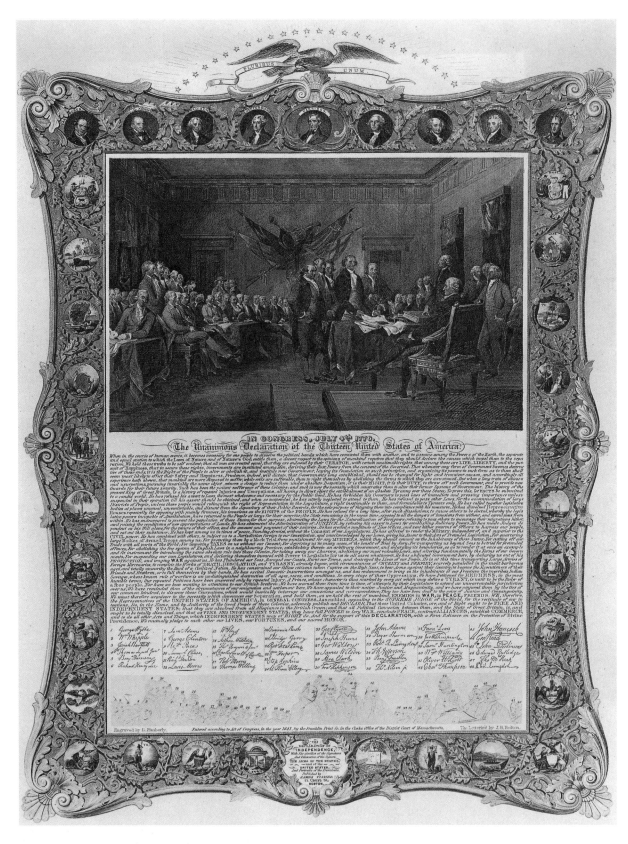

Figure 3–11. *The Declaration of Independence.* Second state of figure 3–10. Published by James Fisher, Boston, 1841. Harvey D. Parker Collection, Museum of Fine Arts, Boston.

Figure 3–12. *The Presidents of the United States*. Lithograph, 29¾ x 50¾ inches. Published by E. B. and E. C. Kellogg, Hartford, 1846. Library of Congress.

which appeared in 1841, restored the presidential portraits to their accustomed prominence (fig. 3–11). The crude medallions of the 1838 print were replaced with carefully engraved miniature portraits. President William Henry Harrison's portrait in the center at the top may indicate that the print was published in connection with his inauguration. In this revised version the national emblem also was given more prominence. The eagle with the banner "E Pluribus Unum" looms over the frame, and a star for each of the twenty-six states helps to tie together the presidents, the Declaration of Independence, and the Union.

By the mid–1840s portraits of the presidents had come to dominate prints of both the text of the Declaration of Independence and Trumbull's painting of the signing. With the increasing popularity of lithography, large posters popularized for the masses the historical roster

of the presidents and their continuing symbolic association with the Declaration of 1776. In 1846 a lithograph published on a sheet over four feet wide and two and a half feet high by the Hartford, Connecticut, firm of E. B. and E. C. Kellogg—a major publisher of popular lithographs—presented the portraits of all the presidents through Polk, who was then in office (fig. 3–12). In the center of the print figures of Justice and Liberty flank a copy of Trumbull's painting. Below, a roster of the presidents lists their life dates and inauguration dates. The lithograph's large size suggests a work designed for display on the wall of a public building or schoolroom.

Somewhat smaller, but still posterlike, is a more popularized version in the same genre published by Phelps, Ensigns, and Thayer in New York in 1846 (plate 12). The large lettering presenting the "Presidents of the United

Figure 3–13. *The Presidents of
the United States.* Litho-
graph, 12⅜ x 9⅜ inches.
Published by James Baillie,
New York, 1844. American
Antiquarian Society.

States," together with brief biographical
sketches and portraits of each president, leaves
no doubt as to the principal subject of the
print. But the positioning of the crudely drawn
copy of Trumbull's work in the center of the
design is symbolically important, visually associating the presidency with independence and
the founding of the nation. The presidential
portraits in this lithograph are also crudely
drawn, and the partial hand-coloring was
quickly applied, indicating an inexpensive production for a mass market.[18]

Nathaniel Currier, who pioneered in the
publication of popular lithographs containing
portraits of all the presidents, also included
Trumbull's scene of the signing of the Declara-

tion on some of his prints (plate 15). Currier's
imitators and competitors did likewise.
Among them was James Baillie of New York,
whose similar print (fig. 3–13) is more crudely
drawn than Currier's and lacks the patriotic
embellishments of waving flags that adorn
Currier's design.[19]

The earlier, more elaborate, and technically
more demanding prints that depict all the presidents, along with Trumbull's painting and the
text of the Declaration of Independence, still
continued to be designed and published. Louis
R. Menger, a New York publisher, released an
elaborate lithograph by J. Britton in 1849 titled
*The Presidents of the United States and Declara-
tion of Independence* (fig. 3–14). The presidents

Figure 3–14. *The Presidents of the United States and Declaration of Independence*. Lithograph, 43 x 33 inches, by J. Britton. Published by Louis R. Menger, New York, 1849. Library of Congress.

Figure 3–15. *The Declaration of Independence and Portraits of the Presidents.* Engraving, 19³/₁₆ x 14½ inches, engraved and printed by Illman and Sons, Philadelphia, circa 1857–1860. Historical Society of Pennsylvania.

Figure 3–16. *The Declaration of Independence and Portraits of the Presidents.* Second state of figure 3–15, [1861]. Library of Congress.

take precedence in the title and are dominant in the print, but the basic design reaches back to the early prints of the Declaration of Independence. The text of the Declaration is encircled by the seals of the states, as in the early prints, and by a larger border of portraits of all the presidents, including the recently inaugurated Zachary Taylor. Trumbull's scene of the signing is reduced in size but clearly discernible on the large poster, which measures three feet seven inches high and two feet nine inches wide. Little space on the print is left unembellished. Figures of Justice and Liberty support the title design, while the national eagle guards the ring of states beneath Washington's portrait. Drawings of the Capitol and the White House decorate the lower corners of the crowded print, and even portraits of a few vice-presidents fill unused space in the border.[20] With the number of states more than double the original thirteen and the roster of presidents numbering twelve, the presidency was firmly enshrined with the Declaration of Independence, shared its symbolic importance, and represented a cordon of protection for the nation's independence and its union.

That cordon appeared to be broken in an elaborate engraved print published by Illman and Sons in Philadelphia while James Buchanan was president (fig. 3–15). The border around the Declaration of Independence is di-vided with portraits of Pierce and Buchanan placed toward the corners of the print, and a vignette of Washington's tomb at Mount Vernon appears beneath the Declaration of Independence. Like some prescient warning that a leader was required to bridge the widening gap that threatened the Union, the print symbolically leaves the Declaration of Independence vulnerable and endangered. In a later state of the print (fig. 3–16), published after Lincoln's election, a portrait of the president-elect is placed in the gap, not quite filling it and leaving unanswered the question of whether the traditions of the presidency that reached back to Washington and the Declaration of Independence would be strong enough to form an unbreakable chain. We have no way of knowing whether such symbolism lurked in the mind of the designer or engraver, but the design portended the tragic years that lay ahead for the nation. We now know that the Union and the presidency survived those years of civil war, and the presidency again became a symbol uniting the states and protecting their common independence. That success was rooted in the values that the visual representations of the presidency reflected and reinforced. Deeply embedded in American political culture was an inseparable association of the presidency with the national independence and union that the Declaration of 1776 begot and nurtured.

CHAPTER IV

The Presidency and the Union

ROM THE beginning of the new republic under the Constitution the presidency served as a unifying force and a symbol of union binding together thirteen recently independent states. George Washington, the leading embodiment of unity during the American Revolution, was uniquely fitted to be the first president, and his unanimous election enabled him to serve, as no other man could have done so well, as the symbol of union. Contemporary artists sensed this crucial role of the presidency and provided visual images that revealed and shaped perceptions of the president as the champion of the Union.

One of the earliest and most politically significant prints to greet the new government under the Constitution and the first president was a large and ambitious engraving published in 1789 by Amos Doolittle of New Haven, Connecticut (fig. 4–1). Entitled *A Display of the United States of America*, the design presents as the central focal point a portrait of President Washington, hailed as "The Protector of his COUNTRY, and the Supporter of the rights of MANKIND." Doolittle, who in another print depicted the scene of Washington's inauguration in an engraving of Federal Hall (fig. 8–4), here celebrated the newly strengthened Union by surrounding the president's portrait with an interlocking ring of the arms, or seals, of the thirteen states, united above Washington's

head by the arms of the United States. In the links of the chain of states, he inscribed statistics on population and congressional representation. In the upper right corner the recently adopted Constitution was given equal recognition with the declaring of independence noted in the upper left corner of the print.

It was appropriate that Washington the president appeared in civilian dress with no military symbolism adorning the print. The likeness of Washington employed by Doolittle, however, was a poor one, copied from an engraving by James Trenchard published in the *Columbian Magazine* in 1787, and when Doolittle revised the plate he offered a different image (fig. 4–2).[1] The new portrait was taken from a recent profile etching of the president by Joseph Wright (fig. 6–3) and showed Washington in military uniform. Various versions of this image appeared in all subsequent editions of the print, which reached a total of six before the end of Washington's second term.[2] A desire to provide a better likeness rather than to add a military presence to the design appears to have been the reason for the alteration, though Jefferson would later criticize Wright as a portraitist "whose eye was so unhappy as to seize all the ugly features of his subject, and to present them faithfully; while it was entirely insensible to every lineament of beauty."[3] In uniform Washington appears as a more commanding figure, but his identity as president of

Figure 4–1. *A Display of the United States of America.* Engraving, 20½ x 16½ inches, by Amos Doolittle, New Haven, 1790. Inscribed: "To the Patrons of Arts and Sciences, in all parts of the World, this Plate is most respectfully Dedicated by their obedient humble Servants Amos Doolittle and Ebnr. Porter." John Carter Brown Library, Brown University.

Figure 4–2. *A Display of the United States of America.* Engraving, by Amos Doolittle, New Haven, October 1, 1791. Later state of figure 4–1. McAlpin Collection, New York Public Library, Astor, Lenox and Tilden Foundations.

Figure 4–3. *A New Display of the United States*. Engraving, 19 x 15½ inches, by Amos Doolittle, New Haven, August 14, 1799. Library of Congress.

the United States remains predominant. The symbolism of the president as the center of the Union of interlocking states was unaltered. In addition to the new portrait, the print issued in October 1791 offered revised population figures based on the census of 1790 and noted the admission of Vermont to the Union as a state.

After John Adams succeeded Washington as president, Doolittle published *A New Display of the United States* (fig. 4–3). Designing the new plate in the wake of aroused national feelings following the XYZ incident with France, he employed symbolism similar to that of his earlier work. President Adams's portrait—derived from the painting by John Singleton Copley in 1783—occupies the center, surrounded by the arms of all the states sketched on tilelike squares.[4] The arrangement conveys an impression of a union of states cemented together to form a whole around the central block of the presidency. Across the top of the print, the American eagle grasps the banner of defiance to France, "Millions for Our Defence—Not a Cent for Tribute."

While Doolittle's new plate is impressive, the earlier device of an interlocking chain of states more forcefully projected an indissoluble union. That symbolism—earlier employed on continental currency during the Revolution—was also widely used by other artists and designers. Contemporaneously with Doolittle's original *Display of the United States*, the design appeared on inaugural buttons made for Washington's first inauguration.[5] The device also was popular on ornamented pottery pieces produced in Liverpool for the American market (fig. 1–2). One artist associated the presidency with liberty, independence, and union by presenting a portrait of Washington supported by figures of Liberty and Independence along with the American flag, the whole scene being encircled by an unbroken ribbon of states (fig. 4–4).

Later presidents shared similar associations. A print inscribed "Maddison: Liberty, Independence, and the Federal Union" was used as a transfer on an earthenware mug (fig. 4–5) and originally had appeared with Washington's name. The theme of union and unity prevails in the design of a Liverpool pitcher made in 1801, following Jefferson's inauguration as

president (fig. 4–6). The familiar ribbon of states frames his portrait with a border that had surely been used before, for it includes only the first fifteen states, omitting Tennessee, which entered the Union five years before Jefferson's inauguration. Prominently inscribed above the frame is an excerpt from Jefferson's first inaugural address calling for unity: "We are all Republicans—all Federalists."[6]

The frequent symbolic identification of the presidency with the Union can also be seen in representations such as that in a pamphlet publication of Jefferson's inaugural address of March 4, 1801 (fig. 4–7). President Jefferson's unflattering image, based on a portrait by Edward Savage, is embellished with the national emblem and a star for each of the sixteen states, while on the facing title page the national eagle displays the banner "E Pluribus Unum."

The first four presidents are depicted as the builders of a Union worthy to be called the Temple of Freedom in a poster-size broadside published by Jonathan Clark in Albany, New York, in 1812 (plate 5). Entitled *The First Great Western Empire: or, The United States of America*, the patriotic print was copyrighted January 15, 1812, and issued in an eighth edition in colored copies "executed with American materials" in June 1812, the month in which the United States declared war on Great Britain.[7] The Federal Constitution supports the arched entrance to the Temple of Freedom presided over by Liberty, while portraits of Washington and Adams on one side, and Jefferson and Madison on the other, are enshrined within the Temple of Freedom as its architects and builders. The bricks of the foundation of the temple provide the inscription:

> These are the Men who, with thousands of others, achieved the Independence of the United States. They laid the foundations of our freedom broad and deep; they constructed her TEMPLE of the choicest materials of past ages; and embellished it with the finest ornaments of modern times. Should this vast fabric be left to decay, or be rent asunder, then the fairest hopes of the friends of freedom throughout the world will be forever lost.

Prominently displayed along with the presidents of the United States within the walls of the temple are symbols of agriculture, domes-

Figure 4–4. *G. Washington.*
Liverpool pitcher, 7¼ inches
high, circa 1790–1796. Henry
Francis du Pont Winterthur
Museum.

Figure 4–5. *Maddison: Liberty, Independence, and the
Federal Union.* Liverpool
mug, circa 1809–1812. Philadelphia Museum of Art, Bequest of R. Wister Harvey.

Figure 4–6. *Thomas Jefferson:
President of the United States
of America.* Liverpool
pitcher, 7¾ inches high, 1801.
National Museum of Ameri-
can History, Smithsonian Institution.

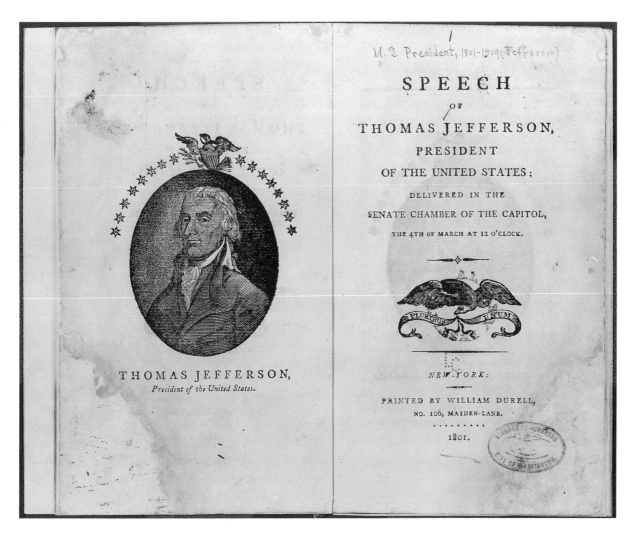

Figure 4–7. Frontispiece and title page of William Durell's printing of Jefferson's first inaugural address, New York, 1801. Library of Congress.

tic manufactures, and commerce. In the temple's tower the arms of the United States guard the roster of the states and territories. Excerpts from the Declaration of Independence and Washington's farewell address fill the corners at the top of the print. Below the temple, the publisher accompanied his own description of the United States with Timothy Dwight's "Columbia" and the words of Washington's address to Congress resigning his commission as commander in chief at the end of the Revolutionary War.

In Clark's print, as in Doolittle's earlier *Displays*, the union of states is basic to the design. Clark provided the population of each state and proudly recorded the grand total of the Union, warning that, should it be rent asunder,

the hopes of freedom throughout the world would be lost forever. Doolittle, with no history of the presidency to draw upon, had featured the portrait of the president then in office as the center of the new Union. Clark, seeing the presidency firmly established under four presidents—each of whom had contributed to the founding of the republic—gave visual interpretation to the institutionalization of the presidency. Employing portraits of the presidents as the most prominent feature of his design, he reinforced public perceptions of the importance of the presidency to the success of the "First Great Western Empire."

In the boldest and most serious challenge to the Union between the adoption of the Consti-

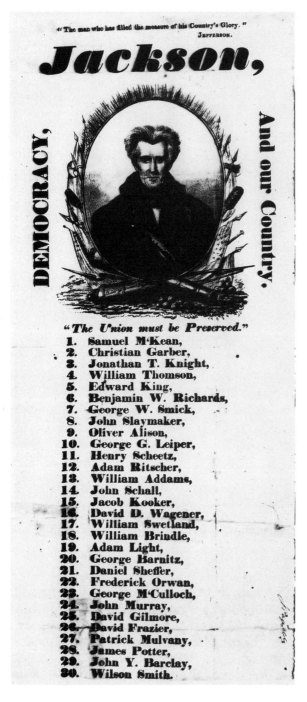

"The man who has filled the measure of his Country's Glory."
JEFFERSON.

Jackson,

DEMOCRACY,

And our Country.

"*The Union must be Preserved.*"

1. **Samuel M'Kean,**
2. **Christian Garber,**
3. **Jonathan T. Knight,**
4. **William Thomson,**
5. **Edward King,**
6. **Benjamin W. Richards,**
7. **George W. Smick,**
8. **John Slaymaker,**
9. **Oliver Alison,**
10. **George G. Leiper,**
11. **Henry Scheetz,**
12. **Adam Ritscher,**
13. **William Addams,**
14. **John Schall,**
15. **Jacob Kooker,**
16. **David D. Wagener,**
17. **William Swetland,**
18. **William Brindle,**
19. **Adam Light,**
20. **George Barnitz,**
21. **Daniel Sheffer,**
22. **Frederick Orwan,**
23. **George M'Culloch,**
24. **John Murray,**
25. **David Gilmore,**
26. **David Frazier,**
27. **Patrick Mulvany,**
28. **James Potter,**
29. **John Y. Barclay,**
30. **Wilson Smith.**

Figure 4–8. Broadside, 15¾ x 6½ inches, from the 1832 presidential campaign. Pennsylvania Democratic electoral slate pledged to Andrew Jackson. This copy was addressed to H. Bachler, Esq., Harrisburg, Dauphin County, Pennsylvania. Tennessee State Library and Archives.

add a new dimension to the iconographic record of the presidency. Jackson chose the occasion of the Democratic party's annual celebration of Jefferson's birthday for a dramatic reaffirmation of the president's role as the protector of the Union. At the dinner at the Indian Queen Hotel in Washington on April 13, 1830, in a room adorned with a full-length portrait of Washington and two bust portraits of Jefferson, President Jackson rose and delivered a toast: "Our Union: It must be preserved." The effect was explosive in the room crowded with members of Congress, cabinet officers, high-ranking military officers, and leading citizens of the city. Secretary of State Martin Van Buren long remembered the "sensation" created in the large assemblage.[8] Jackson's words were soon being quoted throughout the country, and during the presidential election of 1832 the quotation appeared in campaign materials, sometimes with Jackson's likeness. Such a design decorates a ticket containing the names of the Democratic electoral slate pledged to vote for Jackson's reelection in Pennsylvania (fig. 4–8). Framed with the words "Democracy, Jackson, and our Country," the president's portrait has an approving quotation from Jefferson above it, and beneath it is Jackson's toast: "The Union must be Preserved."

Jackson's success in dealing with the nullification crisis, which came to a head just after his reelection in November 1832, turned these words into a major legacy of his presidency, and he would repeat them in his farewell address upon leaving office in 1837.[9] The words would be incorporated into popular prints of Jackson (figs. 5–29, 5–30) and into the symbolism of the presidency. A print published by Thomas Moore's Lithography in Boston in 1839 ties the declaring of independence in 1776 with Jackson's defense of the Union and identifies the presidency with both (fig. 4–9). Between two columns surmounted by Liberty and Hope, General Washington is depicted outside Boston—a view of the Battle of Bunker Hill in the background—presenting the Declaration of Independence to officers representing the thirteen united states. Portraits of General Warren and General Lafayette adorn the bases of the columns, which are described in the legend as intended to represent New England rising out of Old England.

tution and 1850, the opposition of South Carolina to a protective tariff aroused President Andrew Jackson to a vigorous defense of the Union that would be celebrated in print and

Figure 4–9. *Independence Declared 1776. The Union Must Be Preserved.* Lithograph, 23 x 17⅛ inches, designed and published by Joseph A. Arnold, printed by Thomas Moore's Lithography, Boston, 1839. Harry T. Peters "America on Stone" Lithography Collection, Smithsonian Institution.

Figure 4–10. Invitation to the Grand National Inauguration Ball for President James Buchanan, March 4, 1857, 10½ x 7 inches, printed by Toppan, Carpenter and Company, Philadelphia, 1857. National Museum of American History, Smithsonian Institution.

Above this scene the presidents who subsequently served the new nation project the symbolic support of the presidency for Jackson's determination to preserve the Union forged in 1776. President Van Buren, hands joined with Jackson, confirms the pledge on the banner, "The Union Must Be Preserved." Above, the national eagle with the motto "E Pluribus Unum" guards the banner of independence.

Nearly twenty-seven years after Jackson delivered his famous toast, his words appeared on the invitations to the Grand National Inauguration Ball for President James Buchanan, who had served in Congress while Jackson was pres-

ident (fig. 4–10). The design of the invitations for the March 4, 1857, gala depicts two columns connected to form an arch symbolizing the Union, whose future was so uncertain when Buchanan took office. Each column, adorned at the top with the banner "E Pluribus Unum" and stars for each of the thirteen original states, is built of stones representing each state and territory. Solid blocks, they rest on foundations inscribed "Constitution of the United States" and "The Union Must Be Preserved." That such solemn symbolism should be employed for such a festive occasion may have reflected the tenor of the uncertain times. It may also have anticipated the heavy responsibility of preserving the Union facing the new president, whose portrait brightens the print but seems to draw attention to the fragility of the arch joining the two columns together. If such symbolism may be conjectured only in the minds of those who now know what lay ahead, the composition, nonetheless, unmistakably confirmed anew the essential role of the presidency in the preservation of the Union.

Between the presidencies of Jackson and Buchanan numerous popular prints visually portrayed that association. Those years brought the perfecting of lithography and the mass production of popular prints, projecting before the public more frequently than ever before the images of past presidents. In reminding viewers of the historical institution of the presidency, such prints focused attention on the Union and on the relationship of the presidency to its future. The heritages of the presidency and the Union were inseparable, and the art of prints and posters gave strong expression to, and support for, that unity. One of the most impressive such works is a lithograph by George and William Endicott published in New York in 1845, soon after James K. Polk took office as the eleventh president (fig. 4–11). The print was so large that it required lithographing in two sections, each approximately 22 x 31 inches, to be joined together to produce a poster over three and a half feet tall and two and a half feet wide. These dimensions suggest a work expected to be displayed in public buildings or schools.

As a historical record of the presidency and the growth of the Union that had transpired since the inauguration of the first president fifty-six years earlier, the poster is imposing. A traditional Old World style of border embellished with delicate flowers and curling branches projects the United States as a nation that had taken its place among the established powers of the world and had a historical record worthy of being celebrated in art and imagery. Yet the symbolism remains distinctly American. The portrait of the first president occupies the place of honor in the center of the print above a roster of the presidents, the whole enclosed by a chain of state seals. Carefully drawn portraits of Washington's successors in oval frames form a large oval extending to the border.

ders of the print. Below the portrait of incumbent President Polk is inscribed "E Pluribus Unum." Figures of Liberty and Justice, so frequently depicted since the early years of the republic, fill the lower corners. In the corners at the top of the print can be found the newer icons of "Peace and Plenty" and "Industry and Prosperity," increasingly employed as the nineteenth century advanced. The chain of states ties the presidency to the record of the growing union, while the most prominent motto on the poster, "Liberty and Union," reaffirms the role of the presidency in the preservation of the Union.

Less ambitious is an engraved print of the presidents that appeared while Franklin Pierce was in office (fig. 4–12). Figures of Fame in the upper corners of the print herald "The Presidents of the United States," but the cluttered design lacks the unity of the previously described work. Although Washington generally occupies the place of honor in such works, the drawings of the projected Washington Monument, the Bunker Hill Monument, and Washington's headquarters at Newburg, New York, accord more attention to Washington's military fame than is usual in such presidential depictions. Yet these symbols were reminders of a common cause that had brought a Virginia leader to Bunker Hill and Newburg. Moreover, the engraving of the national Capitol in the center of the print provides a unifying symbol, and the highlighting of the still unfinished expansion of the Capitol gives recognition to a growing Union. The emblematic national eagle with a display of the stars and stripes appears prominently at the top of the print, while another eagle stands vigilant at the bottom. For a nation that had weathered the threat of disunion in the crisis of 1850 and still faced unresolved issues, the work was a reminder of the heritage of the presidency in the history of the Union.

A concern for the future of the Union became increasingly evident in a number of prints as the decade of the 1850s progressed. National patriotism exudes from a series of presidential designs with which New York stationer Charles Magnus embellished sheets of elegant stationery. A design with President Pierce in the center surrounded by portraits of all the presidents is dominated by symbols of Union

Figure 4–11. *The Presidents of the United States*. Lithograph printed in two sections, each 22¼ x 31½ inches, by George and William Endicott. Published by T. and E. H. Ensign, New York, 1845. Deposited for copyright May 31, 1845. Library of Congress.

Figure 4–12. *The Presidents of the United States.* Engraving, 24 x 18½ inches, circa 1853–1857. Presidents Washington through Pierce. Metropolitan Museum of Art. Gift of Miss Eleanor and Mr. William J. Mathews, 1956.

Figure 4–13. *Presidents of America.* Decorated stationery sold by Charles Magnus, New York, circa 1853–1856. Engraved surface 6 x 8 inches. American Philosophical Society.

(fig. 4–13). The national emblem appears above the portrait of the first president at the top of the sheet and also on an unfurled banner. The ribbon proclaiming "E Pluribus Unum" is bolder than usual, and a large American flag waves above the heads of Jefferson and Madison. The design, initially titled "Presidents of America," was revised in a later state to hail "The Presidents of Our Great Republic" (plate 24). The new title reflects a heightened concern for a cherished Union. While some purchasers of the decorated stationery may have preferred to preserve a red, white, and blue hand-colored example, or not write on the decorated page of a folded sheet, some letter writers wrote directly on the embellished sheet.[10] The depiction of two different portraits of President Pierce on Magnus's prints also indicates a demand for stationery large

enough to justify such added effort and expense.

An even more patriotic version of the print was published after Buchanan became president (fig. 4–14). An enlarged portrait of President Washington now appears in the center (where the incumbent president had previously been placed), and the figure of Columbia joins the other national symbols at the top of the plate. The same design was used after Lincoln's election, the portrait of the beardless new president replacing the figure of Columbia (fig. 4–15).[11] Magnus later published a more subdued sheet, picturing a bearded Lincoln (fig. 4–16). None of the symbols of union or national patriotism remains in that design. Instead, the White House—a limited symbol of the presidency—is prominently featured. Only the title "The Presidents of Our Great

Figure 4–14. *The Presidents of Our Great Republic*. Decorated stationery sold by Charles Magnus, New York, circa 1857–1860. Engraved surface 6 x 8 inches. American Philosophical Society.

Figure 4–15. *The Presidents of Our Great Republic*. Decorated stationery sold by Lange and Kronfeld, New York, circa 1861. Engraved surface 6 x 8 inches. New-York Historical Society.

Figure 4–16. *The Presidents of Our Great Republic.* Decorated stationery sold by Charles Magnus, New York, circa 1861–1865. Engraved surface 7¼ x 5¾ inches. Library of Congress.

Republic" endures. Decorated envelopes (fig. 4–17) accompanied the new stationery. One envelope offers the portraits of the first eight presidents, with Washington's portrait centered above the White House. The other cover pictures Lincoln along with the seven most recent presidents.[12]

The rising fears for the survival of the Union as the year 1860 opened were vividly expressed on the cover of the *Song of the Union*, by a Pennsylvanian, published in January 1860 (fig. 4–18). Surrounded by the stars of the states of the Union and aided by a distressed national eagle, George Washington is shown in the heavens trying to hold back the black storm clouds that threaten to crumble the portal of the Union and strike down an eagle with a peace branch and the banner "E Pluribus Unum." Below Washington's image are words

extracted from his farewell address: "I shall carry with me to my grave a strong incitement to unceasing vows, that your Union may be perpetual."[13] If the olive branch and banner of union fell to earth, the artist visualized the trampling of the Constitution and the Union and pictured torches from two directions setting fire to the nation's Capitol. A year later, as the president from Pennsylvania to whom the songwriter dedicated his work seemed helpless to stem the tide toward disunion, the artist's vision approached reality.

The year 1861 began with the Union disintegrating. South Carolina had seceded on December 20, 1860, and before the end of January five more lower South states left the Union. The wrenching throes of the nation drew forth an artistic response unmatched in the iconographic record of the presidency. A print en-

Figure 4–17. Decorated envelopes, 3³/₁₆ x 5⅝ inches, sold by Charles Magnus, New York, circa 1861–1865. New-York Historical Society and James W. Milgram, *Abraham Lincoln Illustrated Envelopes and Letter Paper, 1860–1865* (Northbrook, Ill., 1984).

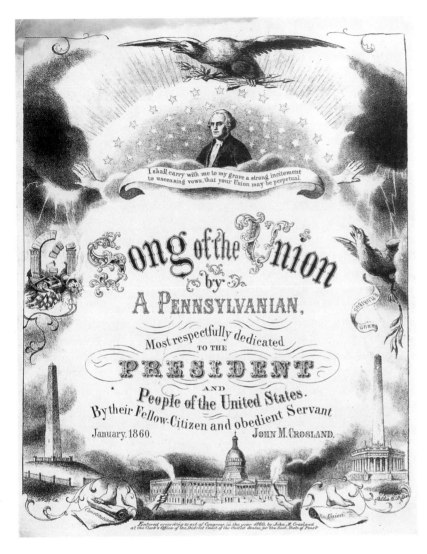

Figure 4–18. *Song of the Union*. Sheet music cover, Philadelphia, 1860. Library of Congress.

titled *Peace* (plate 17), published by the firm of Middleton, Strobridge and Company of Cincinnati, Ohio, brings together as did no other single work the symbolism of the presidency, the Union, and the nation. The print was deposited for copyright on January 21, 1861, two days after Georgia became the fifth state to vote to secede.[14]

In the well-executed, poster-size lithograph, an unidentified artist captured in tones of black and brown the images of the nation and celebrated the Union that only peace would preserve. In the center of the design, the portrait of the first president is surrounded by portraits of all his successors, including Lincoln, who would take office on March 4, 1861. Around the presidents, a cordon of shields bearing the arms of all the states affirms the unity of the presidency and the states. The flags and shield

above the presidential display reinforce the symbolism with the word *Union*, while solicitous angels hold the banner of "Peace" and the national eagle spreads its protective wings. Below, Columbia stands over the continent of North America and "The American Union," her shield emblazoned:

> A UNION OF HEARTS, A UNION OF HANDS,
> A UNION WHICH NONE MAY SEVER,
> A UNION OF LAKES, A UNION OF LANDS,
> THE AMERICAN UNION FOREVER.

The artist superimposed these images of the presidency and the Union upon scenes of the American nation, visualizing peaceful Indians and frontier settlers in a country where agriculture, industry, and commerce work together in prosperous harmony. The city of Washington with the Capitol and the monument to Washington reaching skyward preside over the peaceful vistas. Only the preservation of the Union could preserve this peaceful panorama.[15]

A superb chromolithograph of *Presidents of the United States* by A. Feusier, published in Philadelphia early in 1861, in a different way conveys a similar message (plate 16). An oval border containing the portraits of all the presidents frames a striking drawing of Columbia. At the top of the frame Washington appears slightly larger than his successors, while below a clean-shaven Lincoln completes the latest link in the protective cordon of presidents. Within this cordon a flag-draped Columbia presents a vigorous presence. A spirited American eagle clenching the banner of union beside her, she stands erect with liberty pole and shield of union celebrating the heritage of the presidency in the building of the nation and summoning that heritage for its preservation. In the background the United States Capitol projects a united nation, while a steamboat at full steam portrays its future progress and prosperity. In celebrating the Union and its presidents, the print reminded Americans of a heritage worthy of protecting. A poster-size print, the bright chromolithograph also displayed the technical advancement of that art form.[16]

If many Americans could take pride in such a splendid representation of their Union, the image of the new president was unacceptable to large numbers of Americans in the states of the South. The beard that Lincoln began to grow after his election was not yet full before this print and others like it were rejected in a large section of the country. With the firing on Fort Sumter on April 12, 1861, and President Lincoln's call for troops, the Union, which fifteen earlier presidents had helped to build and whose images symbolically guarded that heritage, collapsed. Four long years of a civil war that neither side had anticipated would be so protracted and so deadly left much of the country in ruins but preserved the Union. In its restoration the legacy of the presidency would be revived to heal the wounds and rebind the ties of union.

The end of the Civil War and the tragedy of Lincoln's assassination on April 14, 1865—six weeks after his second inaugural and five days after Appomattox—combined to elevate Lincoln to a place in the pantheon of American presidents second only to Washington. As printmakers rushed to unite the image of the assassinated president with that of the father of the country, they produced images that symbolically portrayed the restoration of the Union. In a colored lithograph entitled *Washington and Lincoln. The Father and the Savior of Our Country* published in New York in 1865, Currier and Ives pictured Washington and Lincoln standing before the glowing flame of liberty adorned with the American eagle and the shield of union (plate 26). Standing slightly taller than Lincoln, Washington is shown shaking Lincoln's hand, while raising his left hand in a gesture of blessing. In Lincoln's left hand a rolled document may be presumed to be the Emancipation Proclamation.[17]

An even more vivid representation of the presidency and the restoration of national unity can be seen in a lithograph by Charles Shober published in Chicago in 1865 (fig. 4–19). Entitled *National Picture*, the print carries the inscription "Behold Oh! America, Your Sons. The greatest among men." The drawing depicts Washington and Lincoln standing on an America that stretches from sea to sea, weapons of war silent at their feet, holding steady between them the shield of union. In one hand Washington holds the Constitution, while Lincoln, accurately pictured as the taller of the two men, holds the Emancipation Proclamation. The legend proclaims: "Under Providence Washington Made and Lincoln Saved Our Country."[18]

The restoration of the Union revived the historical legacy. Although the unifying force of the presidency had failed to save the nation from civil war, a persevering president had upheld the commitment of his office to the preservation of the Union. That the legacy of the presidency could be marshaled in the rebuilding of the Union was made easier by the images of the presidency and the nation that popular prints had conveyed and reinforced since the inauguration of the first president.

Figure 4–19. *National Picture*. Lithograph, 12½ x 14½ inches, by Charles Shober after drawing by L. Kurz, Chicago, 1865. Library of Congress.

CHAPTER V
The Presidential Stance

T HE STYLE of state portraiture widely followed in Europe since the sixteenth century provided the model that Gilbert Stuart employed to create the official image of the first president of the United States. Having studied in England, Stuart was familiar with those formal portraits, and he carried back to America a portfolio of engravings of some of them, which he would draw upon in creating his full-length portrait of President Washington.[1] In turn, the engravings that derived from Stuart's work established a style of presidential portraiture that would prevail from Washington to Lincoln.

The transformation of the image of Washington as the commanding general and military hero of the American Revolution into that of presidential statesman was swift. Among the portrayals of Washington the statesman, an engraving by Edward Savage was particularly important (fig. 5–1). Published in 1793, the mezzotint titled *George Washington Esqr. President of the United States of America* presents a presidential-looking Washington, dressed in black velvet, seated at a table, and studying a map of the new federal city. Savage's image of a dignified statesman contemplating the future capital became a popular one, judging from the number of copies of the print still in existence, and it played a major role in replacing the image of military leader with that of statesman.[2]

During Adams's presidency H. H. Houston offered a similar image of *His Excellency John Adams President of the United States of America* (fig. 5–2). The engraving, taken from a portrait by William Joseph Williams painted about 1795, depicts a seated Adams holding a volume of the laws of the United States.[3] Embellished with the arms of the Republic, the print is inscribed: "Respectfully Dedicated to the Lovers of their Country and Firm Supporters of its Constitution."[4] Although both Savage's and Houston's prints were designed to present portraits that were presidential, neither had the character of state portraiture in the European style.

The same was true of an engraving of Adams by George Graham (fig. 5–3), who copied from a portrait of the second president by William Winstanley. Henry Adams later observed of Winstanley's full-length painting that the body of his great-grandfather was about a third larger than it should be in relation to the legs.[5] The disproportion is evident in Graham's engraving. Pictured wearing a sword and holding in his hand a scroll labeled "Federal Constitution," Adams appears awkwardly posed, and other ornamentations add little to the portrait. The print, titled *John Adams, President of the United States of America*, is inscribed "Hail! Noble Chief! Protector of the cause of purest Freedom Founded on the Laws." Remarking that the age of sculpture and painting had not yet arrived in the United States, John Adams

Figure 5–1. *George Washington Esqr. President of the United States of America.* Engraving, 17¹⁵⁄₁₆ x 13⅞ inches, by Edward Savage. "From the Original Portrait Painted at the request of the Corporation of the University of Cambridge in Massachusetts," by Edward Savage. Published by Edward Savage, Philadelphia, 1793. National Portrait Gallery, Smithsonian Institution.

His Excellency JOHN ADAMS President
of the United States of America.
Respectfully Dedicated to the   Lovers of their Country
and Firm Supporters   of its Constitution

Figure 5–2. *His Excellency John Adams President of the United States of America.* Engraving, 14¹³/₁₆ x 10½ inches, by H. H. Houston after painting by William Joseph Williams. Published by David Kennedy, Philadelphia, circa 1797. National Portrait Gallery, Smithsonian Institution.

later commented: "Artists have done what they pleased with my face and eyes, head and shoulders, stature and figure and they have made of them monsters as fit for exhibition as Harlequin or Punch."[6] Though Adams did not cite specific examples, he no doubt would have included Graham's engraving among them. As an early example of the employment of the Constitution as an icon in presidential portraiture, however, the work is important. The image of a president with the Constitution or other document in his hand would long endure. In 1865 a lithograph by Charles Shober pictured Washington in a similar pose holding the Constitution in his hand, while Lincoln held the Emancipation Proclamation (fig. 4–19).

Once Gilbert Stuart created his presidential image of Washington, all other depictions of either Washington or Adams paled in comparison and soon faded in popularity. Excelling in the painting of countenances, Stuart disliked the laborious painting of large formal portraits, but his full-length portrait of Washington created a style for presidential portraits that would come to dominate American portraiture.

What became the equivalent of an official state portrait of Washington was painted by Stuart in 1796 for the Marquis of Lansdowne

Figure 5–3. *John Adams, President of the United States of America.* Engraving, 19½ x 14 inches, by George Graham after painting by William Winstanley. Published by John Berkeanhead, 1798. Metropolitan Museum of Art, Bequest of Charles Allen Munn, 1924.

Figure 5–4. *Jacobus Benignus Bossuet Episcopus.*
Engraving, 19⅞ x 13½ inches, by Pierre Imbert
Drevet after painting by Hyacinthe Rigaud,
1723. Library of Congress.

Figure 5–5. *Louis Seize.* Engraving, 27½ x 20½
inches, by Charles-Clement Bervic after painting by Antoine-François Callet, 1790. Library
of Congress.

on order from William Bingham of Philadelphia (plate 2). Stuart copied his likeness of
Washington now known as the "Athenaeum"
head (plate 1), for which Washington sat in
1796, and drew on his portfolio of engravings
of European state portraiture to create the
stance and provide the background. He relied
heavily on an engraving by Pierre Imbert
Drevet of a portrait of Bishop Bossuet painted
by Hyacinthe Rigaud (fig. 5–4).[7] But he replaced the bishop's relaxed pose with the formality displayed in the royal stance of Louis
XVI in an engraving by Charles-Clement Bervic after a portrait by Antoine-François Callet
(fig. 5–5).[8] Callet's work, in turn, followed the
portrait of Louis XIV painted by Rigaud in
1701.[9]

Stuart and other Americans would have
been familiar with Callet's portrait of Louis
XVI not only through Bervic's engraving but

also through a copy of the painting that the
French government gave to the United States
in 1784, together with a portrait of Marie An-
toinette. Both of these portraits hung in the
Senate chamber in Philadelphia while Stuart
was painting in that city. Members and visitors
from time to time commented on the large
paintings, though on occasion the damask cur-
tains that could be closed over them were
drawn. When the capital moved to Washington in 1800, the portraits went with the legislators and remained in the Senate until 1813, at
which time they were removed to committee
rooms.[10] The presence of the portraits of monarchs in a legislative hall of a republic was often
the subject of controversy. But the paintings
displayed to American eyes the formal state
portraiture of Europe, aiding them in recog-
nizing that Stuart provided a state portrait of a
republican president that could rival the work
of the court portraitists of Europe.

The regalia of power and position are present in Stuart's painting of Washington (plate

2). The columns of order, the heavy drapery, the richly designed carpet, and the gilded furniture are accompaniments of court, but unlike Louis XIV in Rigaud's portrait or Louis XVI in Callet's painting, the president is not richly robed. Though Washington wears a sword, no crown and scepter evince power. Instead, the president's chair of authority displays the symbol of the republic with the stars and stripes of the thirteen states painted in red, white, and blue. Replacing the symbols of royal power common in the state portraiture of Europe with emblems of the new republic, Stuart painted a table with legs formed of tightly bound fasces and adorned with national eagles, the table covering raised to reveal golden American eagles prominently in the foreground.

The president of the republic stands by a table used for work. Pen, inkwell, papers, and books fill the top of the table. The books on the table are titled *Federalist* and *Journals of Congress*. Other volumes—*General Orders*, *American Revolution*, and *Constitution and Laws of the United States*—crowd the space beneath the table. Their titles record Washington's past glories and the triumphs of the new nation and define his present responsibilities. The president's black-cockaded hat rests on the table along with his papers associated with the administration of the laws. There is a stiffness in Washington's outstretched arm, and Stuart in a later version of the portrait lowered the arm, resting Washington's hand on a paper on the table (fig. 5–8).[11]

Knowing the popularity of elegant engravings after European state portraits, Stuart planned to have his example of American state portraiture engraved; and he expected to profit from the venture. The portrait was sent to Lansdowne with the stipulation that the artist reserved the engraving rights to the work. But that did not deter its reproduction, and in 1800 James Heath in London engraved a plate that would not only establish Stuart's painting as the official image of Washington but also set a style for portraying Washington's successors in the presidential office.

The English publisher titled the portrait *General Washington* and inscribed it as "Engraved by James Heath Historical Engraver to his Majesty and to his Royal Highness the Prince of Wales from the original Picture in the Collection of the Marquis of Lansdown" (fig. 5–6). The artist was identified as "Gabriel Stuart." When prints reached America, they were widely advertised for sale at eight dollars, with "handsomely framed" copies selling for fifteen dollars and proof prints "elegantly framed" costing twenty dollars.[12]

Gilbert Stuart may have overlooked being misidentified on the plate, but he was furious at the appearance of Heath's engraving because he thought his rights to his work had been violated. Having taken precautions to guard against such an event, he protested his "mortification to observe, that without any regard to his property, or feelings, as an artist, an engraving has been recently published in England; and is now offered for sale in America." While complaining of this invasion of his rights, he expressed some consolation at the inadequate quality of Heath's work. Indicating that Heath's engraving "can not satisfy or supercede the public claim, for a correct representation of the American Patriot," he announced his intention to publish an engraving of his "Mount Vernon" portrait of Washington, "executed upon a large scale, by eminent artists." His print would sell for twenty dollars, ten dollars in advance. Apparently hoping to preempt the market for presidential prints, he announced that engravings of his portraits of Adams and Jefferson were in preparation and would be published in a few weeks.[13]

None of these engravings promised by Stuart ever appeared—not of Washington, nor of Adams, nor of Jefferson. It was thus Heath's engraving of Stuart's Washington that American engravers copied, and it set the style for popular presidential portraits. William Dunlap later denounced the work as "that vile engraving from the *atelier* of Heath, which is unfortunately spread throughout our country, a libel upon Stuart and Washington." Dunlap regarded the "Athenaeum" head of Washington (plate 1) as Stuart's best representation of the first president and thought that Heath's print had misled Americans "in their ideas of the countenance of the man they most revere."[14] While later critics have been less harsh than Dunlap, they have noted a disproportion between the head and the body in the Lansdowne portrait, as well as in the engraving.

GENERAL WASHINGTON.

Figure 5–6. *General Washington*. Engraving, 21 x 14 inches, by James Heath after Stuart's "Lansdowne" portrait (plate 2). Published by James Heath, London, 1800. National Portrait Gallery, Smithsonian Institution.

Figure 5–8. *George Washington*. Oil on canvas, 95 x 60 inches, by Gilbert Stuart. Painted for the State House, Hartford, Connecticut, 1801. Museum of Connecticut History.

Figure 5–7. *General Washington. President of the United States*. Engraving, 19⅞ x 13 inches, by Charles Goodman and Robert Piggot. Published by William H. Morgan, Philadelphia, 1818. Historical Society of Pennsylvania.

Also, in the Lansdowne portrait, Washington gazes off into the distance, while in the "Athenaeum" head, Washington's eyes look directly at the viewer.

Among important American copies of Heath's engraving was a print engraved and published by Cornelius Tiebout in 1801.[15] Charles Goodman and Robert Piggot also later copied it for William H. Morgan's series of presidential portraits, adding "President of the United States" under Washington's name (fig. 5–7).

Although such reproductions of Stuart's Lansdowne portrait made it his best-known depiction of the first president, the artist him-

self modified that presentation of Washington in portraits painted about the same time that Heath's engraving was coming to dominate the American market. In May 1800 the General Assembly of Connecticut ordered from Stuart a full-length portrait of Washington for display in the State House at Hartford (fig. 5–8). Stuart had the painting ready for delivery in February 1801. Soon afterward, the legislature of Rhode Island commissioned the artist to paint similar portraits for the State Houses in Providence and Newport. Stuart delivered both of these paintings to Rhode Island in October 1801. In each of the three paintings Stuart depicted the president with his right hand resting on a document on the table, rather than extending his arm as in the Lansdowne portrait.[16] Stuart also eliminated the carpet and re-

Figure 5–9. *Thomas Jefferson: President of the United States.* Engraving, 19⅞ x 13 inches, by Cornelius Tiebout. Published by Augustus Day, Philadelphia, 1801. Library of Congress.

produced the marble flooring found in Rigaud's portrait of Bishop Bossuet (fig. 5–4).

The first president after Washington to have his portrait published in the style of state portraiture introduced by Stuart was Jefferson. After Adams's defeat in his bid for reelection in 1800, Adams's portraits were no longer in demand. On the other hand, the election stimulated a flourishing of Jefferson portraiture. During the year 1800 presidential candidate Jefferson sat for three portrait painters—Rembrandt Peale, Gilbert Stuart, and Edward Savage—and engravers competed to get likenesses of the candidate and, later, the new president before the public.[17] Among the principal prints contending for public attention were two full-length engravings of Jefferson that appeared within a few months after his inauguration.

First to announce the projected publication of a full-length engraved portrait of Jefferson was George Helmbold, Jr., of Philadelphia, who promised a print 22 x 14 inches that would be a match for the print of Stuart's Lansdowne portrait by Heath.[18] A few months later Augustus Day announced plans to publish a similar print.[19] For months advertisements in the *Aurora* of Philadelphia heralded the merits of each promised print and disparaged the caliber of the competing effort. Helmbold promised a print from a portrait by an "eminent Portrait painter," copied by an engraver of "first rate abilities." Day identified his engraver as Cornelius Tiebout, "an American artist of the first abilities," and promised that the portrait would be taken from Rembrandt Peale's "masterly" painting of Jefferson. Helmbold pledged that the likeness in his print would be striking and the engraving "equal, if not superior to any work of the kind hitherto executed in the United States." He ultimately revealed that the engraver would be David Edwin, "whose abilities were well known in the line of his profession."[20]

Available for purchase on July 4, 1801, both Tiebout's plate for Day (fig. 5–9) and Edwin's engraving published by Helmbold (fig. 5–10) reflected the influence of Heath's engraving of Washington. The background of Tiebout's engraving—columns, drapery, and open vista—was so similar to Heath's print as to indicate that it had been used as a model. Tiebout, however, added originality to his work by picturing Jefferson as both a philosopher and a statesman, surrounding him with things that interested and described him. Jefferson holds the Declaration of Independence in his hand, while the table beside him is crowded with books and a bust of Franklin—like Jefferson a voice of the Enlightenment in America. To Jefferson's left, an electric static machine—described by the publisher as a "philosophical" (scientific) apparatus—and a globe replace the chair in the Washington print.

The background of David Edwin's engraving for Helmbold suggests not only the influence of Heath's print but also that of Bervic's engraving of Callet's portrait of Louis XVI (fig. 5–5). The column, balustrade, and the picture on the wall in the distant chamber are so similar to the earlier work as to make it nearly certain that Edwin employed Bervic's print. But the royal setting of Louis XVI's portrait was altered to fit the American scene. Jefferson, like Washington in Stuart's portrait, stands by a table where pen, inkwell, paper, and books indicate a working president. Books are also under the table and line the wall behind it.

Edwin and Tiebout had each engraved bust portraits of Jefferson after Rembrandt Peale's 1800 life portrait (fig. 2–2), and each employed his version of that image for the head in his full-length engraving.[21] But neither engraver had a model of Jefferson's figure to copy, for no standing portrait of Jefferson had been painted except for John Trumbull's portrait on the uncompleted canvas of the signing of the Declaration of Independence. In neither Edwin's print published by Helmbold nor Tiebout's engraving published by Day does Jefferson wear a sword, and he is even more plainly dressed than Washington in Stuart's portrait, wearing laced shoes instead of silver-buckled slippers.

Both prints are of dimensions similar to Heath's engraving of Washington and suitable for display along with that portrait of the first president. In the competition as to which would enjoy that honor, Tiebout's engraving for Day appears to have won. Edwin's engraving for Helmbold evidently met a cool reception, for it was quickly followed by a revised plate in which Jefferson's stature was altered to show him as taller and slimmer (fig. 5–11). Edwin also added a chair to the picture, though it lacked the symbolism of the presidential chair

Figure 5–10. Thomas Jefferson. Engraving, 20 x 13 inches, by David Edwin. Published by George Helmbold, Jr., Philadelphia, 1801. Virginia Historical Society.

Figure 5–11. *Jefferson*. Engraving by David Edwin, second state of figure 5–10. Published by George Helmbold, Jr., Philadelphia, 1801. National Portrait Gallery, Smithsonian Institution.

painted by Stuart in his Lansdowne portrait of Washington. Even after Edwin's revised print appeared, it was Tiebout's print that most influenced the evolving style of presidential state portraiture initiated by Stuart. Tiebout's plate would be reissued while Madison was president, as part of a series of presidential portraits published by William H. Morgan of Philadelphia.

Morgan had an important role in fostering the emerging tradition of popular prints presenting full-length portraits of the presidents. On the eve of Madison's inauguration, he advertised a proposal to publish a full-length print of Madison to be engraved by David Edwin (fig. 5–13) and "to correspond with those already published of presidents Washington and Jefferson." The announcement stated, "Mr. Madison is represented as a statesman in the hall of the house of representatives, his hand rests on the constitution of the United States which lays open on a table, a globe, books and various concomitants are expressively distributed throughout the print."[22]

Although Morgan's announcement did not reveal the source of the portrait to be engraved by Edwin, he had apparently already contracted with Thomas Sully to paint the portrait (fig. 5–12) and promised "the most accurate likeness hitherto published of Mr. Madison."[23] Sully, however, did not take Madison's likeness from life but copied the head from the portrait painted by Gilbert Stuart in 1804.[24] He placed Stuart's head of Madison on a body posed in

Figure 5–12. *James Madison*. Oil on panel, 27 x 20 inches, by Thomas Sully after Gilbert Stuart, 1809. The Corcoran Gallery of Art, Gift of Frederic E. Church.

Figure 5–13. *James Madison, President of the United States*. Engraving,
19¹³⁄₁₆ x 13⅛ inches, by David Edwin after painting by Thomas Sully.
Published by William H. Morgan, Philadelphia, 1810. National Portrait
Gallery, Smithsonian Institution.

Painted by C.B.King.   Published Dec.r 15.th 1817 by W.H. Morgan, N.194 Chesnut St. Philad.a   Engraved by Goodman & Piggot.

JAMES MONROE L.L.D.

PRESIDENT OF THE UNITED STATES.

Figure 5–14. *James Monroe L.L.D. President of the United States*. Engraving, 19½ x 13 inches, by Charles Goodman and Robert Piggott after painting by Charles Bird King. Published by William H. Morgan, Philadelphia, 1817. Library of Congress.

the manner of Washington in Heath's engraving of Stuart's Lansdowne portrait (fig. 5–6) and of Jefferson in the full-length engraving by Tiebout (fig. 5–9). The background and ornamentations are similar to those earlier prints. The table and chair are less ornate than Stuart's. But, like Stuart, Sully painted the shield of the republic with the stars and stripes on the back of the chair, and he draped Madison's plain outer coat and simple hat over the chair arm and back. A globe that had appeared in both of the full-length prints of Jefferson also found its place on Madison's table. Where Jefferson holds the Declaration of Independence in his hand in Tiebout's engraving, Madison rests his hand on the Constitution, in a manner similar to that of Washington in Gilbert Stuart's later version of his full-length portrait of Washington (fig. 5–8). Madison's stance in Sully's painting and Edwin's engraving (fig. 5–13) is much the same as that of Washington and Jefferson. Morgan's print of

Madison sold for six dollars (twelve dollars with glass and frame) and evidently met with success, for the publisher not only reissued Tiebout's engraving of Jefferson but also published a new engraving of Heath's print of Stuart's Lansdowne portrait of Washington, engraved by Charles Goodman and Robert Piggot (fig. 5–7).

Morgan also published an engraving (fig. 5–14) by Goodman and Piggot of Charles Bird King's portrait of James Monroe—a portrait that departed from the presidential stance common to the prints of Washington, Jefferson, and Madison. The work table and books are present, and there are columns, but Monroe is seated in a chair, paper in hand, in a relaxed pose. At the same time, the vista opening to the Capitol reaffirms the official character of the portrait, and the books leaning against the table leg are titled *Atlas of U.S.* and *Constitution United States.* Inscribed "James Monroe L.L.D. President of the United States," the print is dated December 15, 1817, during the first year of Monroe's presidency. Although this style of presidential portraiture would not replace the popular standing stance, the vista showing the United States Capitol in the distance would become a common feature of many later presidential portraits.

When Morgan added President John Quincy Adams to his series, he followed the style of his Monroe print and published an image of a seated Adams (fig. 5–15). Painted by Thomas Sully, the portrait shows Adams in his library surrounded by books and maps and holding a large volume in his hands. Adams himself may have had some part in the composition of the portrait, because being pictured holding a book was one of his favorite poses.[25] Publisher Morgan appears to have commissioned Sully to paint the portrait, for Sully handled the negotiations with Asher Brown Durand to make the engraving. In a letter revealing details about the making of presidential prints only rarely found in surviving records, Sully wrote from Philadelphia to Durand in New York on March 21, 1825:

> Mr. Morgan of this city has requested me to enquire of you if you can undertake to engrave a whole length likeness of President Adams from a portrait that I am now finishing—the shortest time in which the plate can be delivered from the time you receive the portrait, and your charge for such engraving. The size of the plate is to correspond to that of Washington—Jefferson—Madison and Monroe which he has published, and may be found in all the print shops. I think the size is about 19 x 14. The picture from which you would copy is 32 by 25 inches.
>
> I have made a rough sketch of the composition in order the better to assist your estimate. The back ground you may perceive is very light and would not require much labour.
>
> Mr. M[organ] would wish it executed in your best style, but I should presume that it would be unnecessary to make such observation to one whose excellent works prove him to possess the true spirit of his art—a desire always to do his best.[26]

Durand agreed to make the engraving for $770, and Sully arranged for William Dunlap to deliver his painting of Adams to Durand in New York. The canvas, he said, was "fresh from the easel." Sully sent along his original sketch of the head of Adams to aid Durand and also the print of Monroe from Morgan's series to match the size.[27]

Sully's letters to Durand confirm the important role Morgan played in creating a major series of presidential portrait prints with likenesses taken by talented artists and reproduced by skilled engravers. Sully's casual comment that Morgan's presidential prints could "be found in all the print shops" provides to the modern reader a rare observation on the availability of presidential prints in the marketplace. The fee of $770 that Morgan agreed to pay Durand for engraving the copperplate also indicates something of the considerable investment the publisher had in the venture. Shipping the copper for the plate to Durand in early June 1825, Morgan waited over a year for the painstaking work required for an engraving of such size to be completed.[28] When published, the print was dated October 6, 1826.

Morgan's publication of the prints of Monroe and Adams in his presidential series might suggest that a less formal style of presidential portraiture was replacing the state portrait introduced by Stuart. But that was not the case. Monroe appeared in formal pose in full-length paintings by John Vanderlyn and Samuel F. B. Morse. Neither portrait is known to have been engraved, but both are significant examples of

Figure 5–15. *John Quincy Adams, President of the United States*. Engraving, 20¼ x 14 inches, by Asher B. Durand after painting by Thomas Sully. Published by William H. Morgan, Philadelphia, 1826. New-York Historical Society.

Figure 5–16. *James Monroe.* Oil on canvas, 100 x 64 inches, by John Vanderlyn, 1822. Collections of the City of New York, Art Commission of the City of New York.

Figure 5–17. *James Monroe.* Oil on canvas, 92¼ x 59½ inches, by Samuel F. B. Morse, 1820. Collection of City Hall, Charleston, South Carolina.

early presidential portraiture in the tradition of Stuart without being stylistic copies.

As a young aspiring artist, Vanderlyn had studied for a few months with Gilbert Stuart before going to Europe for years of study and work. Later, after his return to America, he was commissioned by the city of New York to paint President Monroe's portrait and displayed his own striking style in a fresh interpretation completed in 1822 (fig. 5–16). Still, the pose, the furnishings, and the accoutrements are reflective of Stuart's Lansdowne portrait (plate 2). Monroe's vigorous, yet serious, presence and the map of Florida on the table suggest a nation that was secure and expanding while presenting a worthy successor to Washington.

Monroe appears in a similarly traditional, yet less well executed, portrait by Samuel F. B. Morse commissioned by the city of Charleston to honor Monroe's visit there in 1819 (fig. 5–17). Asked to paint a portrait of the president

to hang in City Hall beside John Trumbull's portrait of Washington commissioned to honor Washington's visit to Charleston in 1791, Morse was challenged to offer a fresh presentation within a traditional mode. The influence of Stuart and the style that his painting nourished can be seen in Morse's painting, completed in 1820. Columned government buildings in the background replace traditional columns, but the presidential chair of authority remains, and Monroe's right hand rests on the table before the text of the Constitution, much in the manner in which his predecessors in the high office had been depicted. At the same time, Morse depicted Monroe, the only military veteran to serve as president since Washington, wearing a sword and boots and holding his old Revolutionary hat in his left hand.

Despite the growing interest in presidential

Figure 5–18. *John Q. Adams. President of the United States.* Engraving, 15⅞ x 11⅞ inches, by Thomas Gimbrede after Gilbert Stuart. Printed by Ridley, New York, 1826. New-York Historical Society.

portraiture, neither Morse nor Vanderlyn was able to paint a full-length portrait of Monroe from life. Monroe had sat for Vanderlyn to paint a bust portrait in 1816, and the artist copied from that work for his full-length painting. Morse in 1819 journeyed to Washington to paint the head of Monroe, after the president's short stay in Charleston provided no time to sit for the artist, then living in Charleston. At the White House, Monroe was very hospitable, inviting Morse to dinner three times, but the president's busy schedule provided only fleeting intervals for sittings. The artist found it "very perplexing, for he cannot sit more than ten or twenty minutes at a time, so that the moment I feel engaged he is called away again." Morse cited an example: "I set my palette today at ten o'clock and waited until four o'clock this afternoon before he came in. He then sat ten minutes and we were called to dinner." Still, when finished, Morse was satisfied with the result and pleased that the president, along with Mrs. Monroe and their daughter, thought it the best likeness taken of him.[29] But Morse was less successful in completing the body without a model.[30]

A traditionally styled portrait of President John Quincy Adams appeared in an engraving by Thomas Gimbrede in 1826 (fig. 5–18). Adams is pictured standing at a podium. Behind him the presidential chair is embellished with the emblems of the republic. A cornucopia—increasingly employed to depict a nation of plenty—adorns the fabric of the chair, and "U S" appears in bold letters on the chair back, guarded by eagle and shield. Thirteen arrows and thirteen stars (two concealed) decorate the column. Adams, who sat for Gimbrede to draw the portrait, clearly had a role in the composition, for Gimbrede incorporated into the border of the drapery one of Adams's favorite devices: the lyre. That symbol of harmony drawn from Greek mythology also appears in the eagle and lyre seal in the inscription, where the lyre replaces the shield in the traditional national seal. Twenty-four stars—one for each state then in the Union—encircle the eagle and lyre seal, a device that appeared on United States passports while Adams was secretary of state.[31]

Adams was also painted in a formal standing pose in a portrait begun by Gilbert Stuart and

Figure 5–19. *John Quincy Adams*. Oil on canvas, 95 x 60 inches. Head painted by Gilbert Stuart, 1825; portrait completed by Thomas Sully, 1830. Harvard University Portrait Collection, Bequest of Ward Nicholas Boylston.

completed by Thomas Sully (fig. 5–19). Stuart painted the head in 1825, while Adams was president, and Sully added the body in 1830, after Stuart died and Adams had left office. Eschewing the embellishments of state portraiture employed by Stuart in painting Washington, Sully offered a plainer, more republican president, in accord with Adams's wishes. Although engravers copied Adams's head by Stuart, the full-length portrait never entered the competition of popular prints. It was, however, much admired for its republican character. The *Boston Patriot and Mercantile Advertiser*, reviewing a public display of the portrait, noted: "The Ex-president is represented in the plain costume that best becomes a true republican, and in no other would we wish to see him apparelled. Our own simple dress, it seems to us, if not so becoming in a picture, is far more *appropriate* than the flowing *toga* of the Roman Senator, or the laced and showy suit of the British nobleman. It is in this simple and unostentatious attire, free from all the vain foppery of foreign Courts, that we would wish to see the President of a Republican people attired."[32]

With the presidency of Andrew Jackson the earlier presidential stance returned in popular prints. Indeed, Francis Kearny modeled his engraving of President Jackson (fig. 5–20) directly after a print of President Jefferson. Although the print was inscribed "Engraved from an Original Drawing," the principal source of the drawing was Tiebout's full-length engraving of Jefferson published by Augustus Day in 1801 (fig. 5–9) and later republished by William H. Morgan. Even the costume belonged to an earlier day, for the knee breeches that Jefferson wore in 1801 were no longer in style when Jackson was president. Where Jefferson holds and points to the Declaration of Independence in Tiebout's engraving, Jackson holds and points to the Constitution of the United States in Kearny's print. The presidential chair that had become an essential feature of earlier presidential prints also appears in Kearny's work.

Painters and printmakers pictured Jackson in many different poses. More than any previous president since Washington, Jackson—the foremost military hero of the war of 1812—had been frequently portrayed in portraits and engravings prior to taking office. As with Washington, a transition in Jackson's image from military hero to statesman was reflected in the portraits and popular prints produced during his presidency.

Jackson portraiture is unusual in that Jackson was the first president to have a resident portrait painter at the White House. Ralph E. W. Earl, a portraitist of modest talent, in 1819 married Jane Caffery, a niece of Rachel Jackson. He quickly became a favorite of Mrs. Jackson, and when Jane died not long after her marriage, Mrs. Jackson insisted that Earl take up residence at the Hermitage and paint a series of portraits of her husband. From then until Jackson left the presidency, Earl served as a resident artist, traveling companion, and factotum. Becoming particularly close to Jackson after

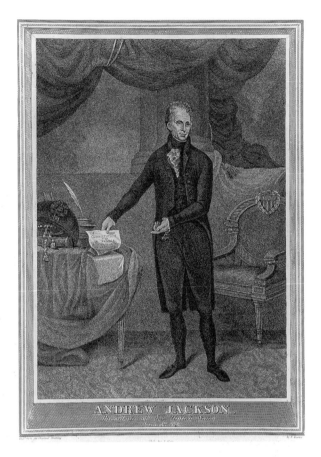

Figure 5–20. *Andrew Jackson, President of the United States. March 4th 1829.* Engraving, 10 x 6¹⁵⁄₁₆ inches, by Francis Kearny. Published by J. How, [1829]. New-York Historical Society.

Rachel's death in 1828, Earl lived in the White House, where he had a painting room, and Jackson paid him fifty dollars for each canvas.[33] Earl also profited from the prints that he had made from his paintings.

Among the more successful of Earl's portraits was a full-length depiction of Jackson at the Hermitage reproduced in a popular lithograph by John Henry Bufford, published in Boston in 1832 (fig. 5–21). Earl had engaged William S. Pendleton, whose Boston firm was one of the earliest American shops to master the new process of lithography, to publish this portrait of Jackson as a country gentleman. The painting had a primitive quality faithfully reproduced by Bufford in the lithograph, which, measuring 22 x 16 inches, was the largest lithograph the Pendleton shop had ever produced.[34]

The artist's correspondence provides un-

Figure 5–21. *Andrew Jackson at the Hermitage, 1830*. Lithograph, 21 x 17 inches, by John Henry Bufford after painting by Ralph E. W. Earl. Published by Pendleton's Lithography, Boston, 1832. National Portrait Gallery, Smithsonian Institution.

common insight into the production and marketing of presidential prints. Earl's friend Dr. George Bates of Boston, who handled the arrangements with Pendleton and kept Earl informed of the progress and problems, forwarded him proof sheets in March 1832. In the accompanying letter Bates relayed Pendleton's hope for a favorable reaction from the artist and said that he and Pendleton would provide every possible aid in the sale of copies. "Our friends hereabouts are urgent in their demands to have a likeness of our venerated President to adorn their parlours," he wrote; "many frames have already been made in anticipation of its publication." [35] Earl's reaction was highly favorable, and he reported to Pendleton from Washington that "the President's family and other friends here who have seen the Print are equally satisfied." Requesting Pendleton to send him two hundred copies of the best impressions, he added: "I hope you and my friend Dr. Bates will be able to have sold as many of the Prints in Boston as will defray the expence of the work." Assuring him that he would pay for any deficiency, he asked Pendleton if five dollars was too much to charge for each print. [36]

In response, Bates reported that Pendleton thought the first impressions might be priced at five dollars and the second impressions at three dollars. Bates's own view was that in Boston only the lower price could be obtained, except in a few instances. He explained, "Most of the Subscribers to the Print and probably most of those who will subscribe are persons not abounding in wealth and not amateurs of the fine arts, but men devoted in heart to our excellent President and who are therefore desirous of possessing the best likeness of him at a cheap rate. . . . The first impressions must be sold to the wealthy, the second to easy in circumstances and the third impressions can be sold at still lower prices to our good country friends, who if not so rich as citizens are not less devoted to Liberty and lovers of her great Champion." [37]

With 1832 an election year in which Jackson was seeking reelection, the publication of the print was well timed. In May, a few days before the Democratic nominating convention opened in Baltimore, Bates sent a hasty note to Earl suggesting that he rush fifty or sixty copies to the city immediately. [38] Earl had already ordered two hundred copies shipped to Nashville, and Bates was soon reporting shipments to New York, Philadelphia, Norfolk, Charleston, New Orleans, Cincinnati, Louisville, and other cities. Advising Earl to write to any friends that he had in these cities, Bates confided: "Whatever may be the merit of a work of art, it will not sell unless the public attention is called to it and purchases solicited." [39] Reporting in August that the shipment to Louisville had been lost when a keelboat sank, Bates urged Earl to try to get additional prints to Kentucky. "Now is the time to sell them," he wrote. "The excitement of the election will help the sale and the presence of the picture will help the election." [40] These revealing letters show the marketing efforts sometimes required to promote popular prints, which in Jackson's case also had to compete with caricatures offering images of the president contrary to that of the serene gentleman depicted in Bufford's lithograph.

Earl's portrait of Jackson most in accord with the tradition of full-length presidential portraiture was a painting picturing Jackson standing erectly by a column with a vista to the Capitol behind him (plate 9). A contemporary description identifies the location as the south front of the presidential mansion and explains that Jackson, wearing a military cloak over his civilian suit and holding a walking stick, is pictured as having returned from a walk. [41] Earl painted two versions of this portrait: a small canvas and the life-size painting reproduced in plate 9. The latter portrait, commissioned to honor Jackson's retirement as president by a popular subscription of one-dollar contributions from one thousand citizens of Washington, D.C., was displayed in the City Hall. An unidentified admirer of the portrait, lauding its merits in a letter to the *Boston Statesman* on the eve of Jackson's retirement, extravagantly claimed that the work "will immortalize Earle, as Washington's portrait has Stewart, and Napoleon's David." [42] Although this prediction was no more accurate than the critic's spelling, the comment provides a contemporary evaluation of Earl's work, while also confirming the recognition of Stuart's premier place as an artist.

The commanding pose and the cape draped

ANDREW JACKSON,
PRESIDENT OF THE UNITED STATES.

Figure 5–22. *Andrew Jackson, President of the United States.* Lithograph, 19⅝ x 14 inches, by Albert Newsam after painting by William James Hubard. Published by Cephas G. Childs, Philadelphia, 1830. National Portrait Gallery, Smithsonian Institution.

over Jackson's shoulders give Earl's portrait a majestical tone rare in presidential portraiture. In contrast, Jackson appears a more pensive president in a striking lithograph by Albert Newsam published by Cephas G. Childs in Philadelphia in 1830 (fig. 5–22). Childs had commissioned William James Hubard to go to Washington to paint Jackson's portrait for the lithograph, and Hubard had recorded a dignified, reflective president, seated in a modest chair, books on the table beside him, and only the column and drapery suggestive of his office of state. The *National Gazette* of Philadelphia

pronounced the print "the most remarkable drawing on stone hitherto achieved in this country."[43] The lithograph must have been successful, for it was subsequently republished at least four times. Hubard's portrait—judged an excellent likeness by the *National Gazette*— was also engraved by John Sartain.[44]

The style of presidential state portraiture introduced by Stuart and popularized by the full-length engravings of Washington, Jefferson, and Madison received important reinforcement from an act of Congress in 1832. To commemorate the centennial of Washington's

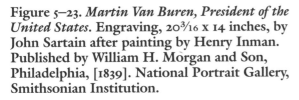

Figure 5–23. *Martin Van Buren, President of the United States*. Engraving, 20³/₁₆ x 14 inches, by John Sartain after painting by Henry Inman. Published by William H. Morgan and Son, Philadelphia, [1839]. National Portrait Gallery, Smithsonian Institution.

Figure 5–24. *Abraham Lincoln, President of the United States*. Engraving, 20¼ x 13⁷/₈ inches, by John Sartain. Published by William Smith, Philadelphia, [1864–1865]. National Portrait Gallery, Smithsonian Institution.

birth, Congress appropriated one thousand dollars to commission the painting of a full-length portrait of Washington to be placed in the chamber of the House of Representatives. After considerable discussion about the choice of the artist, the House voted to commission John Vanderlyn to paint the portrait. In the debate one member argued that Stuart's head "was generally considered the classical likeness of Washington," and another congressman reminded his colleagues that in 1826 Congress had declared that image to be "the standard likeness of Washington." Accordingly, Congress instructed Vanderlyn to copy the head of Washington taken from life by Stuart—the "Athenaeum" head (plate 1). Aside from this

condition, the accessories were to be left to the artist.[45] "Vanderlyn understands that, limited only to Stuart's head, he has *carte blanche* to give us a magnificent picture," wrote Rep. Gulian C. Verplanck of New York, who was one of Vanderlyn's leading promoters.[46] Despite this freedom of artistic presentation, Vanderlyn copied not only Stuart's head of Washington but also much of the style of Stuart's full-length portraits of Washington, though he made important modifications.

Vanderlyn's painting (plate 3), which still hangs in the House chamber, is closer to Stuart's later version of his full-length portrait of Washington (fig. 5–8) than to the Lansdowne portrait (plate 2), but it is more chaste and republican in appearance than any of

Stuart's interpretations. The table leg that was highly ornate in Stuart's painting is concealed; the floor covering is simpler, and the opening vista reveals an expanse of the new and undeveloped country. Washington is more presidential looking. His left hand no longer grasps his sword, and his right hand rests on a document that is clearly inscribed "Constitution." The presidential chair is a close copy of the one in Stuart's painting, except that the seal of the United States now fills the tapestry on the back of the chair, giving it a prominence not found in Stuart's portraiture. Vanderlyn emphasized Washington's presidential role by placing a lettercover addressed to the president on the floor in the foreground. By the time of Jackson's presidency, Heath's engraving of Stuart's Washington presented a somewhat old-fashioned image, but Vanderlyn adapted it to the new age and gave continued life to the presidential stance. He gave the painting a republican tone more in tune with the age of Jackson than with that of Louis XVI. Popular prints continued the tradition.

In 1839, William H. Morgan and Son of Philadelphia added a full-length engraving of President Martin Van Buren (fig. 5–23) to the publisher's series of presidential prints spanning three decades. Engraved by John Sartain from Henry Inman's painting of Van Buren that hung in the New York City Hall, the portrait had been commissioned by the city in 1830 and painted while Van Buren was secretary of state. The painting showed that one did not have to be president to assume a presidential pose. The building in the background is the New York state capitol in Albany, where Van Buren had spent so much of his political career and where he was serving as governor before he resigned in 1829 to join Jackson's cabinet. Van Buren stands with a paper in his left hand rather than in his right hand as is most common in presidential poses, but the overall composition is in the tradition of presidential portraits. Although in December 1838 Inman himself requested the mayor of New York to allow the loan of the painting to Sartain for copying, he failed to win permission, and Sartain made two trips from Philadelphia to New York to copy the portrait.[47] Sartain's engraving of Van Buren corresponded well with earlier presidential prints published by the Morgan firm. This

Figure 5–25. *William Henry Harrison. Late President of the United States.* "Inaugurated March 4th 1841—Died April 4th 1841. Aged 67 Years." Engraving, 20½ x 13¹⁵⁄₁₆ inches, by John Sartain after painting by James R. Lambdin. Published by William Smith, Philadelphia, 1841. Library of Congress.

style of presidential portraiture had become so widely accepted—perhaps expected—that not only were later presidents painted in similar poses but also in several instances the head of a different president appeared in an engraving on the body of an earlier president. Sartain later employed his engraving of Van Buren to produce a print of Lincoln (fig. 5–24). Replacing Van Buren's head with that of Lincoln, he altered the costume and replaced the New York State House with the United States Capitol in the background, but otherwise the plate remained the same.[48]

Although several sets of bust portraits of the presidents were offered to the public, no pub-

Figure 5–26. *John Tyler*. Oil on canvas, 35⅛ x 25¼, by James R. Lambdin, 1841. The White House.

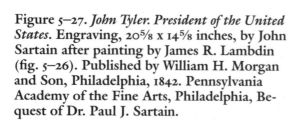

Figure 5–27. *John Tyler. President of the United States.* Engraving, 20⅝ x 14⅝ inches, by John Sartain after painting by James R. Lambdin (fig. 5–26). Published by William H. Morgan and Son, Philadelphia, 1842. Pennsylvania Academy of the Fine Arts, Philadelphia, Bequest of Dr. Paul J. Sartain.

Figure 5–28. *Andrew Jackson. "The Union Must and Shall Be Preserved."* Engraving, 20⅝ x 14½ inches, by John Sartain from plate of John Tyler (fig. 5–27). Published by William Smith, Philadelphia. Library of Congress.

lisher attempted a complete series of full-length presidential portraits. At the same time, portrait painters continued to follow the style that had evolved from Stuart and his imitators, and some of these images were copied in popular prints. John Sartain engraved the portrait of William Henry Harrison painted by James R. Lambdin, picturing Harrison wearing a cape and standing with his hand on his inaugural address (fig. 5–25). A bust of Washington sits on his writing table, and the familiar chair, column, drapery, and vista opening to the Capitol complete the picture. Published in Philadelphia, the print appeared in 1841 after Harrison's death, and the demand for it was strong.

Between April 7 and July 2, 1841, eleven hundred copies were printed.[49]

In the same year, Lambdin painted a similar portrait of Harrison's successor, John Tyler, though without a cape (fig. 5–26).[50] In Lambdin's painting, Tyler's hand rests on a book instead of the frequently pictured document, but the stance is presidential, and the traditional columns and a vista to the Capitol are present. Lambdin's portrait of Tyler was also engraved by Sartain (fig. 5–27). In the manner in which he employed the same plate for portraits of Van Buren and Lincoln, Sartain later used the Tyler plate to make a print of Jackson titled *Andrew Jackson: "The Union Must and Shall Be Preserved"* (fig. 5–28).

It is surprising to find an engraver of Sar-

Figure 5–29. *Andrew Jackson*. Engraving, 26 x 19½ inches, by Alexander H. Ritchie after painting by Dennis M. Carter. Printed by Ritchie and Company, New York, 1860. Library of Congress.

Figure 5–30. *Abraham Lincoln, President of the United States*. Engraving, 26 x 19½ inches. Published by John C. Buttre, New York, [1864–1865]. Library of Congress.

tain's stature being involved in such deception, but he was by no means the only engraver or publisher employing the artifice. A print of Jackson engraved by Alexander H. Ritchie pictures Jackson standing with his hand on a document reading "The Union Must and Shall Be Preserved" (fig. 5–29). Published in New York and copyrighted February 20, 1860, the print conveys a theme appropriate for the times. The plate was later employed by John C. Buttre to publish a print of Lincoln (fig. 5–30). In Buttre's print Lincoln's head appears on Jackson's body, with only minor alterations in dress. Lincoln is even pictured holding Jackson's distinctive eyeglasses. A bust of Washington, not in the Jackson print, sits on the table, serving to tie Lincoln with the first president while blocking from the background the Capitol—larger in Lincoln's day than in Jackson's.[51]

Even after excluding those examples in which he reused old plates to picture different heads on the same body, Sartain remained the most prolific engraver of full-length presidential portraits during the decades of the 1840s and 1850s—a time when lithography was increasingly replacing engraving in the production of popular prints. For his portrait of James K. Polk, Sartain offered a modified version of a traditional presidential portrait (fig. 5–31). Copying the head from a bust portrait of Polk by Thomas Sully, he draped a cape over Polk's shoulders, creating a pose similar to that of Harrison in the portrait by Lambdin, which Sartain had earlier engraved (fig. 5–25). Although Polk holds a document in his hand and the column and drapery are present, the setting lacks the embellishments of office and the symbols of the republic usually found in full-length

Figure 5–32. *Millard Fillmore.* Engraving, 19¹⁵/₁₆ x 14½ inches, by John Sartain. Published by William Smith, Philadelphia, circa 1850. National Portrait Gallery, Smithsonian Institution.

Figure 5–31. *James Knox Polk, President of the United States.* Engraving, 24¼ x 16½ inches, by John Sartain after portrait by Thomas Sully. Published by V. F. and M. F. Harrison, Philadelphia, 1845. Library of Congress.

presidential portraits.

Sartain's engraving of President Millard Fillmore (fig. 5–32) also lacks something of the expected presidential aura, in a time when presidential leadership seemed to have lost some of its strength and inspiration. The presidential chair is adorned with the eagle and shield of the republic, and the table beside the president holds books and papers in the tradition of Stuart's model. Yet the absence of a strong column of order or a vista of power reduces the grandeur of the portrait, and the presidential stance seems subdued. Nonetheless, the basic composition displays a persistence into the 1850s of the style that Stuart had initiated a half-century earlier.

The presidential stance illustrated in this chapter was not unique to presidential portraiture. Any person could have a portrait painted in a similar style, and many statesmen did.[52] Presidential aspirants were not averse to seeing themselves posed in the manner of the presidential image that popular prints had created in the public eye. In this book, prints of presidential candidates have not been included, but a lithograph of Polk that appeared during the campaign of 1844 merits special attention. Published in Nashville, Tennessee, in July 1844, the lithograph by Alfred M. Hoffy of Philadelphia (fig. 5–33) was taken from a painting by W. B. Cooper, the existence of which is not known today. Though the embellishments are spartan and Polk is awkwardly posed, the basic ingredients of the presidential stance are present. Polk stands with his hand on documents and papers on the table beside him against a

JAMES K. POLK.

Published by Barnard & Freeman—Nashville, Tennessee. July 1844.

Figure 5–33. *James K. Polk.* Lithograph, 17⅛ x 13¹⁵⁄₁₆ inches, by Alfred M. Hoffy after painting by W. B. Cooper. Published by Barnard and Freeman, Nashville, 1844. National Portrait Gallery, Smithsonian Institution.

background of columns and flowing drapery. The flag in the background adds to the popularized character of the print. It is a portrait of a candidate in the halls of power, ready to step into the presidential role. The print illustrates both the popularization of the traditional presidential stance and the ubiquity of that image in American culture.

With the growing use of lithography in the 1840s and 1850s, increasing informality was evident in the popular prints offering presidential portraits for a mass market. At the same time, the traditional style of presidential portraiture made popular by formal engraved prints persisted in formal likenesses painted by portraitists. Among them, George P. A. Healy was one of the most active American portrait painters in the two decades before the Civil War.

Born in Boston in 1813, Healy, as a young, aspiring artist, had practiced his skills by copy-

ing portraits of John Adams by John Singleton Copley and of Washington by Gilbert Stuart. Following study in Europe, he rose rapidly to prominence as a portraitist of presidents after King Louis Philippe commissioned him to paint a series of portraits from life of American presidents and other statesmen for the gallery at Versailles. John Tyler was the first American president whom Healy painted from life. In 1845 the artist took the last portrait of Andrew Jackson to be painted before the former president's death, and soon afterward he painted John Quincy Adams. The French monarch also commissioned the American portraitist to copy a series of presidential portraits, the earliest request being to copy Gilbert Stuart's Lansdowne portrait of Washington. In the course of his career Healy painted eleven presidents from life and made a number of copies of these likenesses. He completed at least eight por-

Figure 5–34. *Millard Fillmore*. Oil on canvas, 92⅝ x 56¾ inches, by George P. A. Healy, 1857. The White House.

Figure 5–35. *Martin Van Buren*. Oil on canvas, 59¹⁵⁄₁₆ x 44¾ inches, by George P. A. Healy, 1858. The White House.

traits of Franklin Pierce. He also copied important earlier portraits of American presidents by Stuart, Vanderlyn, and others.[53]

In 1857 Congress authorized the joint committee on the Library of Congress to contract with Healy for a series of portraits of the presidents of the United States for the executive mansion and appropriated five thousand dollars, with the provision that the cost of a full-length portrait should not exceed one thousand dollars.[54] It was no doubt a blow to Healy's pride that the committee was given the discretion to purchase instead of Healy's work such of Gilbert Stuart's portraits of the presidents as might be for sale; but in the end the commission went to Healy.

The chairman of the library committee authorized the first payment of one thousand dollars to Healy on January 30, 1858, for which

the artist delivered a full-length portrait of Millard Fillmore (fig. 5–34).[55] President Fillmore stands in a presidential pose with his right hand resting on a copy of the Constitution—the covering page of which is embellished with a portrait of President Washington. The Capitol of the United States can be seen in the opening vista, while the traditional column, drapery, and presidential chair complete the setting.

In the course of the next eighteen months Healy delivered to Congress portraits of Martin Van Buren, James K. Polk, Franklin Pierce, John Quincy Adams, and John Tyler.[56] All were described by the artist as half-length depictions, but the canvases may be more appropriately considered as three-quarter length. The portraits of Van Buren (fig. 5–35) and Pierce (fig. 5–36) are typical, though John

Figure 5–36. *Franklin Pierce.*
Oil on canvas, 61⅝ x 46½
inches, by George P. A. Healy,
1858. The White House.

Quincy Adams, pictured in old age, was shown seated.[57] Healy painted Van Buren and Pierce in similar standing poses, each standing with his right hand on papers on a table beside him, though the portrait of Pierce contains more embellishments. Under the table leg in the Pierce canvas, a large volume is entitled *Laws and Constitution of the United States.* Healy received eight hundred dollars for each of these five canvases.[58]

While completing the portraits commissioned by Congress, Healy also painted a full-length portrait of James Buchanan (fig. 5–37), which he unsuccessfully tried to get Congress—and later the president—to purchase. In December 1859 he sent the large painting, 100 x 64 inches, to Sen. James A. Pearce, chairman of the joint committee on the Library of Congress, as an example of full-length portraits

that he would like to paint of all the presidents. The artist painted Buchanan standing with his left hand on a copy of the Constitution of the United States. Behind him the column, drapery, and presidential chair offer the required accompaniments of state portraiture, while the opening vista shows the recently erected equestrian statue of Andrew Jackson that could be seen from the White House. If that statue reminded viewers of earlier glories, the darkening clouds above it also must have suggested an uncertain future.

Whatever the merits of Healy's painting, Congress—faced with matters far weightier and more critical than purchasing presidential portraits—declined it. As the crisis of the Union deepened and the artist's personal finances became desperate, Healy wrote plaintively to Buchanan on Christmas Day 1860 ask-

Figure 5–37. *James Buchanan.* Oil on canvas, 100 x 64 inches, by George P. A. Healy, 1859. Dickinson College Collection. Gift of Mrs. Merle White Allen.

ing the president to purchase the portrait for a thousand dollars. With the Union collapsing around him, Buchanan had greater concerns and left office without purchasing the work. By the summer of 1861, with the Union and the Confederacy at war, Healy offered the portrait to the still uninterested Buchanan for five hundred dollars.[59] Although Healy's unwanted painting languished in a country where neither Buchanan nor his portraits stood very high in public estimation, this last presidential portrait before the Civil War clearly displayed the tradition of presidential portraiture that had prevailed since Washington's day. That tradition, which John Vanderlyn codified in his portrait of Washington commissioned by Congress in 1832 (plate 3), is evident in Healy's painting. From Washington to Lincoln the style of state portraiture introduced by Gilbert Stuart dominated the making of presidential portraits.

CHAPTER VI

Heads of State

N 1792 the Senate of the United States included in a bill to establish a mint a provision to put on coins "an impression or representation of the head of the President of the United States for the time being," along with his name and "the succession of the Presidency numerically."[1] When the measure reached the House of Representatives, it touched off a heated debate, and a motion was introduced to substitute for the image of the incumbent president a representation "emblematic of Liberty, with an inscription of the word Liberty." Rep. John Page of Virginia expressed the concern of many members when he deplored the Senate proposal as following the practice of monarchies in exhibiting the heads of kings on their coins. "I am certain," he declared, "that it will be more agreeable to the citizens of the United States, to see the head of Liberty on their coin, than the heads of Presidents." Page told his colleagues that the people needed no added ways to honor Washington. "They have his busts, his pictures everywhere." To put Washington's image on coinage "would be viewed by the world as a stamp of Royalty on our coins."[2]

The House struck the Senate provision from the bill, refused to recede from the change when the Senate returned the bill, and prevailed in the final passage of the act. A die had already been made, and some specimens with Washington's head had been struck when Congress rejected the proposal.[3] But as Rep. James Madison noted: "It was agitated with some fervor and the first vote of the house confirmed by a larger majority."[4] So strong were the feelings against the image of the president appearing on coinage in a republic that the precedent set in 1792 has subsequently been altered only in putting a president's image on a coin after his death. Even that practice did not begin until the twentieth century, and only a few presidents have been so honored.

Although President Washington's image did not appear on the coins of the United States, it had already appeared on commemorative medals. The first portrait medal of Washington to be struck in the United States was offered to the public by James Manly of Philadelphia early in 1790 (fig. 6–1). A notice in New York's *Gazette of the United States*, soliciting subscribers to the medal, began:

> Medals, from the earliest period of time, have been regarded, by every enlightened people, as the greatest help to history, and the best method of transmitting to posterity the memory of the heroes and patriots of the age, and one of the most honorary compliments a grateful people could confer on their favourites;—As the history of mankind furnishes no instance of a hero or patriot who has better deserved, or has been more justly intitled to the affections or esteem of a grateful people, than the President of the United States—an artist is induced to offer the citizens

Figure 6–1. George Washington medal, by James Manly, Philadelphia, 1790. Gold, 48 mm diameter. Massachusetts Historical Society.

of America, a medal with a striking and approved likeness, and such inscriptions or allegorical figures as shall best suit so great a character.[5]

The image of Washington on the obverse of the Manly medal was derived from a likeness taken by Joseph Wright. Manly offered it in white metal for one dollar, in gold-colored metal for two dollars, in silver for four dollars, and in gold according to weight.[6] The latter appears to have been rare, though the example reproduced here was struck in gold. Despite the advertised promise of allegorical figures, the medal lacks such adornments. The obverse is inscribed "Geo. Washington Born Virginia Feb. 11, 1732." The reverse contains the lines "General of the American Armies, 1775. Resigned, 1783. President of the United States, 1789." Above the inscription is a star, and below, "J. Manly &c. 1790."

The gold medal is signed "Brooks" on the edge of the bust of Washington. Some, but not all, impressions in other metals also carry that signature, indicating that Samuel Brooks, a Philadelphia goldsmith and seal engraver, had a role in the execution of the medal.[7] At the same time, Manly's signature is on the reverse, and justification for referring to the work as the "Manly medal" is provided by the following announcement appearing in the editor's column of the *Federal Gazette and Philadelphia Evening Post*, March 20, 1790:

> We have the pleasure to inform our Customers and the Public in general, that a beautiful medal, with *a fine profile* of the venerated PRESIDENT of these states has lately been executed in this city by Mr. James Manly, an Irish artist, who resided a considerable time in London. Mr. Manly has had uncommon difficulties to contend with in executing so capital a branch of the fine arts in a country where the auxiliary arts have not yet arrived at perfection.

This commentary may explain why the promised allegorical figures did not appear on the medal. In the same issue of the *Federal Gazette* the following advertisement from Manly also appeared:

> General Washington's Historical Medals
> A Striking and approved likeness taken from life, in silver, white and gold-coloured metal—from one dollar to four—are now ready to be delivered to those patriotic Gentlemen who have subscribed, and to every citizen throughout the United States, who have virtue to esteem that exalted character, or generosity to patronise the arts and manufactures of America. They are to be had at the Artist's, No. 1, Carter's-alley, Philadelphia.

Since the initial notice had indicated that the medal would be struck in gold, the fact that gold was not mentioned in this announcement may indicate that the gold impressions had not yet been struck.

Similar to the Manly medal was the Twigg medal (fig. 6–2), which offered an image of Washington taken from a profile etching by Joseph Wright (fig. 6–3). Wright's portrait of Washington, printed on a card, was available in New York as early as June 1790, when Jefferson sent a print to his daughter Martha.[8] Twigg signed the bust on the obverse of the medal and inscribed the image simply "George Washington." The reverse carries an inscription similar to that on the Manly medal: "General of

Figure 6–2. George Washington medal, signed "Twigg," circa 1790. White medal, 35 mm diameter. National Numismatic Collection, Smithsonian Institution.

Figure 6–3. *G. Washington*. Etching, 2⁹⁄₁₆ x 1¹⁵⁄₁₆ inches, by Joseph Wright, New York, 1790. I. N. Phelps Stokes Collection, New York Public Library, Astor, Lenox and Tilden Foundations.

Figure 6–4. George Washington medal, by John Reich, commissioned by Joseph Sansom, Philadelphia, 1806. Silver, 40 mm diameter. American Numismatic Society.

the American Armies 1775. Resign'd the Command 1783. Elected President of the United States. 1789."

Artistically the most important medal celebrating the presidency of Washington was struck after his death. In October 1806, *Poulson's American Daily Advertiser*, published in Philadelphia, carried an advertisement for a silver medal with "A Head of Washington as President," executed "by that celebrated Artist John Reich—the likeness from a drawing of Stuart's sketched on purpose."[9] Reich, a tal-

ented German immigrant, already had executed two medals of President Jefferson. The advertisement did not identify the "person of taste" who had commissioned the medal, but Joseph Sansom, a wealthy Philadelphian, was the sponsor of the work.

The design of the medal (fig. 6–4) is striking. The bust of Washington, in civilian dress, is inscribed simply "G. Washington Pres. Unit. Sta." The notice announcing the medal described the reverse as depicting "the ensigns of Authority (civil and military) deposited in laurels, upon the tablet of the United States." These are symbolized by a sword and fasces laid on a pedestal from which a fringed cloth is pulled back to reveal the shield of the United States. The inscription records, "Commiss. Resigned: Presidency Relinq.," with the date, 1797, when Washington relinquished the presidency. The promoters of the medal described the work as "the most splendid monument that has been erected to the memory of Washington."[10] The medal must have been popular, for in the following year it was advertised as being for sale not only in silver but also in bronze and

Figure 6–5. George Washington peace medal, 1792. Silver, 180 x 132 mm. Buffalo and Erie County Historical Society.

white metal.[11]

The same anti-monarchical attitudes that led lawmakers of the young republic to refuse to put the image of the head of state on coinage were also reflected in the design of the earliest peace medals presented by presidential envoys to Indian chiefs. Representatives of European rulers and American colonial emissaries had long followed the custom of presenting medals with the head of a reigning monarch to Indian subjects at the time of making treaties or on other special occasions. The practice, Jefferson wrote in 1793, was "an ancient custom from time immemorial."[12] The new American republic continued the tradition of medal giving, seeking at the same time to persuade Indians to exchange medals with the heads of European monarchs for medals with the image of the American president, thereby demonstrating their loyalty to the new American rulers.

The medals introduced during Washington's presidency are quite unlike the European medals. Instead of being round, they are oval, and

they do not contain the traditional head of a ruler. A silver peace medal made in 1792, inscribed "George Washington President," is engraved with a peaceful scene rather than the head of the president (fig. 6–5). In place of a monarchical image, Washington is pictured standing beside an Indian chief, who is wearing one of the oval medals around his neck and sharing a peace pipe with the president. Washington appears in uniform but wears no hat, and his sword is sheathed. The chief's tomahawk lies on the ground. In the background a farmer is shown plowing his field with oxen, and a distant barn represents the mark of permanent settlement. Engraved on the reverse of the medal is an early version of the seal of the United States. Each Washington peace medal is unique, being individually engraved, but all the medals depict similar scenes. The medal reproduced here was presented to the Seneca chief Red Jacket in 1792.[13]

No Indian peace medals with President John Adams's image were made. When Jefferson be-

Figure 6–6. Thomas Jefferson peace medal, by John Reich, Philadelphia, 1801. Silver, 105 mm diameter. National Numismatic Collection, Smithsonian Institution.

came president, the United States mint for the first time began to strike peace medals with the bust of the president in the manner of European heads of state. No record has been located to explain the change, though the preference of the Indians for the old-style medals may be suspected. Within nine months following Jefferson's inauguration, the mint was shipping a peace medal with the new president's image to the War Department, which administered Indian affairs. The medal, produced in three sizes, was engraved by John Reich.[14] The medal was impressive in all sizes, but the largest version, struck in two sheets of silver united by a silver rim, was particularly handsome (fig.

6–6). All versions of the medal present an image of Jefferson after Houdon's bust, with the legend "Th. Jefferson President of the U.S. A.D. 1801." On the reverse the inscription "Peace and Friendship" is symbolized by a crossed tomahawk and peace pipe and by the clasped hands of an American (showing the cuff of a military uniform) and an Indian (wearing a silver band often worn by Indian chiefs). The American eagle embossed on the bracelet may have caused some confusion, for on a new medal struck after Madison became president, a bare wrist identifies the hand of the Indian (fig. 6–7). This reverse was used until the presidency of Millard Fillmore.

Figure 6–7. James Madison peace medal, by John Reich, Philadelphia, 1814. Silver, 76 mm diameter. American Numismatic Society.

The presidential image in the style of European medals proved popular with the Indians, and the design employed in the Jefferson and Madison medals became the model followed for succeeding presidents until the 1850s. A shorter bust image, such as found on a medal of John Quincy Adams engraved by Moritz Furst (fig. 6–8), replaced the longer bust portraits employed in the Jefferson and Madison medals, but little other change was made until the presidency of Fillmore.

On the new medals introduced under Fillmore, the president's head on the obverse appears in classical style. Fillmore sat for the artist Joseph Willson to model his likeness, though the engraving for the medal was done by Salathiel Ellis (fig. 6–9). Willson himself designed and executed a new reverse to replace the traditional clasped hands. Pictured is an Indian in feathered headdress and blanket facing a white American dressed in modest civilian clothes. They stand before an American flag, which envelops both, a peaceful farmland scene forming the background. Between them a plow and an ax symbolize the industrious pursuits of American society in which the Indians were encouraged to join. Reflecting a transition away from regarding Indians as military foes toward seeing them as future citizens, the words "Labor, Virtue, Honor" above the flag replaced

Figure 6–8. John Quincy Adams peace medal, obverse by Moritz Furst, Philadelphia, 1825. Silver, 51 mm diameter. National Numismatic Collection, Smithsonian Institution.

the "Peace and Friendship" legend that had been the standard inscription on the peace medals for fifty years.[15] The same reverse die was employed on the medal of Franklin Pierce (fig. 6–10), the obverse of which also followed the Fillmore model. The president's image in classical style was taken from life by Salathiel Ellis, who also executed the medal.

By the middle of the nineteenth century, when the images of Fillmore and Pierce appeared on medals originally devised to promote the friendship and loyalty of American Indians, the peace medals had taken on an

Figure 6–9. Millard Fillmore peace medal, by Joseph Willson and Salathiel Ellis, Philadelphia, 1851. Silver, 63 mm diameter. American Numismatic Society.

Figure 6–10. Franklin Pierce peace medal, by Salathiel Ellis, Philadelphia, 1853. Silver, 63 mm diameter. National Numismatic Collection, Smithsonian Institution.

added significance. They had become an iconographic record of the presidency and of unusual historical significance. As early as 1825, Thomas McKenney, the head of the Bureau of Indian Affairs, reminded the director of the mint that "these medals should be as perfect in their resemblance of the original, as the artist can make them. They are intended, not for the Indians, only, but for posterity."[16] The medals, in truth, were becoming of increasing interest to other Americans. In 1831 President Jackson requested three of the small silver medals with his image (fig. 6–11) for his own use, paying three dollars each for them.[17] Moritz Furst, the

diesinker who engraved the peace medals of presidents Monroe through Van Buren, early sensed something of the growing importance of the series. In the 1820s he sought to fill out the set by executing medals of Washington and John Adams in the style introduced with the Jefferson medals. President John Quincy Adams tried to dissuade him, "convinced that in a country where there is no taste for medals he could not expect to be paid for his labor in the die."[18] Though Furst was unsuccessful in getting sufficient support to strike the medals, his die of the Adams medal survived.[19]

In the 1840s the director of the mint sought

Figure 6–11. Andrew Jackson peace medal, obverse by Moritz Furst, Philadelphia, 1831. Silver, 51 mm diameter. Massachusetts Historical Society.

Figure 6–12. Thomas Jefferson inaugural medal, by John Reich, Philadelphia, 1802. Silver, 45 mm diameter. American Numismatic Society.

approval to strike Furst's John Adams medal and also to add a Washington example to the series, but he was unable to obtain funding. Years later, in 1878, the mint finally struck the Adams medal and in 1903 added one of Washington.[20] By then, more than a decade after the medals had ceased to be designed specifically for the Indians, the series had become a record more of the presidency than of Indian relations. The fact that the Treasury Department today still sells restrikes of these medals makes the series unmatched in its place in the iconography of the presidency.

Representing the best of early American medallic art, the striking of Indian peace medals also gave rise to the making of presidential inaugural medals. There were no medals struck for the inaugurations of either Washington or John Adams. The first medal to honor a new president celebrated the inauguration of Jefferson in 1801. In February 1802 the *Aurora* of Philadelphia published an advertisement announcing "A STRIKING LIKENESS of THOMAS JEFFERSON, President of the U. States; on a *Medallion* executed by Mr. Reish, the celebrated German artist, to commemorate, at once, the Era of American Independence, and the auspicious day which raised Mr. Jefferson, to the dignity of President over a free people."[21] The absence of a precedent for an inaugural medal may explain why the design incorporates the commemoration of American

independence with the celebration of Jefferson's inauguration, but the primacy of the honor to Jefferson is demonstrated by the placement of his image on the obverse of the medal.

John Reich had executed the Indian peace medal with Jefferson's image, and he again used the bust by Houdon as the model for the inaugural medal (fig. 6–12). Jefferson's profile faces in the opposite direction from his image on the peace medal, and the shorter bust length of the smaller inaugural medal (45 millimeters in diameter) produced a more attractive portrait. Jefferson himself was impressed with Reich's work. Sending one of the medals to his daughter Martha, he pronounced the artist "equal to any in the world." Confirming that his own image was "taken from Houdon's bust, for he never saw me," Jefferson indicated his approval and remarked, "It sells the more readily as the prints which have been offered the public are such miserable caracatures." Martha Jefferson Randolph judged the medal "elegant," which was the same word that Rep. Samuel Latham Mitchill of New York chose to describe it in sending one of the medals to his wife. Mitchill also wrote, "The likeness is striking."[22]

The reverse of the Jefferson medal would not have disappointed purchasers who had seen it described in the advertisement in the *Aurora* as presenting "emblematical figures, in a style of workmanship never equalled before in this country, and excelled in none."[23] The goddess of Liberty, shown standing by a rock representing the Constitution, holds in her hand the Declaration of Independence—a fitting tribute to its author whose image appeared on the obverse. An eagle bearing a laurel wreath hovers above. The legend proclaims, "Under His Wing is Protection," and in exergue, "To commemorate July 4 1776." The handsome medal sold for $4.25 in silver and $1.25 in white metal, making an example of a work of art and the image of a popular president available to a wide stratum of the populace.[24]

Despite the popularity of Jefferson's inaugural medal, no similar medals were struck for either Madison or Monroe. The delay in the striking of a new Indian peace medal bearing Madison's image may explain the failure to repeat the Jefferson precedent. Although the peace medals with Madison's image (fig. 6–7) bear the date 1809 (designating the beginning of his presidency), the medals did not appear until late in 1814—midway in Madison's second term.[25]

Moritz Furst, who succeeded John Reich as the diesinker at the mint and executed Indian peace medals of the presidents from Monroe through Van Buren, revived the striking of inaugural medals. When President John Quincy Adams sat for Furst to draw his likeness for the peace medal, the artist revealed to him a plan to execute an inaugural medal. In May 1825—not long after his inauguration—Adams recorded in his diary:

> Mr. Furst the Medalist came this morning and I sat to him about half an hour to take a profile of my face, with a pencil on paper from which he is to engrave it on the die for the medals to be distributed to the Indians. In about ten days the die will be so far advanced that he will ask two or three sittings more, and he is engraving a separate medal for himself, the head of which he in-

tends to engrave in the antique costume. In the medals for the Indians the bust is in the modern dress.[26]

Adams encouraged the artist's private undertaking by subscribing for ten silver medals, but despite Furst's care in taking the likeness from life, the president found the result wholly unsatisfactory. When Adams received the ten medals he had ordered, he paid Furst his price of ten dollars each but complained in his diary that they were "intrinsically worth about one dollar each." Adams later referred to Furst as "a wretched Medalist."[27]

The image that Adams so strongly disliked followed the profile on the Indian peace medal (fig. 6–8), but it is an even poorer likeness. The obverse is inscribed "John Quincy Adams President of the United States," together with the date of his inauguration, March 4, 1825 (fig. 6–13). The reverse displays considerable merit, presenting a design that Charles Francis Adams said his father had devised.[28] A figure of Minerva, the goddess of Wisdom, offering an olive branch to an Indian seated on a cornucopia symbolizes the legend "Science Gives Peace and America Plenty."

The reverses of the inaugural medals of Jefferson (fig. 6–12) and John Quincy Adams (fig. 6–13) illustrate the transition of iconographic symbols that Michael Kammen has recognized as taking place between the years following the Revolution and about 1825.[29] The medals display a transition from an emphasis on liberty to an emphasis on prosperity. On the Jefferson medal the protecting national eagle, the Declaration of Independence, and the Constitution accent the theme of liberty. On the Adams medal the eagle is placed in the background, while the cornucopia appears in the foreground to depict the theme of peace and prosperity indicated in the legend.

At the time Furst executed the medal commemorating Adams's inauguration, he apparently had instigated a plan to expand—perhaps complete—the series of inaugural medals to which he was contributing the second example. In 1825 Adams recorded that he had been shown casts made by Furst for medals "of Mr. Monroe, Mr. Madison, and the second Presidency of G. Washington 1796 all badly executed."[30] Furst must have received no more

Figure 6–13. John Quincy Adams inaugural medal, by Moritz Furst, Philadelphia, 1825. Silver, 51 mm diameter. National Numismatic Collection, Smithsonian Institution.

Figure 6–14. Andrew Jackson inaugural medal, by unknown artist, 1833. Silver, 18 mm diameter. Massachusetts Historical Society.

encouragement from others than he did from Adams to pursue the work, for there is no evidence that the pieces were struck at the time.[31]

The next inaugural medal known today honored the second inauguration of Andrew Jackson in 1833 (fig. 6–14). The small silver medal, about the size of a dime, is unusual, and little is known about it. The image of Jackson on the obverse was taken from an engraving by James Barton Longacre, but the medalist is unknown.[32] The reverse is ornately inscribed: "And. Jackson Inaugurated Presidt. U.S. Second Term Mar. IV. 1833."

With the inauguration of Jackson's successor, a sequence began of four similar medals commemorating the inaugurals of Martin Van Buren, John Tyler, James K. Polk, and Zachary Taylor. The medals were private ventures, but they were struck at the United States mint by mint employees. The obverse of each example was struck from the die used for the respective middle-size Indian peace medal.[33] The new reverse dies were similar in design, providing the inauguration date within a wreath.[34] The image of Van Buren (fig. 6–15) was engraved by Moritz Furst, who had done all of the peace medals beginning with Monroe.

With the medal for Tyler (fig. 6–16), the mint introduced a new process for engraving medallic portraits and gave new attention to artistic merit. Dispensing with the services of diesinkers, the mint in 1841 installed a mechanized engraving device known as a portrait lathe. The process required the portrait image to be modeled in wax or clay. A plaster cast made from this was then cast in iron and that casting used to produce reduced facsimiles on the mechanical portrait lathe.[35] In introducing the new process, the director of the mint sought out talented artists to make the models to be copied.

The artistic quality of the portraits on the medals of Tyler (fig. 6–16) and of Polk (fig. 6–17) is high. Tyler's image was the work of Ferdinand Pettrich, a German-born sculptor, who was paid fifty dollars for two medallion likenesses, one in wax and one in plaster of paris.[36] The model of Polk's head was made by the American artist John Gadsby Chapman, who went to Washington to take the president's likeness from life. In February 1846 Polk recorded in his diary sittings "for Mr. Chapman, an artist, who at the instance of the Secretary of War is taking my likeness for the purpose of having medals prepared to be presented to the various Indian tribes."[37] Three and a half hours of sittings over three days were required before Chapman was satisfied with the likeness. He then completed the wax model on a plate about four inches in diameter and received two hundred dollars for his work. Previous to delivering the model to the mint, Chapman took two plaster casts from the wax as security against

Figure 6–15. Martin Van Buren inaugural medal, by Moritz Furst, Philadelphia, 1837. Bronze, 62 mm diameter. National Numismatic Collection, Smithsonian Institution.

Figure 6–16. John Tyler inaugural medal, by Ferdinand Pettrich, Philadelphia, 1842. Bronze, 62 mm diameter. National Numismatic Collection, Smithsonian Institution.

Figure 6–17. James K. Polk inaugural medal, by John Gadsby Chapman, Philadelphia, 1846–1847. Bronze, 62 mm diameter. American Numismatic Society.

Figure 6–18. James Buchanan inaugural medal, by Anthony C. Paquet, New York, 1857. White metal, 60 mm diameter. DeWitt Collection, University of Hartford.

Figure 6–19. Medal of first eight presidents, by W. H. Bridgens, New York, circa 1837–1840. White metal, 48 mm diameter. American Numismatic Society.

any risk in the production of the medal.[38]

President Polk did not know that the image made for the peace medal would also be employed for the obverse of a commemorative medal of his inauguration (fig. 6–17). Although the inaugural medal, like the peace medal, carried the date 1845 on the obverse, neither was struck before 1846. The Indian medal was ready by July 1846.[39] Within the next year the inaugural medal had been struck, for on June 24, 1847, when President Polk and several government officers visited the mint in Philadelphia, they were presented with gilded specimens.[40]

A similar medal commemorated the inauguration of Zachary Taylor. The die for the Taylor peace medal was used for the obverse in the same way as the dies of the Van Buren, Tyler, and Polk peace medals. The reverse copied the design found on the inaugural medals of Tyler and Polk. Taylor's medal was the last inaugural medal to be struck from Indian peace medal dies. The use of the mint's dies and government facilities to strike inaugural medals for private profit was exposed along with other irregular practices at the mint, leading to the firing of the chief engraver by President Pierce in 1853.[41] The rarity of the medal of Taylor, who died sixteen months after taking office, may indicate that it never reached the public before the scandal halted the production of inaugural medals at the mint.

Though interrupted, the tradition of making inaugural medals did not cease. A handsome specimen celebrated the inauguration of James Buchanan (fig. 6–18). The work of Anthony C. Paquet, the medal was struck in New York. Paquet departed from the profile images traditional on earlier medals by presenting a nearly

(1) George Washington   (5) James Monroe

(2) John Adams   (6) John Quincy Adams

(3) Thomas Jefferson   (7) Andrew Jackson

(4) James Madison   (8) Martin Van Buren

Figure 6–20. Medals of the first sixteen presidents, by George Hampden Lovett, New York, completed in 1861. The medals, 36 mm diameter, were struck in both white metal and copper. The reverse of each medal pictures the home of the president shown on the obverse. National Numismatic Collection, Smithsonian Institution.

(9) William Henry Harrison

(13) Millard Fillmore

(10) John Tyler

(14) Franklin Pierce

(11) James Knox Polk

(15) James Buchanan

(12) Zachary Taylor

(16) Abraham Lincoln

full-faced portrait of the new president. The observe is inscribed "James Buchanan, XVth President of the United States. Born April 23rd 1791. Inaug: March 4th 1857." The eye-catching reverse offers the seal of the United States in the center, from which lines interspersed with the names of all the states extend outward to create a sunburst effect. The encircling inscription proclaims the timely words of President Jackson: "The Union Must and Shall Be Preserved." The roster of the thirty-one states dates the medal as appearing in 1857—prior to the admission of Minnesota in 1858.

Just as engravers and lithographers offered portraits of all the presidents on a single sheet, at least one medalist took up the challenge of putting the images of the first eight presidents on a single medal. W. H. Bridgens, of New York, struck a medal only 48 millimeters in diameter with portraits of all the presidents through Martin Van Buren (fig. 6–19). Washington's portrait—slightly larger than the others—fills the center, encircled by his seven successors. Only a few of the crudely executed, miniature likenesses would be recognizable without the names inscribed above their portraits. On the reverse, within a wreath in the style used on contemporaneous inaugural medals, a roster lists the presidents pictured on the obverse. Nothing has been discovered regarding the making or distribution of the medal. It undoubtedly appeared during the presidency of Van Buren, at a time when collective likenesses of the presidents were widely popular. The medal was included in the cabinet of Washington medals assembled in the United States Mint in 1859.[42] Clearly not the work of a skilled medalist, yet remarkable in conception and effort, the medal gives expression to the historical tradition of the presidency in popular culture.

Also included among the Washington medals in the mint in 1859 was a small medal, 36 millimeters in diameter, with Washington's image on the obverse (fig. 6–20). The piece was signed "G. H. Lovett N. Y." The image derived from Washington's likeness on the "Evacuation of Boston" medal struck in France after the end of the Revolutionary War. That image, taken from Houdon's bust, had become the most popular medallic image of the first president.[43] Lovett's head of Washington is encircled by a

wreath of flowers and leaves and inscribed "George Washington, First President of the Ud. States." For the reverse Lovett engraved a picture of "Washington's Residence at Mount Vernon," signed "G.H.L. N.Y."

This Washington medal is one of a series of the presidents of the United States through Lincoln (fig. 6–20). On each medal, the president's image appears on the obverse, encircled by a wreath of the same design and similarly inscribed with the president's name and numerical designation—though the inscriptions are not always consistent in the abbreviations used. On the reverse is an engraved picture of the home of each president. Only the medals of Washington, John Adams, Jefferson, Madison, and John Quincy Adams are signed, which may indicate that Lovett did not perform all of the work for the series; but he created the style of a distinctive series.[44]

The beardless face of President Lincoln on Lovett's medal suggests that the final example in the series was struck early in 1861. All of the medals after Washington's are listed in the catalogue of medals struck in honor of the presidents of the United States from John Adams to Lincoln compiled by Alfred H. Satterlee, published in 1862.[45] The date by which Lovett's series had been completed can thus be firmly fixed, but the date when the first example may have been struck has not been determined with equal certainty, though sometime in the 1850s prior to 1859 seems a reasonable conjecture.

Some of the presidential likenesses on Lovett's medals derived from Indian peace medals, which were the likely models for the images of Jefferson, Madison, Monroe, Jackson, and Van Buren. Images of other presidents appear to have derived from a variety of sources. Among the pictorial sources for the residences of the presidents, Benson Lossing's *The Lives of the Presidents of the United States* (1848) was a possibility for many of the homes of the presidents prior to Zachary Taylor.

Lovett's series reflects an interesting transformation in the presentation of presidential images. The contrast of these medals with earlier medals of Washington, Jefferson, or John Quincy Adams is revealing. Classical or allegorical designs adorn the earlier works, connecting the president with symbols of the nation or public service. Lovett's medals associate the presidents with their private lives, reflecting a domestication of the presidency that already could be seen in such publications as Lossing's *Lives of the Presidents*, where each president's portrait is accompanied by a drawing of his home (figs. 9–20 and 9–21). Public interest in the homes of the presidents had grown with the mass production of inexpensive drawings. Lovett's medals—struck in copper and white metal—made widely available inexpensive works of artistic merit, combining traditional medallic portraits of the presidents with well-executed engravings of presidential homes. While contributing to the historical record, the medals reminded Americans that the men who temporarily occupied the White House had permanent roots among the people.

CHAPTER VII

Presidents Caricatured

N APRIL 1789, while New Yorkers anxiously awaited the arrival of President-elect George Washington in the temporary capital for his inauguration, John Armstrong described the preparations for his reception. "All the world here and elsewhere are busy in collecting flowers and sweets of every kind to amuse and delight him in his approach and at his arrival," the former member of the Confederation Congress reported. "Even Roger Sherman has set his head at work to devise some style of address more novel and dignified than Excellency." Yet amid the adulation of the new president, Armstrong found skeptics "who doubt its propriety and wits who amuse themselves with its extravagance." He offered as an example the appearance of a caricature entitled *The Entry*, which he said was "full of very disloyal and profane allusions." It pictured Washington in the arms of a mulatto servant mounted on an ass, led by Washington's aide David Humphreys chanting "hosannas and birthday odes." A couplet provided the motto of the drawing:

> The glorious time has come to pass
> When David shall conduct an Ass.

Armstrong thought the caricature demonstrated "that wit spares nothing—neither Washington nor God—and that the former like the latter will have something to suffer and

much to forgive."[1] Clearly, Armstrong expected that even the heroic Washington would soon be suffering at the hand of caricaturists. But Washington was largely spared such representations, partly because the art of caricature was not yet far advanced in the United States. Little evidence of the caricaturing of Washington has survived. Armstrong's description is the only reference located relating to Washington in caricature while president. *The Entry*, which Armstrong fortunately described so fully, is not known to be extant today, and no contemporaneous caricature of President Washington has been located.

A caricature commonly identified as depicting Washington can, on close study, more convincingly be interpreted as picturing President John Adams. Entitled *The Times; a Political Portrait* (fig. 7–1), the caricature contains the legend:

> Triumph Government: perish all its enemies.
> Traitors be warned: justice though slow, is sure.

These words and the content of the drawing portray the country at the time of the war crisis with France following the XYZ affair in 1798. The print depicts the mobilization of the army to repulse a feared French invasion, the Republican opposition to the president's actions, and the administration's determination to sup-

180

Figure 7–1. *The Times; a Political Portrait.* Engraving, 12¼ x 17¾ inches, by unknown artist, circa 1798. New-York Historical Society.

press internal subversion. Benjamin Franklin Bache, the young Republican editor of the Philadelphia *Aurora*—the opposition newspaper most detested by the Federalists—is shown being trampled by the troops while a dog demonstrates its disrespect for his newspaper. The artist was remarkably successful in offering a political portrait of the United States in 1798, effectively displaying how the two parties viewed each other. On the one hand, he presented the Federalists' view of their vigorous efforts to defend the country against enemies foreign and domestic, while hampered by Republican obstructionism. On the other hand, he revealed the Republicans' alarm that the administration was using an imaginary threat of foreign invasion to expand the army unnecessarily and to pass the alien and sedition acts to suppress internal dissent and run roughshod over the freedom of the press.

The figure in the carriage leading the troops does not resemble Washington either in size or in features, which were widely known through portraits and engravings. Though Washington would be named commanding general of the expanded army by President Adams in July 1798, he never took the field. Nor did Adams. But beneath the military hat is a countenance similar to many contemporary engraved portraits of Adams, and the officer's size is appropriate for Adams's stature. While Adams is rarely thought of as having worn a military uniform, it is of peculiar interest in interpreting this print to note that in May 1798 when twelve hundred young men marched to the president's house in Philadelphia to offer their services against France, Adams appeared to address them wearing full military uniform and a sword.[2]

More easily recognized are the figures of Jefferson pulling a rope attached to the carriage and Albert Gallatin clinging to a spoke of a wheel. William Cobbett, writing as "Peter Porcupine," had earlier used the phrase "Stop de

Figure 7–2. *Look on This Picture, and on This*. Engraving, 9⅞ x 12¼ inches, by unknown artist, New York, June 1807. New-York Historical Society.

Wheels of de Government" to ridicule Gallatin's speeches in Congress and had even published a caricature of Gallatin mouthing the words.[3] In June 1798 New York Federalist Robert Troup in commenting on the Republican leader in Congress had remarked, "Gallatin continues to clog the wheels of government, but he has not sufficient strength to stop its motion."[4] The identity of the accomplice of Jefferson and Gallatin in trying to stop Adams's carriage is not clear. As this example indicates, the deciphering of early American caricatures is rarely easy and sometimes impossible, but these ephemeral materials offer an opportunity to view popular perceptions of the presidency not elsewhere available.

Not until the presidency of Andrew Jackson,

when the techniques of lithography permitted the speedy production of large numbers of inexpensive prints, did political caricatures become widespread in the United States.[5] Prior to Jackson's presidency, the president most frequently depicted in caricature was Jefferson, though the number of extant Jefferson caricatures is small in comparison to the large number of Jackson cartoons. In artistic quality, Jefferson's presidency provides some of the best examples of early American caricatures. One striking print contrasts Washington and Jefferson by employing well-executed engraved portraits of both presidents, embellished by contrasting symbols and comparisons disparaging of Jefferson (fig. 7–2). The portraits, derived from Gilbert Stuart, are described in words ex-

Figure 7–3. Cartoon by unknown artist, circa 1808–1809. Etching, 12⅞ x 17 inches, titled in ink above first frame "An old Philosopher teaching his mad Son economical Projects." Free Library of Philadelphia.

tracted from William Shakespeare, presenting a harsh portrayal of the incumbent president. While Washington's portrait is crowned by a laurel wreath radiating halolike rays, a burning candle produces a darkening cloud above Jefferson's head. Washington's portrait rests on books inscribed *Order*, *Law*, and *Religion*. Jefferson's image rests on volumes entitled *Sophisms*, *Notes on Virginia*, *Tom Paine*, *Condorcet*, and *Voltaire*. A stately lion and an American eagle support Washington's portrait, in contrast to a coiled snake and a sinister lizard beneath the portrait of Jefferson. In capital letters the artist printed a line from Hamlet asking viewers to compare the pictures, and under Washington's picture continued with Shakespeare's words:

See what a grace was seated on this brow:
An eye like Mars to threaten and command,
A combination and a form, indeed,
Where every God did seem to set his seal,
To give the world assurance of a man.[6]

In a parallel column under Jefferson's portrait, the artist continued to quote Shakespeare, presenting the president "like a mildew'd ear, / Blasting his wholesome brother." The print is dated New York, June 1807, but the artist or circumstances that produced it have not been discovered.

In the last years of Jefferson's presidency, deteriorating relations with Great Britain increasingly offered subjects for caricaturing the president. The embargo act of 1807 prohibiting all

Figure 7–4. *Intercourse or Impartial Dealings.* Etching and engraving, 11³⁄₈ x 13³⁄₄ inches, by "Peter Pencil," 1809. Houghton Library, Harvard University.

exports from the United States—the most unpopular measure of Jefferson's eight years in office—especially provoked ridicule. In the style of eighteenth-century English caricature, an unusual print with a sequence of frames shows President Jefferson and Secretary of State Madison hauling a ship into drydock at the bequest of Napoleon, while behind the curtain a disgruntled Congress debates the embargo bill in closed session (fig. 7–3). When one member, suspicious of the hand of Napoleon in the embargo bill, protests that the president is concealing everything from Congress, another member brandishes a gun to prevent the curtain from being raised.[7]

Two prints by "Peter Pencil," an artist not otherwise identified, also satirize Jefferson's embargo policy. Dated 1809, the prints constitute a pair, presenting similar figures of both Jefferson and Napoleon. In each print the head of Jefferson is copied from a widely circulated engraving by David Edwin of Rembrandt Peale's 1800 portrait of Jefferson, offering a more faithful image than characteristic of most caricatures. The print entitled *Intercourse or Impartial Dealings* (fig. 7–4) shows Jefferson submitting to a club-wielding George III, while Napoleon empties his pockets. *Non Intercourse or Dignified Retirement* (fig. 7–5) pictures Jefferson in shirtsleeves and ragged breeches, his coat on the ground, saying how fine it feels to be independent of all tailors. "I have stript my-

Figure 7–5. *Non Intercourse or Dignified Retirement*. Etching and engraving, 11¾ x 13¾ inches, by "Peter Pencill," 1809. Houghton Library, Harvard University.

self rather than submit to London or Parisian Fashion!" he exclaims. To one side, Napoleon applauds and says that Jefferson now has only to take off his shirt of Irish linen.[8]

The War of 1812 generated an unprecedented number of caricatures, especially from the pen of the prolific William Charles, a Scottish-born engraver who employed the techniques and vocabulary of English caricature for an American audience.[9] President Madison, however, was only rarely pictured in these prints. A notable exception is a print by Charles entitled *A Boxing Match, or Another Bloody Nose for John Bull* (plate 10), in which Madison appears as the embodiment of the nation in a boxing match with King George III. One of a series of

prints celebrating American naval victories over the British, *A Boxing Match* recalls the battle between the HMS *Boxer* and the USS *Enterprise* off the coast of Portugal on September 5, 1813. Sketching the two ships in the background, Charles pictured a bloodied-nosed John Bull (in the personage of George III) pleading with Brother Jonathan (represented by Madison) to stop the attack. To which, Madison replies: "Ha-Ah Johnny! you thought yourself a *Boxer* did you!—I'll let you know we are an *Enterprize*ing Nation, and ready to meet you with equal force any day." Although presidents were generally the subject of ridicule when depicted in cartoons, that was not always the case, as this print demonstrates.

Figure 7–6. *The Pedlar and his Pack or the Desperate Effort, an Over Balance.* Etching, 11 x 16½ inches, by unknown artist, 1828. American Antiquarian Society.

It is unlikely that Madison, who suffered harsh treatment at the hands of British caricaturists, would have objected to being easily recognized in Charles's drawing.[10]

The partisanship so strongly manifest in the caricatures of President Jefferson diminished in the years following the War of 1812, as the Federalist party faded from the national scene. But the "era of good feelings" under President Monroe was short-lived, and political parties revived in the 1820s. With the renewed partisan competition, satirical drawings came to be more widely employed in political campaigns than ever before. The presidential election of 1828 displayed clearly that presidents seeking reelection could expect to be attacked in caricatures. Campaign caricatures are beyond the scope of this study except insofar as they portray the presidency, but they serve to illustrate that incumbent presidents were not treated differently from other candidates. One interesting print from the presidential campaign of 1828 depicts the Jacksonian version of President John Quincy Adams's efforts to retain the presidential chair. Entitled *The Pedlar and his Pack or the Desperate Effort, an Over Balance* (fig. 7–6), the etching was the Jacksonian response to the "coffin handbill." That broadside, published by Philadelphia newspaper editor John Binns, portrayed presidential candidate Jackson as a murderer for having signed the order for the execution of six militiamen convicted of desertion during the Creek War. The black-bordered print was headed "Some Account of some of the Bloody Deeds of Gen. Jackson" and pictured at the top six large black coffins with the names of the executed militiamen; smaller black coffins were scattered throughout the print.[11] In responding to this attack on Jackson, the unknown artist of *The Pedlar* pictured editor Binns staggering under the weight of the coffins, Henry Clay, and President Adams. Secretary of State Clay, who was managing Adams's campaign for reelection, is

A GRAND FUNCTIONARY.
"The Lord High Keeper."

APARTMENT FOR T. WATKINS CRIMINALS

Have you no feeling in your Vocation.

Feeling? no! I'm acting in my MAGISTERIAL Capacity !!!! D—n the fellow he opposed my election and if he is released he'll set up a News-paper against me - Here let him rot !!!

———— Man proud man | ———— like an ANGRY APE.
Drest in a little BRIEF authority. | Plays such fantastic tricks before high heaven,
  | As make the Angels weep.

Figure 7–7. *A Grand Functionary. "The Lord High Keeper."* Lithograph, 11½ x 9¼ inches, by Edward Williams Clay, 1829. American Antiquarian Society.

shown warning Adams to hold on "for I find that the people are too much for us, and I'm sinking with Jack and his Coffins!" Editor Binns complains that he is feeling faint under the load and asks for an extra dose of Treasury patronage, while President Adams vows to hold on to the presidential chair in spite of the coffin handbills or the wishes of the people.

The proliferation of caricatures evident during the campaign of 1828 continued after Jackson's election to the presidency. Jackson's strong personality, his rough-hewn character, and the controversial policies of his administration provided inviting subjects for ridicule and satirical barbs, while the recently perfected techniques of lithography supplied the means for rapid publication of the caricaturist's draw-

ings. "This pictorial commentary was often unfriendly and frequently crude in inspiration and execution," one student of Jacksonian caricature has written, "but it marked the first major flowering of American political caricature."[12] A year after Jackson left office, Ralph Waldo Emerson would note in his journal: "Caricatures are often the truest history of the time for they only express in a pointed unequivocal action what really lies at the bottom of a great many plausible, public, hypocritical manoeuvres."[13]

Few restraints guided the hands of caricaturists as they portrayed a president who evoked both admiration and contempt. Jackson was portrayed not only as a crowned tyrant and a Napoleon but also as an pugilist, a jackass, and

Figure 7–8. *Exhibition of Cabinet Pictures*. Etching, 8 x 11 inches, by David Claypoole Johnston, 1831. American Antiquarian Society.

an ape.[14] However much Americans revered the office of the presidency and enshrined its occupants in the historical memory of the nation, presidents were never spared criticism while in office, and Jackson was subjected to more abuse than most.

A cartoon from early in his presidency depicts Jackson as a hooded, craggy-faced man incarcerating a political opponent. In *A Grand Functionary. "The Lord High Keeper"* (fig. 7–7), Edward Williams Clay pictured Jackson placing a double lock on the prison cell of Tobias Watkins, former fourth auditor of the Treasury, one of his earliest dismissals from office. The caption reads:

> Man proud man
> Drest in a little BRIEF authority.
> like an ANGRY APE.

Plays such fantastic tricks before high heaven,
As make the Angels weep.

Jackson is recorded as claiming to be acting in his magisterial capacity and saying "D——n the fellow he opposed my election and if he is released he'll set up a Newspaper against me—Here let him rot!!!" The facts of the case were that Watkins's accounts in the Treasury Department were seven thousand dollars short, and he had fled the city when the shortage was discovered. Subsequently apprehended, tried, and convicted, he became the first example of Jackson's promise to reform the government and a case widely celebrated by Jackson's admirers.[15] This caricature makes it clear that from the outset of his administration Jackson could expect no deferential treatment from political artists.

Perhaps no print is more expressive of the caricaturing of President Jackson than the extraordinary etching by David Claypoole Johnston entitled *Exhibition of Cabinet Pictures* (fig. 7–8). A wall hung with cartoons offers a visual impression of caricatures characteristic of Jackson's day, while a closer examination of the work provides a revealing view of President Jackson as seen by a major caricaturist. The print is also one for which a rare contemporary commentary survives. The *Boston Patriot and Mercantile Advertiser* for August 17, 1831, reported that the print was displayed in the windows of bookstores and "draws crowds of the curious of all classes." The reporter described it as exhibiting twenty-two pictures, "the prominent figure of which, bears a strong resemblance to the 'Greatest and best.'" Offering details about several of the drawings, the writer pointed out that "one picture represents a 'Splendid Crisis,' where certain members of the late Cabinet are at hard blows, and from the nose of one on the floor there flows a stream of pure 'red ink.'"

The elaborate print contains allusions to Jackson's opposition to the Bank of the United States, to nullification, to broken Indian treaties, and to other issues, but the contemporary viewer would have grasped immediately that the artist's central theme was the crisis in Jackson's cabinet. The design of the drawing itself is a play on the word *cabinet*, which in one sense means a small exhibition room in a museum. Both the cartoons on the wall and the titles of the books in the Cabinet Library also make it clear that the cabinet crisis stemmed from the "petticoat war" within the administration centering around Peggy Eaton, the wife of Secretary of War John H. Eaton. The marriage of Eaton to the twenty-nine-year-old daughter of a Washington tavern keeper and recent widow of a navy purser, after rumors of an affair, was the talk of Washington. When cabinet wives snubbed Mrs. Eaton and the controversy became embroiled in political rivalries within Jackson's administration, a major imbroglio ensued, climaxing in 1831 in the breaking up of Jackson's first cabinet.

Johnston's print is filled with allusions to the Eaton episode and rich in characterizations of President Jackson. The Cabinet Library on one side of the room is filled with books, only three

of which, covered with cobwebs, appear not to have been read. They are titled *Political Economy*, *Johnson's Dictionary*, and *Murray's Grammar*, a dig at Jackson's lack of literary skills. Among the books more frequently taken from the shelves are volumes entitled *School for Husbands*, *Slave of Passion*, *Innkeeper's Daughter*, *Secrets of the Tavern*, *All for Love*, and others that poke fun at the Eaton affair.

The cartoons on the wall are replete with depictions of the cabinet crisis. In the upper right corner, a petticoated figure puts a torch to Troy. In the center of the display a *New design for the Arms of the U.S.* is composed of corsets, petticoats, and a booby gannet. To the right, Jackson tries to scrub a petticoat clean, while being told by the washerwoman that he will never get the dirt out and had better dry and whitewash it. Prominent in the foreground is a drawing entitled "Scene from the comic farce of TURN OUT as played by the Administration company," showing Jackson shoving members of the cabinet out the door. The caricature in the lower right corner pictures Jackson tripping over a lady's petticoat in a skating race with Henry Clay, his expected rival in the election of 1832. Although the Boston reviewer did not describe all of the pictures, he found them "full of meaning" and advised "those who love a hearty laugh to sit down and carefully study out this unique production."

The print abounds with unflattering portrayals of Jackson. The president is shown as an ape wearing a crown, as an "enraged granny," as a blind man, and as Don Quixote attacking the Bank of the United States. An intriguing drawing at the lower right of the print contains a self-portrait of D. C. Johnston with palette in hand and a portrait of Washington on the wall behind him. The artist is displaying a portrait of a dour-faced Jackson titled "The 2d Washington" and saying that it is ridiculous to call his work a failure for "Stuart himself never made a better copy." One careful scholar has also noted that on the wall behind Jackson in the washerman scene is a miniature drawing of the full-length portrait of President Jackson, with cane and hat in hand, by Ralph E. W. Earl, soon to appear in a lithographic reproduction (fig. 5–21).[16]

Another important caricature of Jackson inspired by the cabinet change attracted the at-

The Rats leaving a Falling House.

Figure 7–9. *The Rats leaving a Falling House.* Lithograph, 18¼ x 11¾ inches, by Edward Williams Clay, 1831. American Antiquarian Society.

tention of ex-president John Quincy Adams, recently elected to the House of Representatives. Passing through Philadelphia in April 1831, Adams noticed that there was scarcely any topic of conversation other than the recent breaking up of the president's cabinet in Washington. "There was a caricature published here on Saturday upon this incident, called 'the rats leaving a falling house'" (fig. 7–9), he recorded. "Four sleek rats, with faces of recognizable likeness to the four Secretaries, are scampering away upon the floor. Jackson is struggling to sustain himself in a chair that is breaking under him; and his right foot is pressing upon Van Buren's tail, as if to detain him.

An altar of reform is falling over, with an imp having the head of an ass, the body of a monkey, and the wings of a bat, armed with a broom. The room is hung round with papers, on each of which is inscribed 'Resignation;' and the President's spitting-box and broken tobacco-pipe are on the floor."[17]

Contemporary descriptions of caricatures are so exceptional that Adams's explanation has been quoted in full. It leaves little to be added except to note that the heads of the fleeing cabinet members are, from left to right, those of Secretary of War John H. Eaton, Secretary of the Navy John Branch, Secretary of State Martin Van Buren, whom Jackson is trying to re-have been the first president to be pictured wearing spectacles, was frequently shown in caricatures with eyeglasses on his forehead or in his hair, as sketched in pencil by Clay in 1831 (fig. 7–10). Adams also supplied rare information on the circulation of presidential caricatures, reporting that ten thousand copies of the print had been struck off and that two thousand copies had been sold in a single day. He regarded this as an indication of the low estimation in which Jackson and his administration were held—a not surprising assessment from the man denied a second presidential term by Jackson's electoral victory in 1828.[19]

During Jackson's campaign for reelection in 1832, political artists depicted the president as both a tyrant and the champion of democracy. In artistic quality and boldness of attack on an incumbent president, the most impressive print is a lithograph titled *King Andrew the First* (fig. 7–11). The drawing, by an unknown artist, pictures Jackson in regal robes, a crown on his head and a scepter in his right hand, standing before a throne. Trampled beneath his feet are the Constitution of the United States, a coat of arms proclaiming "Virtue, Liberty and Independence," and the tattered remains of "Internal Improvements and the Bank of the United States," while in his left hand King Andrew holds the scroll of a veto message. Also on the floor is a discarded volume titled *Judiciary Statutes.* The legend "Born to Command," above Jackson's head and below the title, is supported by a list of charges that include the indictment "A King born to command, as he has shown himself by appointing men to office contrary to the will of the People." In bold print, a final question asks, "Shall he reign over us, or shall the people rule?"

In a Democratic party broadside (fig. 4–8), Jackson's supporters offered an opposing picture of the president, though it has not been determined whether it was in answer to the above assault or whether *King Andrew* was inspired by the Democratic picture of Jackson. In any case, a Democratic ticket for electors in Pennsylvania frames a portrait of Jackson with the words "Democracy, Jackson, and our Country." Above the portrait is an endorsement from the departed Jefferson hailing Jackson as "the man who has filled the measure of

Figure 7–10. *Andrew Jackson.* Pencil on paper, 8 x 3¼ inches, by Edward Williams Clay, 1831. National Portrait Gallery, Smithsonian Institution.

strain from leaving, and Secretary of the Treasury Samuel D. Ingham. The artist was Edward Williams Clay, America's most prolific political caricaturist.[18] Jackson, who appears to

Figure 7–11. *King Andrew the First.* Lithograph, 26 x 10¼ inches, by unknown artist, 1832. New-York Historical Society.

Figure 7–12. *Americans! Behold your hero.* Lithograph, 20½ x 19⅝ inches, by James Akin, [1832]. Houghton Library, Harvard University.

his Country's glory," while below the portrait is Jackson's famous toast, "The Union must be Preserved."

Another print from the campaign of 1832 employed words and pictures to project to Pennsylvania voters an image of Jackson as the defender of his country, the preserver of the Union, and the champion of the people against the special interests of the Bank of the United States (fig. 7–12). A drawing by James Akin pictures Jackson in two poses. In one he is defending his country at the Battle of New Orleans. In the other he is holding high a banner proclaiming "Our Federal Union Must Be Preserved," while affirming his duty to veto the rechartering of the bank. In the background the bank is pictured "lavishing its bribes on the hirelings who vilify him," while in the foreground a workingman in humble dress doffs his hat in salute. An appeal to Americans to "support the virtuous Jackson" at the polls is printed below in both English and German.[20]

Some Americans were uncomfortable with the caricaturing of presidents. When editor

Duff Green published a series of anti-Jackson caricatures in the *United States Telegraph Extra* during the presidential campaign of 1832, he felt compelled to justify pictorial satire as standing on the same ground as written satire. To illustrate "A New Song for the Political Nursery"—a parody on the old nursery song "Hushaby, baby, on the tree-top"—he published a woodcut caricature of "Granny Jackson's Lullaby to Little Martin" (fig. 7–13). While separately published caricatures were popular, their appearance in newspapers or magazines was unusual, and a few weeks later Green published a lengthy justification of his innovation. In regard to the drawing of Jackson and Van Buren, he wrote:

> If we should wish to show that he cherishes and indulges the caprices of this individual, with the unlimited indulgence of a *granny* for an infant; if we might with moral propriety make such a charge in words, . . . it may, with as much justice, with as much moral propriety, be made by the pencil, by appropriate personifications, and with all the appropriate emblems of *the rocking-*

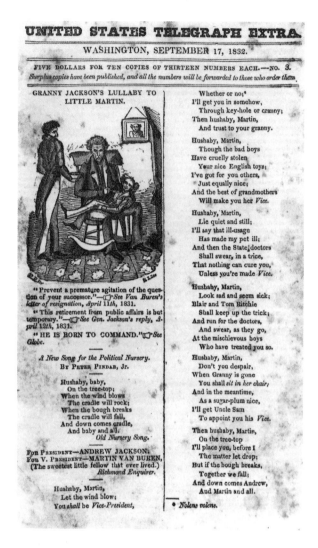

UNITED STATES TELEGRAPH EXTRA.

WASHINGTON, SEPTEMBER 17, 1832.

FIVE DOLLARS FOR TEN COPIES OF THIRTEEN NUMBERS EACH.——NO. 3.
Surplus copies have been published, and all the numbers will be forwarded to those who order them.

GRANNY JACKSON'S LULLABY TO LITTLE MARTIN.

"Prevent a premature agitation of the question of your successor."——☞ *See Van Buren's letter of resignation, April 11th, 1831.*

"This retirement from public affairs is but temporary."——☞ *See Gen. Jackson's reply, April 12th, 1831.*

"HE IS BORN TO COMMAND."☞ *See Globe.*

A New Song for the Political Nursery.
BY PETER PINDAR, JR.

Hushaby, baby,
  On the tree-top;
When the wind blows
  The cradle will rock;
When the bough breaks
  The cradle will fall,
And down comes cradle,
  And baby and all.
        Old Nursery Song.

FOR PRESIDENT——ANDREW JACKSON.
FOR V. PRESIDENT——MARTIN VAN BUREN,
(The sweetest little fellow that ever lived.)
        Richmond Enquirer.

Hushaby, Martin,
  Let the wind blow;
You *shall* be Vice-President,

Whether or no;*
  I'll get you in somehow,
    Through key-hole or cranny;
  Then hushaby, Martin,
    And trust to your granny.

Hushaby, Martin,
  Though the bad boys
  Have cruelly stolen
    Your nice English toys;
  I've got for you others,
    Just equally nice;
  And the best of grandmothers
    Will make you her *Vice.*

Hushaby, Martin,
  Lie quiet and still;
  I'll say that ill-usage
    Has made my pet ill;
  And then the State doctors
    Shall swear, in a trice,
  That nothing can cure you,
    Unless you're made *Vice.*

Hushaby, Martin,
  Look sad and seem sick;
  Blair and Tom Ritchie
    Shall keep up the trick;
  And run for the doctors,
    And swear, as they go,
  At the mischievous boys
    Who have treated you so.

Hushaby, Martin,
  Don't you despair,
  When Granny is gone
    You shall *sit in her chair;*
  And in the meantime,
    As a sugar-plum nice,
  I'll get Uncle Sam
    To appoint you his *Vice.*

Then hushaby, Martin,
  On the tree-top
  I'll place you, before I
    The matter let drop;
  But if the bough breaks,
    Together we fall;
  And down comes Andrew,
    And Martin and all.

* *Nolens volens.*

Figure 7–13. *United States Telegraph Extra,* Washington, September 17, 1832. Caricature of Jackson is 2⅞ x 2³⁄₁₆ inches. Ellis Library, University of Missouri–Columbia.

chair and the *pap-spoon.* But, it is said, this is placing these persons in a ridiculous light; holding them up to laughter and contempt. Granted. But do we not do the same by preferring verbal charges? It is the *truth* which makes the ridicule, and not the representation.[21]

Andrew Jackson greatly expanded the power of the presidency. He used the veto more extensively than all the previous presidents combined, and he asserted the novel claim that the president was the direct representative of the American people—a concept that would be more expansively articulated in the next decade by President James K. Polk. While Jackson maintained the support of a majority of the American people, his expansion of presidential authority aroused strong opposition in Congress and provoked vigorous protests from the opposition Whig party. After he ordered the removal of the government's deposits from the Bank of the United States, following his veto of the bank's rechartering, the Senate in March 1834 passed a vote of censure of the president. In response, Jackson sent to the Senate a solemn protest, upholding his actions and presidential authority. The heated debate that ensued in the Senate was continued in newspapers throughout the country.[22] The issue also provided inviting material for political caricaturists, who already had directed their barbs at Jackson's expansive presidential role.

In *The Model of a Republican President* (fig. 7–14) New York caricaturist Anthony Imbert depicted Jackson as having adopted Napoleon as his model, picturing him in military uniform, a Napoleonic headpiece replacing the hat that the portraits of Ralph E. W. Earl had made familiar. As Jackson tries on the uniform, Secretary of the Treasury Roger B. Taney, who had carried out the president's directive in removing the deposits from the bank, is suggesting that he should be "a little more *pursey*" to resemble Napoleon. At his side, Van Buren indicates approval, saying that Jackson has the sword and should have the purse to go with it. To the right, Attorney General Benjamin F. Butler and Amos Kendall, Jackson's speech writer, are preparing to get Jackson to sign the protests they have prepared to send to the Senate.

One unusual and widely reported incident during Jackson's presidency provided the opportunity for a clever caricaturist to present Jackson as a "blockhead." While the frigate USS *Constitution* was being rebuilt at the Boston Naval Yard in 1834, Commodore Jesse D. Elliott, commandant of the Boston yard and an ardent admirer of the president, received the approval of the Navy Department to have a figurehead of Jackson carved and placed on the prow of "Old Ironsides." When reports of the plan circulated in Boston, at a time of low presidential popularity following Jackson's removal of government deposits from the Bank of the United States, there was an outcry of disapproval.[23] One handbill protested, "Old

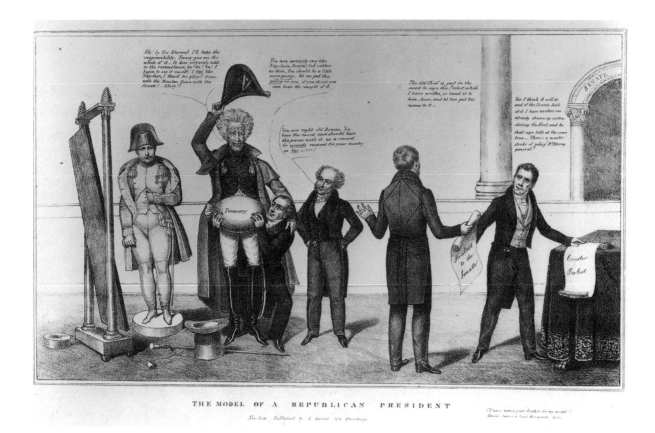

Figure 7–14. *The Model of a Republican President.* Lithograph, 13 ½ x 20⅜ inches, by Anthony Imbert, New York, 1834. New-York Historical Society.

'Glory President,' has issued his special orders for a Colossean Figure of his *Royal Self* in Roman Costume, to be placed as a figure head on OLD IRONSIDES!!! ... Shall this Boston built ship be thus disgraced without remonstrance. Let this *Wooden God*, this Old Roman, building at the expense of 300 dollars of the People's money, be presented to the *Office Holders* who glory in such worship, but for God's sake SAVE THE SHIP from this foul disgrace."[24] In more restrained language, *Niles' Weekly Register* in Baltimore argued that the *Constitution* ought to be preserved as far as possible "as she was when she met and humbled the British *Guerriere*" and commented, "Independent of *political* sentiments involved, the propriety of placing on the bows of a national ship the head of any *living* person, is earnestly questioned."[25] But as feelings mounted in Boston and Commodore Elliott received threats of tar and feathers, he felt he could not back down, and the figurehead was mounted.

In New York, Anthony Imbert ridiculed the action in a cartoon titled *Fixing a block-head to the Constitution or putting a wart on the nose of old Ironsides* (fig. 7–15). The commodore is pictured directing black workers in hoisting the figurehead to the ship, while one worker mutters that "dey'd better run him up to the yard arm like dey do de pirate," only to be rebuked by his coworker to hold his tongue because "you don't know nothin bout politics." Meanwhile, the military drummer rebukes the fife player for piping the "Rogue's March" instead of "Hail Columbia." The figure of Jackson, with an uncarved block as a head, holds a scroll labeled "my interpretation of the Constitution."

On July 4, 1834, the *Boston Courier* reported "considerable excitement in the city yesterday, in consequence of the decapitation of the figure of general Jackson, recently placed as a figure-head on the frigate Constitution. It appears that during the night of Wednesday, the head of this wooden image was sawed off, by

Figure 7–15. *Fixing a block-head to the Constitution or putting a wart on the nose of old Ironsides*. Lithograph, 12½ x 19 inches, by Anthony Imbert, New York, 1834. American Antiquarian Society.

Figure 7–16. *The Decapitation of a great Block-head by the Mysterious agency of the Claret coloured Coat*. Lithograph, 13 x 19½ inches, 1834. American Antiquarian Society.

some person or persons unknown. It is rather a mysterious affair." The *Courier* went on to explain that a guard was on watch and other frigates were nearby, but the night was dark and stormy.[26]

Soon another caricature appeared, perhaps also by Imbert, though the lithograph is unsigned. *The Decapitation of a great Block-head by the Mysterious agency of the Claret coloured Coat* (fig. 7–16) pictures a stormy night, a sentinel asleep at his post, a bolt of lightening decapitating the figure with the aid of devils armed with saw and ax, and Jackson's head being carried off by an anthropomorphic coat. While the agency of the claret-colored coat appears mysterious, one scholar has linked the term to an election riot in New York in April 1834, where a Whig leader was identified in later reports as "the fellow with the claret colored coat on." The term was seized upon by New York Whigs as a means of poking fun at Jacksonians.[27] If published in New York, as appears likely, the caricature would have been readily understood there. But even if the reference remained mysterious to Bostonians, they could still appreciate the representation of the incident that was the talk of Boston in the summer of 1834. As for Commodore Elliott, he ordered a new Jackson head carved and moved the *Constitution* to New York. The plain carving of a stern, rough-hewn man of the people, holding a scroll and his familiar hat, survives today in the Museum of the City of New York (fig. 7–17).

Like Jackson, Martin Van Buren, his successor in the presidential chair, was the frequent subject of caricature. In a number of those drawings, Jackson also appeared. The practice of caricaturists attaching human heads to non-human forms, common while Jackson was president, continued while Van Buren was in office. Jackson's successor was pictured as a dragon, a monkey, and a kangaroo—among other representations.[28] But some of the best caricatures of President Van Buren pictured him in presidential dress, generally depicting—and sometimes exaggerating—his diminutive size.

A caricature (fig. 7–18) published in anticipation of Henry Clay's challenge to Van Buren's bid for reelection probably had a short life, for Clay failed to get the Whig party presiden-

Figure 7–17. Andrew Jackson, wooden figure-head, 108 inches, from the frigate USS *Constitution*, 1834. Museum of the City of New York.

tial nomination in 1840. Filled with dialogue that politically knowledgeable viewers of 1839 would have understood and modern viewers may ignore, the drawing, published by Henry R. Robinson, the Whig party's most active publisher of political cartoons, conveys an immediate and clear message. Seated on a scale with Clay, the smaller Van Buren is *Weighed and Found Wanting*, and even the presence of a nearly invisible Jackson trying to offset the weight of Clay is insufficient to balance the scale.[29]

In a cartoon entitled *Bubble Bursting* (fig. 7–

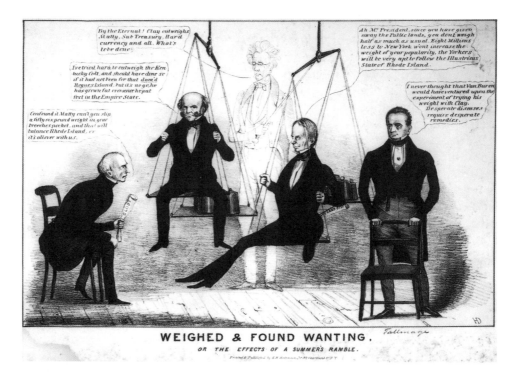

Figure 7–18. *Weighed and Found Wanting*. Lithograph, 13½ x 18 inches. Published by Henry R. Robinson, New York, 1839. American Antiquarian Society.

Figure 7–19. *Bubble Bursting*. Lithograph, 14 x 17½ inches, by Edward Williams Clay. Published by John Childs, New York and Washington, [1840]. American Antiquarian Society.

Figure 7–20. *Winter Amusement 1841 Going Down Hill*. Lithograph, 12 x 16½ inches, by Edward Williams Clay, [1841]. American Antiquarian Society.

19), Edward Williams Clay pictured Van Buren as a failed follower of Jackson. Perched in a large hickory tree, Jackson blows bubbles from a patronage bowl while advising: "If any one desires to ascend to the Regions of Glory, let him attach himself firmly to one of these bubbles." The *Globe* bubble has burst and fallen into the "Salt River"—a river of doom— where editor Francis Preston Blair and Amos Kendall, who was the key figure in launching that Jacksonian newspaper, are struggling to survive. President Van Buren, who promoted the plan for a subtreasury as a replacement for the defunct Bank of the United States, is suffering a milder, but no less certain, descent, as his balloon settles to the ground in the vegetable garden at his home at Kinderhook.

Van Buren was commonly referred to as "Old Kinderhook" and sometimes as "O K," but E. W. Clay turned the letters around in 1841 to picture Van Buren as "Kicked Out" of the

White House in a cartoon titled *Winter Amusement 1841 Going Down Hill* (fig. 7–20). Blair and Kendall again appear in this drawing, along with Sen. Thomas Hart Benton of Missouri, another Van Buren supporter. All are aboard a sled speeding down the snow-covered hill from the White House—the *Globe* already having preceded them down the slippery slope. When Kendall remarks that "this is an expeditious mode of conveyance," Van Buren replies, "It is provided specially for our use, by the sober second thought of the dear people."

Another carefully drawn caricature, published by John Childs in New York, is entitled *Notice to Quit. March 4th 1841* (fig. 7–21). William Henry Harrison's name is already affixed to the White House door, as the downcast former president, with the subtreasury bill tucked under his arm, is being shown out the door. When President Harrison suggests that Van Buren be served a glass of cider before he

Figure 7–21. *Notice to Quit. March 4th 1841.* Lithograph, 12¾ x 9⅜ inches. Published by John Childs, New York, [1841]. Library of Congress.

Figure 7–22. *Polk's Dream.* Lithograph, 12⅞ x 17 inches, by Edward Williams Clay. Published by J. Baillie, New York, 1846. Library of Congress.

leaves, Van Buren, who has heard enough about cider in the campaign, mutters a curse against Harrison's hard cider.

Not surprisingly, political caricaturing surged in presidential election years, but the art was more dormant in nonelection years than might be expected. The compiler of one scholarly checklist has identified some eighty caricatures as appearing during the election year 1844, while locating only five published in 1845.[30] Because so many caricatures were products of election campaigns and there was so much turnover in the presidential office in the two decades after Van Buren, presidential caricatures—as distinct from caricatures of presidential candidates—were not numerous in the 1840s and 1850s.

James K. Polk was more the object of caricature as a presidential candidate than as president, but some of his key policies did provoke the satirist's pen. A striking example is *Polk's*

Dream (fig. 7–22), in which President Polk is depicted struggling with the issue of the boundary of the Oregon territory—an object of heated dispute with Great Britain when the lithograph was published in 1846. Having fallen asleep after studying the map of Oregon and reading the conflicting wisdom of the books on his night table—the *Art of War* and *Life of Napoleon* versus *Calvin's Works* and *Practical Piety*—the president's foot rests on the map of Oregon, his toe pointing to the line 54°40′, for which he has vowed to fight. In his dream Polk is confronted by a demonic apparition hiding behind the mask of the deceased Andrew Jackson, pleading: "Child of my adoption, on whom my mantle hath fallen, swear never to take your toe off that line should you deluge your country with seas of blood, produce a servile insurrection and dislocate every joint of this happy and prosperous union!!!" Polk vows to obey with a Jacksonian, "by the

Figure 7–23. *The Presidential Harlequin.* Lithograph, 14⁹/₁₆ x 11⁹/₁₆ inches. Published by James Bailley, New York, 1851. Henry E. Huntington Library and Art Gallery.

OUR NATIONAL BIRD AS IT APPEARED WHEN HANDED TO JAMES BUCHANAN. MARCH. 4. 1857.

THE IDENTICAL BIRD AS IT APPEARED .A .D. 1861.

"I was murdered i' the Capitol"
Shakespere

Depot . 98. Nassau St. N.Y.

Figure 7–24. *Our National Bird.* Lithograph, 7⅝ x 13 inches, by Michael A. Woolf. Published by Thomas W. Strong, New York, 1861. American Antiquarian Society.

eternal!" Aroused by the noise in Polk's bed-chamber, three members of his cabinet come to investigate. Neither Secretary of the Navy George Bancroft nor Secretary of State James Buchanan (brandishing a packet of correspondence with the British minister, Richard Pakenham) is certain what is happening or what the president intends to do. Buchanan detects the smell of brimstone but is unable to discern its source. Treasury Secretary Robert Walker raises his finger to point out Polk's toe fixed firmly on the line 54°40′ and exclaims, "Patriotic, even in dreams!"[31]

By the 1850s the number of separately published cartoons was declining both in presidential campaigns and in nonelection years. The rise of illustrated magazines may partially explain this, but a series of weak presidents, without the strong leadership qualities of a Jackson or the keen political abilities of a Van Buren, must also have contributed to the decline. Millard Fillmore, Franklin Pierce, and James Bu-

chanan were not presidents who much inspired or provoked the caricaturist's interest. In *The Presidential Harlequin* (fig. 7–23), published by James Bailley in New York in 1851, President Millard Fillmore is pictured as a monkey controlled by Secretary of State Daniel Webster on the slavery issue. The president's private secretary, shown as an organ-grinder, protests that he has played the tune "Black Joke" long enough and suggests a change now that it has calmed the South. Under Webster's direction, Fillmore agrees, saying that the North begins to be uneasy, and instructs the organ-grinder to play the "Free Soil March."[32]

In a time of weak presidential personalities, one of the most devastating caricatures derided President James Buchanan by not picturing him at all. Instead, the artist, Michael A. Woolf, drew a proud and vigorous national eagle as it appeared when handed to Buchanan on inauguration day in 1857 (fig. 7–24). Facing it is a crippled and emaciated eagle, identified

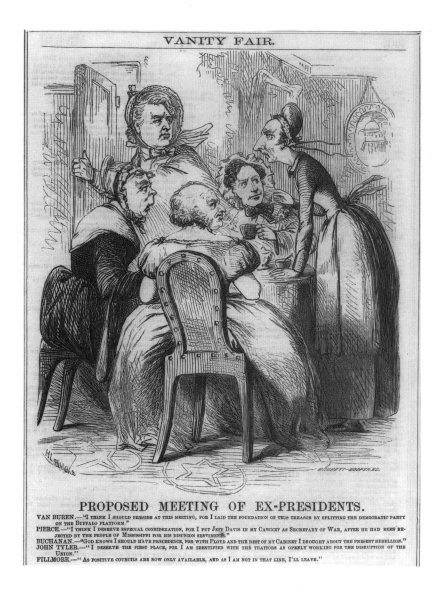

VANITY FAIR.

PROPOSED MEETING OF EX-PRESIDENTS.

VAN BUREN.—"I THINK I SHOULD PRESIDE AT THIS MEETING, FOR I LAID THE FOUNDATION OF THIS TREASON BY SPLITTING THE DEMOCRATIC PARTY ON THE BUFFALO PLATFORM."

PIERCE.—"I THINK I DESERVE ESPECIAL CONSIDERATION, FOR I PUT JEFF DAVIS IN MY CABINET AS SECRETARY OF WAR, AFTER HE HAD BEEN REJECTED BY THE PEOPLE OF MISSISSIPPI FOR HIS DISUNION SENTIMENTS."

BUCHANAN.—"GOD KNOWS I SHOULD HAVE PRECEDENCE, FOR WITH FLOYD AND THE REST OF MY CABINET I BROUGHT ABOUT THE PRESENT REBELLION."

JOHN TYLER.—"I DESERVE THE FIRST PLACE, FOR I AM IDENTIFIED WITH THE TRAITORS AS OPENLY WORKING FOR THE DISRUPTION OF THE UNION."

FILLMORE.—"AS POSITIVE COUNCILS ARE NOW ONLY AVAILABLE, AND AS I AM NOT IN THAT LINE, I'LL LEAVE."

Figure 7–25. "Proposed Meeting of Ex-Presidents." Wood engraving, 9¾ x 7⅛ inches, by Henry Louis Stephens. Published in *Vanity Fair*, May 11, 1861. American Antiquarian Society.

as the identical bird as it appeared in 1861. Around its neck hangs a broken chain of the type frequently used to symbolize the union of states, many of its links now broken. Hobbled by "Anarchy" and "Secession," shorn of its sharp talons, its once defiant beak and vigorous wings now limp, the pathetic bird mutters a Shakespearean line, "I was murdered i' the Capitol."[33]

That presidential leadership bore weighty responsibility for the crisis of the Union in 1861 was a point sharply made in a cartoon appearing in *Vanity Fair*, May 11, 1861 (fig. 7–25). In a drawing entitled *Proposed Meeting of Ex-Presidents*, artist Henry Louis Stephens depicted the five living ex-presidents—Van Buren, Tyler, Fillmore, Pierce, and Bu-

chanan—as women around a tea table bickering over who should preside at the proposed meeting to try to avert disunion. Their leadership in the time of crisis is lampooned, as each president asserts a claim for having made the greatest contribution to the disruption of the Union.

Having long enjoyed the image of champions of the Union, presidents had to share in the blame for the nation's failure to maintain peace and preserve the Union. From the outset of the republic, caricaturists had reminded viewers of the frailties of American presidents, whose nobler images the people eagerly enshrined, but they had not prepared Americans for the ordeal that faced the Union when Lincoln took office.

CHAPTER VIII
The Drama of the Presidency

THE INAUGURATION of an American President is an event that has no parallel in ancient or modern times. It is the great distinctive characteristic of the age, the nation, and its institutions." Thus proclaimed the editor of the *Baltimore Sun* on March 5, 1849, the day of Zachary Taylor's inauguration. By Taylor's time the inauguration of the president had become an occasion of enormous popular interest and public involvement and a symbol of the importance of the presidency in American culture. The event, indeed, had never been without great symbolic significance, and it early became a major dramatic experience in American life. The popularity of the first man elected to the presidency, and Washington's own considerable presence in establishing the dignity of the office, gave to the first inauguration a dramatic character that was never lost, despite the efforts of some later presidents to reduce the ceremonies and pageantry of the presidency.

Washington's journey from Mount Vernon to New York in 1789 to assume the presidential office was itself high drama, with celebrations along the road through Baltimore, Philadelphia, and Trenton—a route that only a few years earlier had been the scene of Revolutionary War battles. The journey also inspired some rare contemporaneous illustrative material that appeared in the *Columbian Magazine*, published in Philadelphia by James Trenchard, an engraver who started the magazine in 1786 and engaged Charles Willson Peale to draw illustrations for publication. One early product of that cooperation was Peale's drawing of a view of Gray's Ferry on the Schuylkill River at Philadelphia, where a floating bridge had been constructed during the occupation of the city by the British army during the Revolution. Engraved by Trenchard, the print appeared as the frontispiece of the August 1787 issue.[1] In anticipation of Washington's crossing of Gray's Ferry bridge on his journey northward in 1789, Philadelphians elaborately decorated the bridge, and Trenchard recorded the view for his readers by redoing the earlier plate. "An East View of Gray's Ferry, near Philadelphia; with the Triumphal Arches, &c. erected for the Reception of General Washington, April 20th 1789" (fig. 8–1) appeared in the May 1789 issue of the *Columbian Magazine*, where the scene was described in detail. The arches, twenty feet high, were made of laurel and evergreens, and the railings on each side of the bridge were similarly decorated. Along one side of the bridge, flags of the eleven states that had ratified the Constitution waved in the breeze, while at one end of the bridge a liberty pole, twenty-five feet high, surmounted by a striped liberty cap, displayed the Revolutionary banner "Don't Tread on Me."[2]

In the same issue, Trenchard also published another scene from Washington's journey to

205

An East View of GRAY'S FERRY, near Philadelphia; with the TRIUMPHAL ARCHES, &c. erected for the Reception of General Washington, April 20th 1789.

Figure 8–1. "An East View of Gray's Ferry, near Philadelphia; with the Triumphal Arches." Engraving by James Trenchard. Published in the *Columbian Magazine*, May 1789. American Antiquarian Society.

his inauguration, titled "View of the Triumphal Arch, and the manner of receiving General Washington at Trenton, on his Route to New-York, April 21st 1789" (fig. 8–2). In the town where Washington's troops had overwhelmed a Hessian garrison after crossing the Delaware River on Christmas night of 1776, the women of Trenton had erected a triumphal arch. Interwoven with laurel and evergreens, the arch stood eighteen feet high, supported by thirteen pillars entwined with laurel. In depicting the arch and Washington's arrival on a white horse, the print published in the *Columbian Magazine* fails to do justice to his reception at Trenton. Not shown was the scene between the arch and the town, where—as described by an observer—the women of Trenton lined one side of the street with their daughters, dressed in white and carrying flowers, standing in front of them. As soon as Washington passed through the arch, the girls advanced to greet the president-elect with song and flowers. The scene was such as to move Washington to respond to their tribute by ac-

knowledging the "exquisite sensation" he had experienced and remarking at "the astonishing contrast between his former and actual situation on the same spot."[3]

Although Trenchard's engraving—rushed to completion for exceptionally quick publication—presented only a limited representation of the scene at Trenton, other artists in later years would draw on contemporary descriptions to offer more elaborate imaginary drawings of the event. In 1845 Nathaniel Currier published a popular lithograph titled *Washington's Reception by the Ladies, on Passing the Bridge at Trenton, N. J. Aprill 1789, on His Way to New York to Be Inaugurated First President of the United States* (fig. 8–3). The print must have been widely admired, for Currier issued no less than four versions of it dated 1845.[4] More than half a century after the event, popular prints kept alive the drama of the first presidential inauguration.

Washington's journey to New York was surpassed by the spectacle of his inauguration. The president-elect rode to his inauguration in

View of the *TRIUMPHAL ARCH*, and the manner of receiving *General Washington* at **Trenton**, on his Route to *New-York*, *April 21.st* 1789.

Figure 8–2. "View of the Triumphal Arch . . . at Trenton." Engraving by James Trenchard. Published in the *Columbian Magazine*, May 1789. American Antiquarian Society.

a carriage pulled by four horses and preceded by troops of horse, artillery, grenadiers, and infantry.[5] Contemporary drawings do not survive to depict the procession, but a view of Washington taking the oath of office was published in an engraving by Amos Doolittle in New Haven in 1790 (fig. 8–4). Entitled *Federal Hall: The Seat of Congress*, the scene of the inauguration is less notable than the details of the building, reproduced from a drawing by Peter Lacour.[6] Doolittle's print records the administering of the oath of office to Washington by Robert R. Livingston, chancellor of the state of New York, on the balcony of Federal Hall at the corner of Broad and Wall streets, but the drawing gives no sense of the crowd of people witnessing the event.

One eyewitness, who watched the proceedings from the roof of a nearby house, later recalled, "The windows and roofs of the houses were crowded; and in the streets the throng was so dense, that it seemed as if one might literally walk on the heads of the people."[7] The firing of a salute by thirteen cannons and loud

shouts of acclamation from the crowd followed the oath-taking ceremony and began a celebration that continued throughout the day, concluding in the evening with an illumination of the city and a display of fireworks. "The transparent paintings exhibited in various parts of the city," declared the *Gazette of the United States*, "were equal at least, to any thing of the kind ever before seen in America. . . . The portrait of 'The Father of His Country' exhibited in Broad-Street, was extremely well executed, and had a fine effect."[8] Such transparent paintings have not survived, but the description indicates the popular interest in visual images, which would increase with the widening public attention directed toward the presidency.

Unfortunately the *Columbian Magazine*, which had taken the lead in publishing illustrated issues, did not continue the practice. From 1790 until its demise in 1792, the magazine rarely featured engravings.[9] Amos Doolittle continued to celebrate the presidency and the new union with his engravings of *A Display of the United States of America* (figs. 4–1 and 4–

Figure 8–3. *Washington's Reception by the Ladies, on Passing the Bridge at Trenton.* Lithograph, 13¼ x 9¼ inches, by Nathaniel Currier, New York, 1845. Library of Congress.

FEDERAL HALL
The Seat of Congress
Printed & Sold by A. Doolittle New-Haven. 1790

Peter Lacour delin.　　A. Doolittle Sculp.

Figure 8–4. *Federal Hall: The Seat of Congress.* Engraving, 16¹⁵⁄₁₆ x 13½ inches, by Amos Doolittle, New Haven, 1790, after drawing by Peter Lacour. I. N. Phelps Stokes Collection, New York Public Library, Astor, Lenox and Tilden Foundations.

2) and *A New Display of the United States* (fig. 4–3). But Doolittle's works were exceptional, and the presidential drama would be sparsely recorded in the visual record until new technologies for printing illustrations were perfected on the 1840s.

The style of Washington's successors in the high office influenced the display of the presidency. John Adams sought to continue the practices instituted by the first executive, but when Jefferson replaced Adams as president in 1801, he sought to reduce the ceremonies of government. He began by walking to his inauguration and by sending written messages rather than addressing Congress in person, as Washington and Adams had done. He replaced the formal receptions, or levees, that Washington and Adams had given with small and informal dinners, and he reduced the formalities of

diplomatic relations to such an extent as to offend some diplomats of the old world.[10] Though Jefferson curtailed the ceremonies of the executive, his supporters showed little inclination to refrain from their celebrations of the presidency. New Yorkers heralded Jefferson's inauguration, like Washington's, with fireworks and illuminations, and in the years ahead Jefferson's supporters throughout the country held annual celebrations of his inauguration on March 4.[11]

Jefferson's efforts to lessen the spectacle of inaugurations had, in fact, little lasting impact. The public never lost interest in presidential inaugurals, and with the election of Andrew Jackson a new upsurge of popular participation in the drama of inaugurations began. Margaret Bayard Smith (Mrs. Samuel Harrison Smith), who had watched Jefferson inaugurated, witnessed the popular pageantry of Jackson's inaugural. Writing under transparent anonymity for the *Ladies Magazine and Literary Gazette*, Mrs. Smith observed:

> The Inauguration was not a ceremony of minute details or many forms. No, it was one grand whole—grand, in simplicity—majestic, from the principles it developed—and, to a reflecting mind, offered a spectacle of moral sublimity. Thousands and thousands of freemen, without distinction of rank, collected in an almost compact mass—silent, orderly and tranquil, awaiting the appearance of the first magistrate. At last, preceded by the marshals with their staves of office—surrounded by the venerable judges of the Supreme Court—the old man with his grey locks, that crown of glory, advances—bows to *the People*, who greet him with a shout that rends the air and thrills every heart. The cannons, from the heights around, from Alexandria and Fort Warburton, proclaim the oath he has taken, and the hills reverberate the sound. It was grand—it was sublime![12]

The scene of disorder that followed at the public reception at the White House moderated Mrs. Smith's exuberance but did not destroy her faith in the people. And the people did not lose their interest in inaugural spectacles.

The inauguration of William Henry Harrison in 1841—following a campaign unrivaled in popular participation in the drama of electioneering—was celebrated with a popular enthusiasm "unexampled since that of Washington in 1789," observed John Quincy Adams. Watching the inaugural procession from the window of his house, the ex-president—then a member of Congress—described "a mixed military and civil cavalcade," consisting of militia companies, Tippecanoe clubs, college students, schoolboys, and a few veterans who had served under the general thirty years earlier. Harrison rode up Pennsylvania Avenue on a white horse, but he wore a plain frockcoat, which, Adams said, made him "undistinguishable from any of those before, behind, or around him." Adams commented on the "sundry awkward and ungainly painted banners, and log cabins" in the parade and the absence of carriages. He did not compare the day to his own inauguration in 1825 but remarked that it lacked the pomp and circumstance of the reception of Lafayette at Baltimore in 1824, and he used the words *showy-shabby* to sum up the day. Still, he recognized the event as "characteristic of the democracy of our institution" and commended the "perfect order with which the whole scene was performed."[13]

The Washington correspondent of the *Baltimore Sun* wrote more enthusiastically about what he saw than did the former president. Describing the "grand procession" to the Capitol, the reporter declared:

> The drums beat, the bugles sounded, the trumpets issued forth their thrilling tones, the banners fluttered in the breeze, and on the people marched, with pleasure beaming from their eyes, and patriotism glowing in their hearts. I am no party man, but I caught the enthusiasm, and joined in the throng, not in honor of a partizan, but out of respect to General Harrison, as the Chief Magistrate of this great and glorious Republic.[14]

An artist who drew the scene of the inauguration at the Capitol pictured an event more in harmony with the report of the *Baltimore Sun* correspondent than with that of Adams (plate 13). His drawing depicts a greater display of military pageantry than Adams described and reflects the exuberance of the crowd. The work, attributed to Charles Fenderich, was published in an unsigned, colored lithograph, offered for sale at Taylor's Bookstore in Washington.[15] The print shows military units in front of the steps of the Capitol, where Harrison delivered a lengthy address and took the oath of office before members of Congress in top hats and others crowded onto the steps of the Capitol. The artist caught the democratic aspects of the day, picturing families dressed in their finest clothes bringing their children and even their dogs to the spectacle.

Philip Hone, a New York businessman present at the Capitol for the inaugural ceremony, shared the artist's impressions. "The display of ladies with military officers and the *corps diplomatique* was very brilliant," he observed, "but the multitudinous mass of sovereigns below and round about was the most imposing part of the pageant."[16] For those American who could not witness the happenings on the steps of the Capitol, the lithograph of the inauguration sold at Taylor's Bookstore offered a vivid glimpse of the presidential drama.

Plate 10. *A Boxing Match, or Another Bloody Nose for John Bull.* Hand-colored engraving, 9¼ x 13 inches, by William Charles, 1813. Library of Congress.

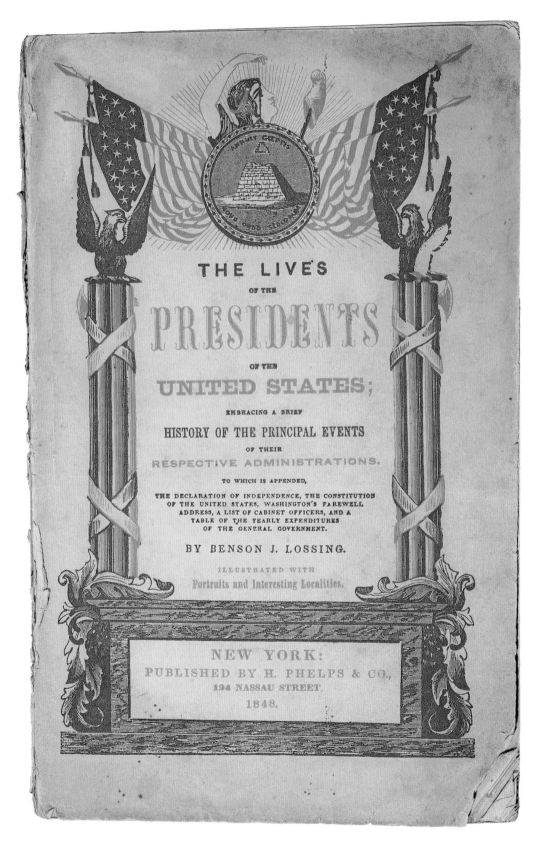

Plate 11. Cover of Benson J. Lossing's *The Lives of the Presidents of the United States* (New York: H. Phelps and Company, 1848). College of William and Mary.

Plate 12. *Presidents of the United States*. Hand-colored lithograph, 28½ x 21 inches, by Phelps, Ensigns, and Thayer, New York, 1846. Harry T. Peters "America on Stone" Lithograph Collection, Smithsonian Institution.

PRESIDENTIAL INAUGURATION OF Wᴹ. H. HARRISON,

IN WASHINGTON CITY, D.C. ON THE 4ᵀᴴ OF MARCH, 1841.

For Sale at Mr. F. Taylor, Bookseller, Washington.

Plate 13. *Presidential Inauguration of Wm. H. Harrison, in Washington City, D.C. on the 4th of March, 1841.* "For Sale at Mr. F. Taylor, Bookseller, Washington," 1841. Attributed to Charles Fenderich. Colored lithograph, 9¾ x 13⁵⁄₁₆ inches. Stokes Collection, Prints Division, New York Public Library, Astor, Lenox and Tilden Foundations.

Plate 14. Presidents fan. Heavily decorated ivory and paper fan, with lithographic portraits of all the presidents of
the United States through Polk. American, circa 1845. National Gallery of Art.
Gift of Ethel G. Tolman.

Plate 15. *The Presidents of the United States.* Hand-colored lithograph, 13 x 9 inches, by Nathaniel Currier, New York, 1844. Library of Congress.

Plate 16. *Presidents of the United States.* Chromolithograph, 27 x 21 inches, by A. Feusier. Published by F. Bouclet, Philadelphia, 1861. Library of Congress.

Plate 17. *Peace*. Lithograph, 28 x 22 inches, printed in black and brown. Published by Middleton, Strobridge and Company, Cincinnati, Ohio, January 1861. Library of Congress.

On the day of Harrison's inauguration, the *Daily National Intelligencer* in Washington carried the following advertisement:

THE INAUGURATION MARCH.—Just received at Stationers' Hall, the Grand Inauguration March composed by Mr. Dielman, which was presented to and accepted by Gen. W. H. Harrison, and will be played by the Marine Band on the Day of the Inauguration. Persons can be supplied with copies by applying as above.
    Mar. 3   W. Fisher

This announcement would have not have been surprising to readers of the newspaper, for by the time of the ninth president's inauguration the tradition of presidential inaugural marches had become well established.

No new presidential march greeted the first president at his inauguration. But a *Washington's March* had already been published and popularized during the Revolutionary War, and in the course of his presidency so many Washington marches were composed as to confuse compilers of music bibliographies for years.[17] During John Adams's presidency an *Adams March* was published, although not before his inauguration.[18]

In the course of Washington's and Adams's administrations *The President's March* became the country's most popular national musical piece. Composed by Philip Phile, the march gained enduring fame when Joseph Hopkinson put words to the music to create *Hail Columbia*.[19] First sung by Gilbert Fox at the New Theatre in Philadelphia on April 25, 1798—at a time of high excitement over the XYZ crisis with France—*Hail Columbia* was an immediate sensation and rapidly became a national song. Abigail Adams, who had gone to the theater to hear the words sung, wrote her sister that "the House was very full, and at every Choruss, the most unbounded applause ensued." After the end of the play, Fox was repeatedly called back to sing the song again, and by the fourth time "the whole Audience broke forth in the Chorus," Mrs. Adams reported, "whilst the thunder from their Hands was incessant."[20]

Both the president and Mrs. Adams must have been pleased two days later to read in *Porcupine's Gazette* that Carr's Musical Repository in Philadelphia would publish the new piece "ornamented with a very elegant portrait of the President," at a price of twenty-five cents.[21] The miniature portrait of President Adams was a separate engraving, trimmed and mounted on the music sheet above the words "Behold the Chief who now commands!" which opened the last stanza of the piece (fig. 8–5).[22] The Adamses undoubtedly were less pleased later to see Washington's portrait affixed in the same manner on other copies of the music, probably after July 1798 when Washington was given command of the new army being raised against the French threat (fig. 8–6).[23]

During the early years of the republic such examples of presidential portraits appearing on sheet music were exceptional. Indeed, illustrated sheet music in general was infrequent before lithography was applied to sheet music in the 1830s and 1840s.[24] The composition and publication of music for presidential inaugurals, however, early had become a part of American political culture.

Several new marches greeted Jefferson's election to the presidency. The *Aurora* of Philadelphia in January 1801 advertised: "Just published at George Willig's Musical Magazine, No. 185 Market Street, Thomas Jefferson's March." The music was composed by George Emrick.[25] In February the *American Citizen* of New York printed a notice soliciting subscriptions for a "Jefferson's March" composed for the piano by G. K. Jackson. The following month the *New York Daily Advertiser* carried advertisements for *Jefferson's March* just published by J. Hewitt, Musical Repository, 23 Maiden Lane.[26] Of these pieces, the march by George Emrick, published by George Willig in Philadelphia (fig. 8–7), became the most widely known. It was performed at a grand procession in Philadelphia on the day of Jefferson's inauguration, March 4, 1801, and it was probably the "Jefferson's March" that Margaret Bayard Smith reported being played eight years later when retiring President Jefferson entered the room at Madison's inaugural ball. Mrs. Smith also reported "Madison's March" being played when the new president made his entrance. Thus, by the time Jefferson left office in 1809 the playing of presidential marches had become a traditional part of inaugural activities.[27]

Though several compositions honored Madison's inauguration, the piece that Mrs.

Figure 8–5. *The Presidents March.* Sheet music, with portrait of John Adams. Published by Carr's Musical Repository, Philadelphia, [1798]. Library of Congress.

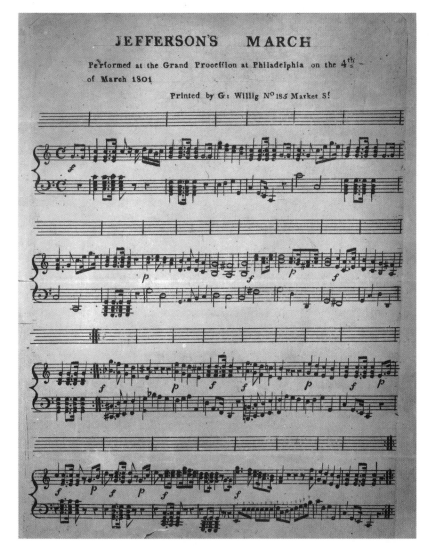

Figure 8–6. *The Presidents March.* Sheet music, with portrait of Washington. Philadelphia, [1798]. Library of Congress.

Figure 8–7. *Jefferson's March.* Sheet music. Published by George Willig, Philadelphia, [1801]. Library of Congress.

Figure 8–8. *Madison's March.* **Sheet music. Published by Carr's Music Store, Baltimore, [1809]. Library of Congress.**

Smith heard at Madison's inaugural ball was probably the march by P. Mauro, of Washington.[28] When printed and sold at Carr's Music Store in Baltimore, Mauro's music carried the note: "This is the March, that the President and his Lady were Serenaded with, by the City Band, the 4th of March 1809, the day of his Inauguration" (fig. 8–8). Among other marches honoring Madison's inauguration was a composition by Louis Dubois, a Charleston "Professor of Music." Writing to Madison on the day after the inaugural, he enclosed a copy of the piece and asked the president to "give me leave to Stamp my march with your name, then with such flattering recommendation, it will go to posterity."[29] Madison's response, if any, has not been found, but the march is not known today and may never have been published. In the years ahead, requests for presidential endorsements would become common and the custom established for presidents to give their approval to musical pieces composed in their honor.

An advertisement for the celebration of the Fourth of July in New York in 1817—the first year of Monroe's administration—announced:

The concert will open with President MONROE'S MARCH, composed by Mr. Gilles, sen. dedicated and presented to the President on his late visit to this city, and accepted by his excellency as his adopted March; arranged expressly for this occasion, with accompaniments for a completely full Military Band, in the style of the imperial music of France—by the author.[30]

Figure 8–9. *President Jackson's Grand March.* Sheet music cover. Published by J. L. Hewitt and Company, Boston, [1829]. American Antiquarian Society.

Figure 8–10. *President Harrison's Grand Inauguration March.* Sheet music cover. Published by George Willig, Jr., Baltimore, [1841]. Library of Congress.

As this notice indicates, by the time of Monroe's presidency musical compositions were receiving the president's mark of approval, and music had become a major part of the theater of the presidency.

By the administration of Andrew Jackson, with the techniques of lithography mastered, the president's portrait on a sheet-music cover would not only honor the president but also attract purchasers. A portrait of Jackson appeared on *President Jackson's Grand March*, published in Boston in 1829 (fig. 8–9). Based on a painting by John Vanderlyn, engraved by Asher Brown Durand in 1828, the Pendleton lithograph by M. E. D. Brown presented the general of the Battle of New Orleans in dress uniform—not Andrew Jackson, the president of the United States.[31] Nevertheless, the music cover was certain to attract attention.

The cover of *President Harrison's Grand Inauguration March*, composed by Henry Dielman, reached new heights in the decorative design of inaugural marches (fig. 8–10). The *Baltimore Sun* lauded the "spirited musical composition" and praised "the neatness and beauty of the embellishments," with a nod to "the taste and capacity of the artists employed at the lithographic establishment of E. Weber & Co." of Baltimore. The large sheet, about 14 x 11 inches, is adorned with a drawing of an inaugural crowd before the Capitol, shown in full view. Above the drawing of the Capitol is a small portrait of President Harrison.[32]

That this memento of the inaugural drama of 1841 was preserved by some Americans for many years can be seen from the handwritten note, dated July 21, 1888, at the bottom of the cover illustrated here. Addressed to William Henry Harrison's grandson Benjamin Harrison, who less than a month earlier had been nominated as the Republican candidate for president of the United States, the note was written by Carrie May Dockery, the thirteen-year-old daughter of Oliver H. Dockery, a former member of Congress and at that time the

Figure 8–11. *Harrison and Tyler Grand Military Waltz.* Sheet music cover. Published by Osbourn's Music Saloon, Philadelphia, [1841]. American Antiquarian Society.

Figure 8–12. *Grand Inauguration March*. Sheet music cover. Published by George Willig, Jr., Baltimore, 1849. American Antiquarian Society.

Republican candidate for governor of North Carolina. Presenting the well-preserved piece from William Henry Harrison's inaugural, found "among a lot of old family music," the young Miss Dockery expressed the wish that "it may likewise commemorate the inauguration of his ellustrious Grandson."

The music and excitement surrounding William Henry Harrison's inauguration in 1841 extended beyond the nation's capital. Philadelphians held a grand ball honoring President Harrison and Vice-President Tyler and dedicated a *Grand Military Waltz* to the new president. The lithograph by Thomas Sinclair decorating the cover of the sheet music was highly political and may have been left over from the recent campaign rather than designed anew for the publication. The artist pictured Harrison, riding on horseback, leaving a log cabin—the dominant symbol of the Whig campaign—being directed to the White House by an American eagle flying overhead. Meanwhile, Van Buren is departing the White House by stately carriage, pulled by four horses, headed for retirement at Kinderhook Hotel (fig. 8–11).

No inaugural music was more elaborately adorned than the cover published by George Willig, Jr., of Baltimore, to celebrate Zachary Taylor's inauguration in 1849 (fig. 8–12). The artwork was done by Edward Weber and Company of Baltimore, who had also lithographed the illustration for *President Harrison's Grand Inauguration March* in 1841 (fig. 8–10). Henry Dielman, professor of music at Mount Saint Mary's College in Maryland, the composer of President Harrison's inauguration march, also composed the music for Taylor's *Grand Inauguration March*. The inscription on the cover indicates that the march had been accepted by the president, adopted by the committee of arrangements, and performed by the Marine Band of the United States at Taylor's inauguration.

The lavishly decorated cover presents, at the top, Taylor's profile on a medallion suspended from a ring held in the beak of the national eagle. The borders contain vignettes of scenes from Taylor's military career. Pictured on the left are Fort Harrison, Matamoras, and Palo Alto; on the right are Buena Vista, Monterey, and Resaca de la Palma. The scene at Fort Harrison goes back to the War of 1812, when the

young Captain Taylor had commanded the defense of his post on the Wabash River from capture by the Indians. The other scenes celebrate victories in the War with Mexico, in which Taylor had won the fame that gained him the presidency. The cover illustrated here is stamped with the name of a New Orleans agent, W. T. Mayo, indicating something of the national distribution of the sheet music.[33] At the price of twenty-five cents, the piece was inexpensive enough to be widely purchased and was no doubt popular as a memento of the inauguration.

In the 1840s, when the rapid spread of the electrotype process of reproducing pictures from large wood engravings made possible long-run printing of illustrations for popular magazines, the visual horizons of Americans expanded enormously.[34] The weekly *Illustrated London News* in 1842 demonstrated the successful application of the process, and by 1851 *Gleason's Pictorial Drawing Room Companion*, published in Boston, was bringing to Americans the drama of the presidency through pictorial reporting.

Americans had seen what could be done with the new technology when the *Illustrated London News* sent its artist-reporter from New York to Washington to cover the inauguration of President James K. Polk on March 4, 1845. The first of two drawings that the London periodical provided its readers on April 19 pictured invited dignitaries arriving at the west entrance to the Capitol, where spectators crowded every available space (fig. 8–13). The figures of the British and Russian ministers shown in the foreground were probably not what most viewers first noticed, for the dominant theme of the picture was the sea of umbrellas raised against a driving rain that "spoiled the display of the day."[35] John Quincy Adams, who previously had witnessed the inaugurations of five presidents besides his own, recorded in his diary that Polk delivered his inaugural address "to a large assemblage of umbrellas." The aging Adams stayed indoors out of the rain, but he noted in his diary that "an unusual degree of pomposity paraded in the inauguration," and as a Whig, he blamed it on the Democrats.[36]

The second drawing published by the *Illus-*

INAUGURATION OF PRESIDENT POLK.—APPROACH TO THE CAPITOL.

Figure 8–13. "Inauguration of President Polk—Approach to the Capitol." Published in the *Illustrated London News*, **April 19, 1845. Ellis Library, University of Missouri–Columbia.**

trated London News shows Polk taking the presidential oath of office in the ceremony on the steps of the east front of the Capitol (fig. 8–14). The figure of Columbus more than Polk dominates the drawing, for the viewer's eye is directed more toward the *Discovery Group* than to the president. That recently emplaced sculpture was the work of Luigi Persico, whose figures of Columbus and the Indian Girl were described by the artist-reporter as "magnificent." He also acknowledged that he had traced his drawing of the sculpture from a daguerreotype.[37]

In describing the oath-taking scene on the platform, the artist indicated that the figure on the left holding the Bible and administering the oath was the chief justice, Roger B. Taney. On the right, Polk, holding his hat and inau-

gural address in his left hand while placing his right hand on the Bible, appears to have a beard, which he did not have on inauguration day. The artist identified the tall man between the chief justice and the new president as Vice-President George M. Dallas, "upwards of six feet high, with a profusion of long white hair."[38] Although offering an unrecognizable likeness of President Polk, the drawing was designed more to convey an impression of the occasion than to present portraits. From the two pictures, viewers in London, only six weeks after the event, could sense something of the excitement of the day that not even the rain could dispel. A few weeks later, copies of the *Illustrated London News* would also be circulating in America.

Polk's journey from Nashville to Washing-

INAUGURATION OF PRESIDENT POLK.—THE OATH.

Figure 8–14. "Inauguration of President Polk—The Oath." Published in the *Illustrated London News*, April 19, 1845. Ellis Library, University of Missouri–Columbia.

ton to take the oath of office had attracted as much public interest and attention as Washington's journey from Mount Vernon to New York for the first inauguration.[39] On the day of Polk's inaugural the streets of Washington were crowded with residents and visitors—including a large number of people who had come by special trains from Baltimore—gathered to watch the parade to the Capitol. The Washington *National Intelligencer* reported that "the city had been filling up for days, and even for weeks, in anticipation of the approaching Inauguration, with strangers of every rank in life, and every variety of personal appearance."[40] The inclement weather did not prevent them from turning out for the proceedings.

Describing his reaction upon seeing the crowd on the Capitol grounds, the *Illustrated London News* artist-reporter wrote: "On the procession coming in sight of the Capitol grounds, there was a new scene for wonder; for every conceivable foot of space on the elevated terraces of these grounds, where a spectator could have a chance of seeing the procession and the President and suite, was crowded to suffocation." On the east front of the Capitol, "the whole area, from the platform erected in front of the eastern portico of the Capitol, to the iron railing of the garden in the rear, was one dense mass of human beings."[41] The scene pictured in word and drawing by this observer would be often repeated in the years ahead.

Americans outside Washington also took keen interest in the events in the capital. Samuel F. B. Morse added to the excitement by transmitting the proceedings by wire to Baltimore. "Professor Morse brought out the Magnetic Telegraph to the platform, close to one side of it," it was reported, "from which point he could hear every thing that went on, having under review all the ceremonies performed, communicating results to Baltimore as fast as they transpired."[42] As the first presidential inaugural reported by telegraph wire and the first sketched by an artist on the scene for rapid publication, Polk's inauguration is notable in illustrating wide interest in the American presidency.

In the collections of the National Gallery of Art is a lavishly decorated ivory and paper ladies' fan, which, when open, displays miniature lithographic portraits of all the presidents through Polk (plate 14).[43] Hand colored, but indifferently drawn, the portraits are in the style of contemporaneous popular prints of the presidents. President Washington's portrait occupies the place of honor in the center at the top of the fan, with crossed banners bearing the seal of the United States beneath the portrait. On the ivory sticks of the fan, a hand-colored picture of the signing of the Declaration of Independence is based on Trumbull's much admired work. The oval lithograph has been cut into strips and pasted on the sticks to form the picture when the fan is open. The seal of the United States adorns the other side of the fan, which is decorated with a block-printed leaf motif, complementing the designs carved on the ivory sticks.[44] On eight of the twenty ivory sticks the letters *P* and *D* are alternately carved to honor President Polk and Vice-President Dallas.

Every space on the paper of the fan is filled. The national eagle and stars decorate the border where the paper joins the sticks. The frames of presidential portraits alternately either rest on bases decorated with eagles or are topped by the figure of Minerva, the goddess of Wisdom, often used to represent America. With arms extended, she holds crowns of laurel in each hand. The frames of the portraits and the decorative design between them appear to have once been silver, now tarnished nearly black. The total effect of the heavily decorated fan, when new, may have been more gaudy than artistic, but within the twenty-inch span of the open fan is a pictorial representation of the presidency embellished with the iconographic symbols of the new nation, its birth, and its growing historical record.

As at Polk's inaugural, an artist was present to record Zachary Taylor's inauguration in 1849 (fig. 8–15). The scene offered in a large wood engraving was "drawn on the spot by Wm. Croome," and the print was "Dedicated to the Various Rough and Ready Clubs throughout the Union." The inaugural platform did not appear so crowded with diplomatic representatives from other nations as at Polk's inauguration four years earlier, but the list of invited guests for the platform and Capitol steps was no less in 1849 than in 1845 and included all members of Congress, cabinet members, the Supreme Court, and the diplomatic corps.[45] The drawings of the participants in the center of the platform at Taylor's inaugural were more carefully done than in the illustration of Polk's inauguration. President Taylor is clearly recognizable, as is Vice-President Millard Fillmore standing behind him. Though less clear, outgoing President Polk appears seated at Taylor's left. Many of the others present would no doubt have been identified by contemporaries. The *Discovery Group* sculpture is again prominently featured in the drawing, which depicts an event more sedate in appearance than the lively scenes published of the inaugurations of William Henry Harrison (plate 13) and James K. Polk (fig. 8–14). The artist's failure to include any of the crowd witnessing the ceremonies—estimated by the Washington *National Intelligencer* at twenty thousand—may partially explain the difference in tone.[46] The bust portrait of Taylor in uniform and the summary of his military career below the inaugural picture also suggest that the print was more a tribute to Taylor than a recording of the inauguration.

President Washington had initiated the practice of making trips through parts of the country to visit towns and cities and to meet with his fellow-citizens. Travel was difficult, however, in the early republic, and Washington's precedent was not repeated until Monroe became president. When travel became easier with the building of railroads in the 1830s and 1840s, presidents were more willing to leave the capital for trips other than returning to

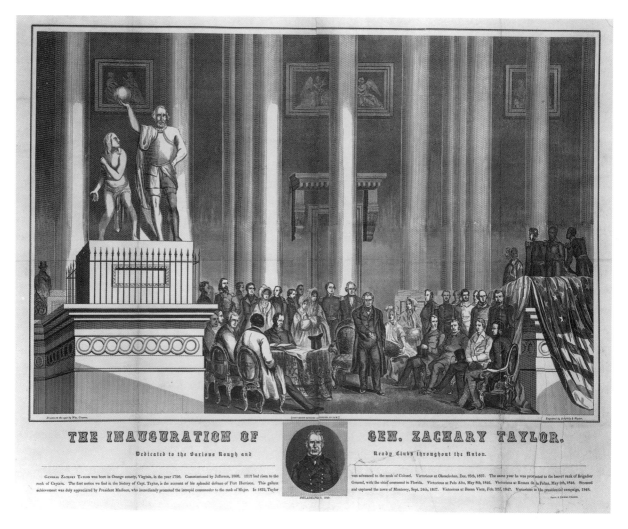

Figure 8–15. *The Inauguration of Gen. Zachary Taylor.* Wood engraving, 23 x 27¼ inches, by Brightly and Keyser after drawing by William Croome. Printed by Smith and Peters, Philadelphia, 1849. Library of Congress.

their homes for vacations. With the appearance of illustrated magazines in the United States in the early 1850s, the travels of presidents became a subject to be reported in pictures as well as in words, offering as never before a visual record of the presidential drama.

In the fourth number of the weekly *Gleason's Pictorial Drawing Room Companion*, launched in Boston on July 5, 1851, Frederick Gleason announced that the illustrations for the next issue would record President Fillmore's recent journey from Washington to New York State to attend the opening of the Erie Railroad. He fulfilled the promise in the issue of August 2 with a series of drawings offering timely images of the president's trip. A scene of Fillmore's re-

ception at the United States Naval Yard in Philadelphia (fig. 8–16)—which the editor had promised would be "a splendid and lively picture, truthful and timely"—depicts a large and enthusiastic crowd and only a minimal display of military ceremony.[47] The view of the president's arrival by the steamer *Erie* at Castle Garden, New York (fig. 8–17), is, according to the caption accompanying the illustration, "a spirited scene indeed, and is given with remarkable accuracy by our artist. All the way up the bay, cannon saluted the progress of the President's party in the steamer." At Castle Garden a large military honor guard awaited the president's arrival. The editor lauded that drawing as "a very expressive picture."[48]

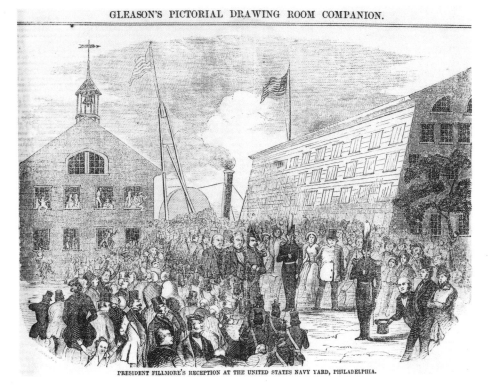

Figure 8–16. "President Fillmore's Reception at the United States Navy Yard, Philadelphia." Published in *Gleason's Pictorial Drawing Room Companion*, Boston, August 2, 1851. Ellis Library, University of Missouri–Columbia.

Figure 8–17. "Landing of President Fillmore from the Steamer Erie, at Castle Garden, New York." Published in *Gleason's Pictorial Drawing Room Companion*, Boston, August 2, 1851. Ellis Library, University of Missouri–Columbia.

THE NEW YORK PROCESSION IN HONOR OF PRESIDENT FILLMORE'S ARRIVAL PASSING THROUGH BROADWAY.

Figure 8–18. "The New York Procession in Honor of President Fillmore's Arrival Passing through Broadway." Published in *Gleason's Pictorial Drawing Room Companion*, Boston, August 2, 1851. Ellis Library, University of Missouri–Columbia.

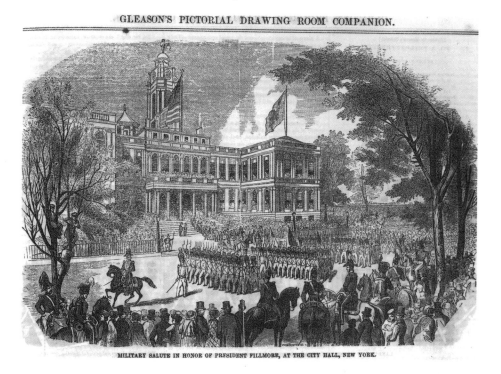

GLEASON'S PICTORIAL DRAWING ROOM COMPANION.

MILITARY SALUTE IN HONOR OF PRESIDENT FILLMORE, AT THE CITY HALL, NEW YORK.

Figure 8–19. "Military Salute in Honor of President Fillmore, at the City Hall, New York." Published in *Gleason's Pictorial Drawing Room Companion*, Boston, August 2, 1851. Ellis Library, University of Missouri–Columbia.

PENNSYLVANIA AVENUE, WASHINGTON CITY, WITH A VIEW OF THE PROCESSION ON THE DAY OF INAUGURATION.

Figure 8–20. "Pennsylvania Avenue, Washington City, with a View of the Procession on the Day of Inauguration." Published in *Gleason's Pictorial Drawing Room Companion*, Boston, March 26, 1853. Ellis Library, University of Missouri–Columbia.

From Castle Garden the president's party proceeded up Broadway, which is depicted by a drawing of the procession passing Barnum's Museum, where viewers lined the street and filled overhanging balconies (fig. 8–18). How promoter Phineas T. Barnum managed to get his museum pictured as the background for the president is not known. "Returning from a long route, the President's party took their stations at the City Hall," *Gleason's* reported, "where they received a marching salute from the military, who filed in review before them."[49] The artist sketched this scene in the most elaborate of the drawings engraved and electrotyped for this issue (fig. 8–19).

The style introduced in reporting the president's trip would be repeated in illustrating subsequent journeys. In November 1851, Gleason devoted most of the issue to President Fillmore's visit to Boston in September for the Great Railroad Jubilee.[50] Gleason's publication met with immediate success. The initial huge pressrun of twenty-five thousand copies was al-

most immediately doubled to fifty thousand, and at a subscription rate of three dollars a year *Gleason's* was a popular bargain.[51] One reader expressed a sense of national pride in the publication. "It evinces, unmistakably, that John Bull is not destined to be ahead of us a great while in the elegance and cheapness of pictorial illustrations," the admirer wrote.[52]

Gleason's magazine played an important role in widening the visual horizons of Americans. One consequence was a greater exposure of the public to the ceremonial role of the president of the United States. That role—performed by Washington and, to a lesser or greater degree, by all his successors—had never before been so widely observed. It was a role that lent itself more to pictures than to words, and it was one that could create a false sense of well-being in the presidential office in a time when the challenges of preserving the Union had never been greater.

Gleason's magazine also covered the inauguration of Franklin Pierce as president on

March 4, 1853. The most visually revealing of the illustrations in the issue of March 26, 1853, was the scene of the procession up Pennsylvania Avenue to the Capitol for the inaugural ceremonies (fig. 8–20).[53] Pierce is pictured riding in an open barouche accompanied—according to the report in the Washington *National Intelligencer*—by outgoing President Fillmore and two members of the arrangement committee. The newspaper reported that the president-elect sat uncovered, "frequently rising to the greeting of the people"—as shown in the drawing. The president's barouche was surrounded by the marshal of the District of Columbia and his aides. Numerous military units with flags flying preceded the president's carriage, which is pictured in the drawing as about to pass in front of the National Hotel at the corner of Pennsylvania Avenue and Sixth Street. The *National Intelligencer* claimed, "The military array was on a scale grander than any that has preceded it in Washington."[54]

The view toward the Capitol on the hill at the end of the avenue provided many Americans who had never seen the nation's capital with a sense of the city that had developed since the government moved to Washington, now more than half a century earlier. The picture conveys images of a colorful, patriotic, yet simple and dignified procession that drew enthusiastic well-wishers to the street. The crowd, however, does not appear to be as large as reported in the newspapers. The *National Intelligencer* estimated that twenty thousand visitors packed the city's hotels, rooming houses, and private homes. Counting spectators from surrounding areas, the editor projected that as many as seventy or eighty thousand people were within the city limits for "the pageant of the day."[55] Among the interesting details of the drawing in Gleason's magazine are telegraph lines connected by only three poles, beginning near the left edge of the picture and ending at the National Hotel.

Four years later, in 1857, *Frank Leslie's Illustrated Newspaper*, reporting on its first presidential inauguration, sought to outdo any previous inaugural coverage. The editor dispatched "a corps of artists" to record the event, sending them first to Wheatland, Buchanan's home in Pennsylvania, and then to travel with the president-elect to Washington. Promising

to devote an entire number to the "great national festival," the editor announced his determination to make the issue "the most brilliant illustrated paper in every respect ever issued from the press." He continued:

It will present a daguerreotyped representation of the great *fête* . . . . An effort will be made to produce something worthy of the occasion, something truly national, something that will live and be preserved as a historical record of the times. By so doing, the people throughout the Union can sit down at their firesides and almost literally witness the imposing ceremonies attending the sublime but simple installation of an American President into office.

Indicating that the number would be electrotyped, the publisher promised to be able to fill all orders and appealed "to the national and to the patriotic feeling of the country" for support "commensurate with the vast outlay attending the production."[56]

The first page of the issue of March 14, 1857, presented a picture of Chief Justice Roger Taney administering the oath of office to the new president, James Buchanan (fig. 8–21). Between them stood John C. Breckinridge, the new vice-president (standing next to Taney), and the outgoing president, Franklin Pierce. The portraits in the engraving were taken from ambrotypes by Mathew Brady. The caption above the picture noted: "Contrasted with the coronation of the rulers of despotic countries, the Inauguration of an American President is simple and unpretending. But the want of theatrical display is more than compensated by the moral grandeur which accompanies the act."[57]

Six additional pages in the sixteen-page number were filled with pictures, beginning with Buchanan's home, Wheatland, including drawings of the library, the parlor, and his "sleeping apartment" (fig. 8–22). The latter page includes pictures of his dog, his favorite rocking chair, his walking stick, his library inkstand, and even a pair of eagles from California living free on the grounds. There were also drawings of the president-elect's departure from Wheatland, of a stop at the Exchange Hotel in Lancaster, and of his boarding the train at Lancaster for the trip to Washington.[58]

Accompanying Buchanan to Washington, the artist-reporters recorded his arrival at the

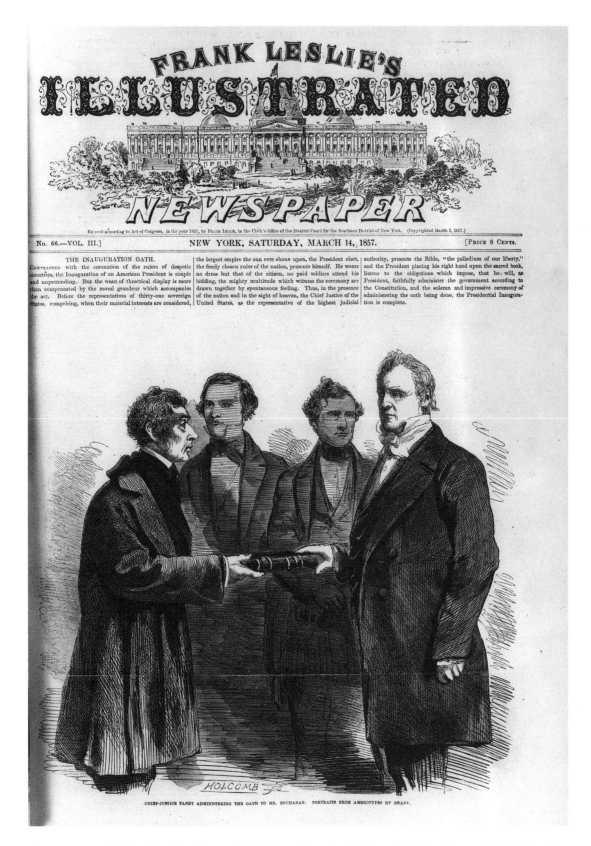

FRANK LESLIE'S ILLUSTRATED NEWSPAPER

Entered according to Act of Congress, in the year 1857, by FRANK LESLIE, in the Clerk's Office of the District Court for the Southern District of New York. (Copyrighted March 2, 1857.)

No. 66.—VOL. III.] NEW YORK, SATURDAY, MARCH 14, 1857. [PRICE 6 CENTS.

THE INAUGURATION OATH.

CONTRASTED with the coronation of the rulers of despotic countries, the Inauguration of an American President is simple and unpretending. But the want of theatrical display is more than compensated by the moral grandeur which accompanies the act. Before the representatives of thirty-one sovereign States, comprising, when their material interests are considered, the largest empire the sun ever shone upon, the President elect, the freely chosen ruler of the nation, presents himself. He wears no dress but that of the citizen, no paid soldiers attend his bidding, the mighty multitude which witness the ceremony are drawn together by spontaneous feeling. Thus, in the presence of the nation and in the sight of heaven, the Chief Justice of the United States, as the representative of the highest judicial authority, presents the Bible, "the palladium of our liberty," and the President placing his right hand upon the sacred book, listens to the obligations which impose, that he will, as President, faithfully administer the government according to the Constitution, and the solemn and impressive ceremony of administering the oath being done, the Presidential Inauguration is complete.

HOLCOMB

CHIEF-JUSTICE TANEY ADMINISTERING THE OATH TO MR. BUCHANAN. PORTRAITS FROM AMBROTYPES BY BRADY.

Figure 8–21. "Chief-Justice Taney Administering the Oath to Mr. Buchanan." Published in *Frank Leslie's Illustrated Newspaper*, New York, March 14, 1857. American Antiquarian Society.

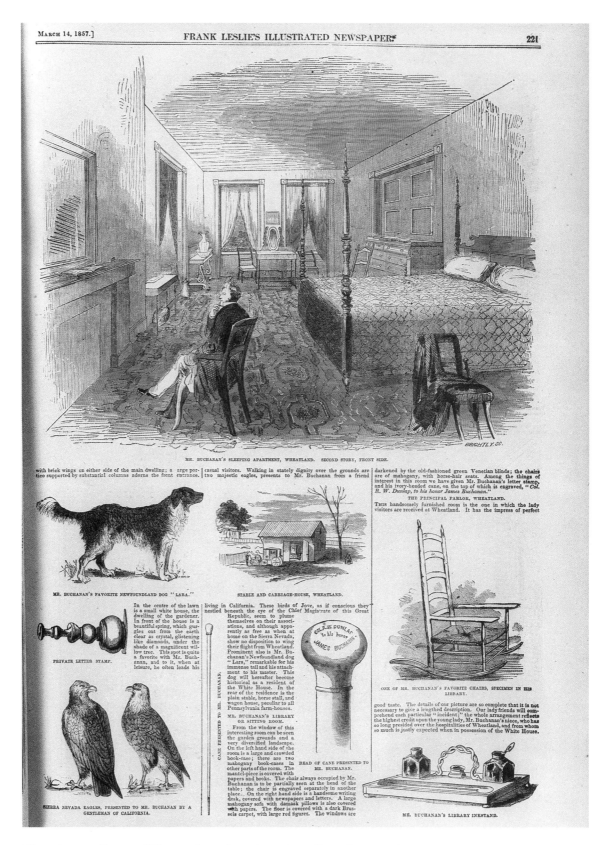

Figure 8–22. Page of illustrations from *Frank Leslie's Illustrated Newspaper*, New York, March 14, 1857. American Antiquarian Society.

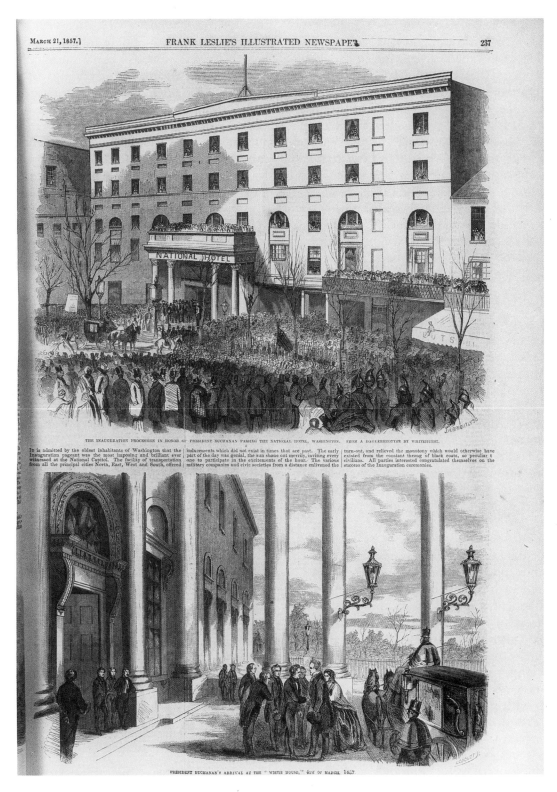

THE INAUGURATION PROCESSION IN HONOR OF PRESIDENT BUCHANAN PASSING THE NATIONAL HOTEL, WASHINGTON.   FROM A DAGUERREOTYPE BY WHITEHURST.

It is admitted by the oldest inhabitants of Washington that the Inauguration pageant was the most imposing and brilliant ever witnessed at the National Capitol. The facility of transportation from all the principal cities North, East, West and South, offered inducements which did not exist in times that are past. The early part of the day was genial, the sun shone out merrily, inviting every one to participate in the excitements of the hour. The various military companies and civic societies from a distance enlivened the turn-out, and relieved the monotony which would otherwise have existed from the constant throng of black coats, so peculiar t civilians. All parties interested congratulated themselves on the success of the Inauguration ceremonies.

PRESIDENT BUCHANAN'S ARRIVAL AT THE "WHITE HOUSE," 4TH OF MARCH, 1857.

Figure 8–23. Above, "The Inauguration Procession in Honor of President Buchanan Passing the National Hotel, Washington." Engraved by Joseph H. Brightly from a daguerreotype by Jesse H. Whitehurst. Below, "President Buchanan's Arrival at the 'White House,' 4th of March, 1857." Published in *Frank Leslie's Illustrated Newspaper*, New York, March 21, 1857. American Antiquarian Society.

Washington railroad station. They drew sketches of his bedroom and parlor at the National Hotel and made a drawing of the inaugural scene in the style of the illustrations of Polk's inauguration that had appeared in the *Illustrated London News*.[59] The hastily drawn sketches, appearing ten days after the inaugural, gave subscribers eyewitness impressions of the recent event, supplementing the written accounts appearing in all the newspapers. With an additional week of preparation, *Frank Leslie's Illustrated Newspaper* provided more finished reproductions in the issue of March 21. A view of the president-elect leaving the National Hotel for the inauguration was accompanied by a picture of Buchanan arriving at the White House to be greeted at the portico by President Pierce (fig. 8–23)—a familiar scene little altered in the inaugural rituals of the late twentieth century. A drawing of a view of the inaugural procession offers the artist's impression of an immense crowd and a very long procession, which included a horse-drawn ship made by mechanics at the Washington Navy Yard (fig. 8–24). "As the pageant moved along," *Leslie's* reported, "sailors were engaged in the rigging and on deck in their various duties as if at sea," providing "an object of curious admiration."[60]

Certain to attract viewers' interest was the drawing of the inaugural ball held in a large, elaborately decorated, temporary building constructed on Judiciary Square (fig. 8–25). Red, white, and blue drapery covered the walls decorated with the flags of many nations, and huge chandeliers lighted the room. From a balcony "tastefully ornamented and graced by a tolerable portrait of Mr. Buchanan," a forty-piece orchestra played for a crowd pictured as far too large to permit much dancing, though *Leslie's* reporter insisted that "the dancing was kept up with spirit until long after midnight." When President Buchanan arrived at the ball about eleven o'clock, the orchestra struck up *Hail to the Chief*. The reporter thought the president looked well, "although a shade of anxious thought appeared at times to cross his fine countenance."[61]

Leslie's was not the only illustrated publication to report the inauguration, but it was the most enthusiastic in its reporting and the most extensive in the scope and scale of its illustra-

tions. *Harper's Weekly*—in its first year of publication as a weekly—offered what was primarily a historical review of inaugurations. The piece was illustrated with drawings of Washington's and Buchanan's inaugurations, together with their portraits and those of their vice-presidents (fig. 8–26). The drawing of Buchanan's inaugural appears to have been no more produced by an artist who had witnessed the scene than was the picture of Washington's inauguration. Harper's commentator mused:

> The ceremony was imposing in a moral aspect only. The long and somewhat tawdry procession; the score of military companies in various developments of 'lace, feathers, and flummery;' the liberty-car with Mrs. Liberty and her pole, fifty feet high (the pole, not the goddess); the full-rigged ship, with the sailors proceeding to double-reef topsails as the horses trotted up Pennsylvania Avenue; Mr. Buchanan and Mr. Breckinridge riding quietly and in a business-like way in their carriage from the hotel to the Capitol, walking into the Senate Chamber to muster forces for the inauguration, and then repairing in company with other dignitaries to the platform under the portico; the inaugural itself, from the first word to the last—all this strikes us as the most perfect—because the least glittering—transmission of power from one administration to another that has ever been witnessed in the history of the country. It is the nearest approach to a quiet common-sense performance of a very practical, though unquestionably momentous, ceremony, that we remember.

Still, the *Harper's* critic could not resist another remark about the parade:

> Of course no argument would convince the gentlemen of the Lancaster Fencibles, or the Peddlington Invincibles, or the John Smith Guards, that their presence on an occasion of this kind, in full armor and marching order, with three days' provisions in their knapsacks, and sixty rounds of ball-cartridge within reach of the hand, was not of the highest consequence, or indeed that the inauguration ceremony could actually be achieved without them.[62]

The *Harper's* critic, while appreciative of the vast importance of the peaceful transfer of political power, was less impressed with the pageantry of inaugurations. At the same time, his comments reveal a recognition of how fully immersed the American people were in the drama of the presidency.

Figure 8–24. "The Inauguration Procession in Honor of President Buchanan Passing through Pennsylvania Avenue, Washington City, March 4th 1857." Published in *Frank Leslie's Illustrated Newspaper*, New York, March 21, 1857. American Antiquarian Society.

Figure 8–25. Buchanan's "Inauguration Ball, in the Immense Building Erected for the Purpose in Judiciary Square, Washington City, March 4th 1857." Published in *Frank Leslie's Illustrated Newspaper*, New York, March 21, 1857. American Antiquarian Society.

Figure 8–26. Pages from *Harper's Weekly*, New York, March 14, 1857, reporting the inauguration of President Buchanan, with illustrations of Washington's and Buchanan's inaugurals. Ellis Library, University of Missouri–Columbia.

CHAPTER IX
The Presidency Popularized and Exploited

I N 1804 Raphaelle Peale offered the public a silhouette profile of "either of our three illustrious Presidents"—Washington, John Adams, or Jefferson—with the purchase of a twenty-five-cent frame (fig. 9–1).[1] At a time when engraved portraits of the presidents commonly cost from two to five dollars, silhouettes offered an inexpensive way for the ordinary person to obtain a presidential profile, just as silhouettes provided affordable likenesses of family members and friends. Presidential images also became popularly known on medals, decorated English earthenware, and elegant porcelain cups (fig. 9–2).[2] They appeared on common mugs (figs. 9–3 and 9–4), snuffboxes (fig. 9–5), sewing boxes (fig. 9–6), tags for yard goods (fig. 9–7), and whiskey flasks (figs. 9–8 through 9–11). The likenesses of numerous American presidents were printed on bank notes.[3] Portraits of presidents decorated the borders of travelers' maps of the United States (fig. 9–12) and embellished informational charts on post roads and post offices (fig. 9–13).

The faithfulness of presidential images on popular pieces varied greatly. Washington's well-known likeness was surely the most readily recognized image in the country. McFarland, Evans and Company had no need to identify his portrait on their yard-goods tag of 1858 (fig. 9–7). Presidential portraits were likely to be more carefully rendered on expen-

Figure 9–1. Thomas Jefferson. Silhouette by Raphaelle Peale, taken from life while Jefferson was president, 1804. The silhouette is 2⅞ x 1¾ inches, cut from paper 4½ x 3⅞ inches, embossed "Peale" below the bust. Thomas Jefferson Memorial Foundation, Monticello.

241

Figure 9–2. Porcelain cups, 2½ inches high, each decorated with a hand-painted portrait of a president: Monroe, Jackson, John Quincy Adams, John Adams, and Madison, circa 1840s. National Museum of American History, Smithsonian Institution.

Figure 9–3. *Thomas Jefferson, President of the United States of America.* Transfer design on earthenware mug, 4⅝ inches high, Liverpool, circa 1801. Robert H. McCauley Collection, National Museum of American History, Smithsonian Institution.

Figure 9–4. Earthenware mugs, 2½ and 2⅝ inches high, decorated with transfer designs: John Quincy Adams, Jefferson, Monroe. Made in England, circa 1800–1825. Henry Francis du Pont Winterthur Museum.

Figure 9–5. Snuffbox, 3½ x 2⅜ x ⅝ inches, with portrait of President Jefferson, taken from engraving by Saint-Mémin made in 1805. National Museum of American History, Smithsonian Institution.

Figure 9–6. Sewing box, 3¼ x 4¾ x 2⁹⁄₁₆ inches, with engraving of John Quincy Adams, circa 1825–1829. Made of colored cardboard, the box is trimmed with colored and gold-embossed paper. On the top is a velvet pincushion decorated with a shield, crossed flags, and the legend "Adams and Liberty." Ralph E. Becker Collection, Smithsonian Institution.

Figure 9–7. Yard goods tag, 3 x 2¼ inches, with portrait of Washington. McFarland, Evans and Company, Philadelphia, 1858. Library of Congress.

Figure 9–8. Whiskey flask, 6⅝ inches high, with image of John Quincy Adams. John Taylor and Company, Brownsville, Pennsylvania, circa 1828. Corning Museum of Glass.

sive porcelain cups than on earthenware mugs. The images of John Adams, Madison, Monroe, John Quincy Adams, and Jackson on the porcelain examples illustrated here (fig. 9–2) could be identified without their names. All derived from important and widely known likenesses. The portraits of John Adams, Madison, and Monroe were all after Gilbert Stuart, from the lithographs taken from the series painted for John Doggett (see figs. 2–23, 2–25, 2–26). The image of John Quincy Adams came from the portrait painted by Asher B. Durand for Luman Reed (see fig. 2–43), and Jackson's portrait followed the likeness by James Barton Longacre for his *National Portrait Gallery of Distinguished Americans*.[4] On the other hand, the images on earthenware mugs were sometimes unrecognizable without a name. For example, the English drawing of Jefferson on the mug shown here (fig. 9–3) bears no resemblance to any of his life portraits. In contrast, the likeness of Jefferson on the snuffbox (fig. 9–5) was derived from the Saint-Mémin profile taken while he was president (fig. 2–7).[5] The crude portraits of Washington, John Adams, Jefferson, and Madison on the post-roads print of 1815 (fig. 9–13) fortunately are identified, though the Scottish printer near Glasgow spelled the incumbent president's name "Mad-

dison." The more recognizable presidential portraits on the traveler's map of the United States of 1850 (fig. 9–12) also are identified; and scattered among the presidential likenesses are portraits of William Penn, Benjamin Franklin, Roger Williams, and Lafayette.

Portrait images were commonly poor on decorated whiskey flasks, the making of which flourished in America between 1820 and 1850. The portraits of only five presidents have been identified on such flasks: George Washington, John Quincy Adams, Andrew Jackson, William Henry Harrison, and Zachary Taylor. With the exception of John Quincy Adams, whose image has been found on only one flask (fig. 9–8), all were military heroes, suggesting that individuals more than the office of the presidency were the object of celebration. Washington was by far the most popular person to be pictured on whiskey flasks; only the American eagle was a more popular motif. Washington and the national emblem commonly appeared on the same flask (fig. 9–9). The example illustrated here is also historically interesting because the edge of the flask contains the inscription

Figure 9–9. Whiskey flask, 6¹⁵⁄₁₆ inches high, with images of Washington and the national emblem. The initials indicate the glass manufacturer, Thomas W. Dyott. Kensington Glass Works, Philadelphia, circa 1826. Corning Museum of Glass.

Figure 9–10. Whiskey flask, 5¾ inches high, with image of Washington on one side and Jackson on the other. Coventry, Connecticut, Glass Works, circa 1829–1836. Smithsonian Institution.

Figure 9–11. Whiskey flask, 8⅝ inches high, with images of Washington, "The Father of His Country," and General Zachary Taylor, circa 1846–1848. Corning Museum of Glass.

"Adams and Jefferson July 4. A.D. 1776." This appears to have been added to the original mold after the extraordinary coincidence of the deaths of both Jefferson and Adams on July 4, 1826—the fiftieth anniversary of the Declaration of Independence.[6] Glassmakers found Jackson's portrait to be popular, and one manufacturer decorated a flask with images of Washington and Jackson on opposite sides (fig. 9–10). As this example illustrates, Washington and Jackson were commonly depicted in military uniform. In the 1840s, however, Washington appeared as a statesman rather than a general in a classical bust titled "The Father of His Country," which appeared on a flask offering the image of Gen. Zachary Taylor on the other side (fig. 9–11).[7]

As the nineteenth century advanced, Americans in their everyday lives increasingly encountered images of their presidents, past and present. By 1825 Americans could purchase a volume containing the inaugural and annual messages of the presidents, with an engraved frontispiece presenting portraits of all the presidents (fig. 9–14).[8] Published in Philadelphia by Robert Desilver, the book also contained the texts of the Declaration of Independence,

the Constitution, and Washington's farewell address. The idea of such collections came to be widely copied. A New York publisher offered a similar volume in 1839 with a frontispiece, engraved by M. A. Moses of Connecticut, featuring miniature portraits of the presidents framing a drawing of the president's house in Washington (fig. 9–15).

In 1846 Edwin Williams, author of the *New York Annual Register*, edited a two-volume compilation of presidential messages, which he soon renamed *Statesman's Manual*. Publisher Edward Walker adorned the title page of each volume with the seals of the states and the Union and included frontispieces presenting crudely drawn portraits of the presidents, accompanied by a picture of the White House and small drawings featuring ocean commerce, railroads, and canals (figs. 9–16 and 9–17). Numerous reviewers praised the work. The *Argus* of Albany called it a "truly national work—a work not only for statesmen and legislators, but for the public generally, and for every intelligent citizen."[9] The reviewer in *The American Review: A Whig Journal of Politics, Literature, Art and Science* concluded, "Of the real value of this work to the people of this country, too

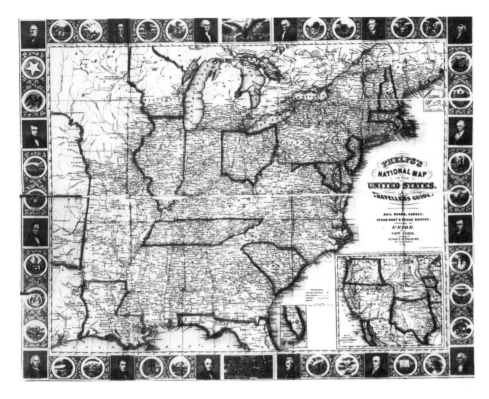

Figure 9–12. "Phelps's National Map of the United States, A Travellers Guide." A colored, foldout map, 20⁷/₁₆ x 25³/₄ inches, drawn and engraved by J. M. Atwood, New York. Published in *Phelps's Travellers' Guide through the United States* (New York: Ensign and Thayer, 1850). Rare Book Room, Cornell University Library.

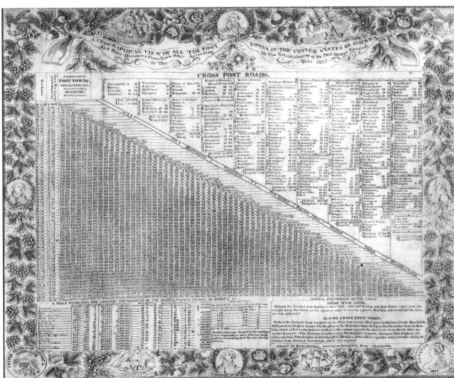

Figure 9–13. *A Geographical View of All the Post Towns in the United States of America and Their Distances from Each Other According to the Establishment of the Post Master General in the Year 1815.* Textile broadside, 20¼ x 26 inches, printed by R. Gillespie, Anderston Printfield, near Glasgow, 1815. Henry Francis du Pont Winterthur Museum.

Figure 9–14. Frontispiece and title page of a volume of addresses of the presidents (Philadelphia: Robert Desilver, 1825). College of William and Mary.

Figure 9–15. Frontispiece and title page of *Addresses and Messages of the Presidents of the United States from 1789 to 1839* (New York: McLean and Taylor, 1839). Engraving by M. A. Moses, 1837. State Historical Society of Missouri.

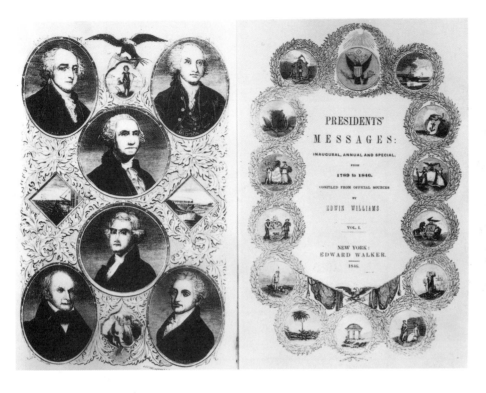

Figure 9–16. Frontispiece and title page of *Presidents' Messages*, edited by Edwin Williams, volume 1 (New York: Edward Walker, 1846). Engraving by Lossing and Barritt. College of William and Mary.

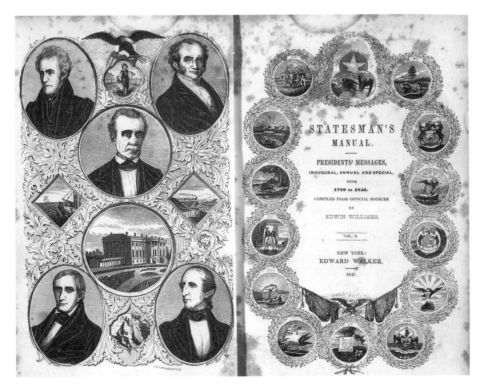

Figure 9–17. Frontispiece and title page of *Statesman's Manual*, edited by Edwin Williams, volume 2 of *Presidents' Messages* (New York: Edward Walker, 1847). Engraving by Lossing and Barritt. Ellis Library, University of Missouri–Columbia.

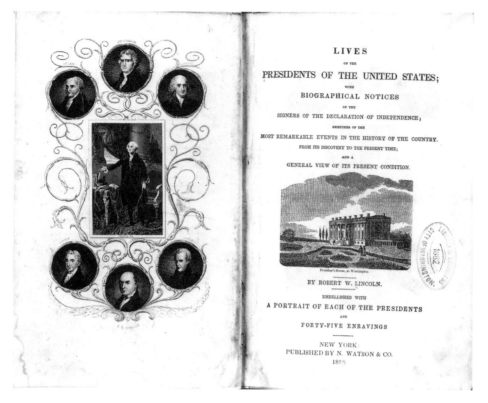

Figure 9–18. Frontispiece and title page of Robert W. Lincoln's *Lives of the Presidents of the United States* (New York: N. Watson and Company, 1833). Engraving by J. H. Hillis. Library of Congress.

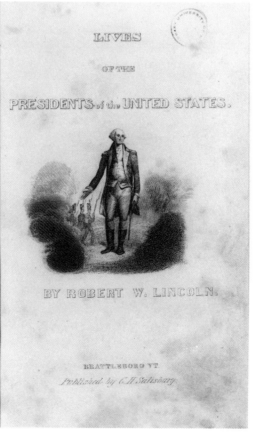

Figure 9–19. Frontispiece and title page of Robert W. Lincoln's *Lives of the Presidents of the United States* (Brattleboro, Vt.: G. H. Salisbury, 1850). Ellis Library, University of Missouri–Columbia.

high an estimate can hardly be formed." But, pointing to a major fault, the critic wrote:

> One thing only, in these volumes, strikes us as worthy of censure: and that is utterly wretched. We refer to the engraved heads of the Presidents, placed as frontispieces. We have never seen anything more absurd and abominable. They look as if they had been etched on clay and moulded of cast iron; and even in that case, they must have been badly done. By the way they look, the cares of State must have made terrible inroads upon them. We should think the old bald eagle at the top would scream over them worse than he appears to be doing; and we only wish the blaze of glory around him would consume the whole infamous combination together. Seriously, it is unjust, and altogether unprofitable, in an age so accustomed to good engravings, to put out such miserable caricatures of our most eminent men; and we frankly advise the publisher to change the plates as soon as possible.[10]

There were, of course, other equally crude presidential likenesses offered to the public. But the reviewer's reference to "an age so accustomed to good engravings" should be noted, for it recognizes the advancement in the art of engraving made during the half-century of the republic and reveals a growing appreciation of the fine arts in America. Williams's publisher accepted the critic's advice and in a new, four-volume edition published in 1849 replaced the earlier frontispieces with individual engraved portraits. The title page proclaimed the work to be "Embellished with Portraits of the Presidents, engraved on steel, by Vistus Balch." Washington's portrait appeared as the frontispiece in volume 1, Jefferson's in volume 2, Jackson's in volume 3, and Zachary Taylor's in volume 4. Individual portraits of the remaining presidents accompanied biographical sketches preceding their addresses.[11] The change won approval from the reviewer in the *American Review*, where the artwork of the earlier edition had been lambasted. Praising the new edition, the critic noted that it was "adorned with really excellent Engravings of all the Presidents."[12]

Williams's *Statesman's Manual*, in the initial two-volume edition of seventeen hundred pages, was offered for sale in "strong muslin binding" at the price of five dollars. Despite the lack of critical acclaim for the artwork in that edition, the publisher could boast of selling four thousand copies of the set during the first year.[13] The rapidity with which new editions appeared attests further to the success of the work.

Another popular type of book celebrating the presidency was the collective biography. In 1833 Robert W. Lincoln published his *Lives of the Presidents of the United States*. The volume was embellished with miniature portraits of the presidents grouped around a reproduction of Stuart's Lansdowne portrait of Washington (fig. 9–18).[14] Lincoln brought out new editions of his work as the roster of presidents grew, adding new portraits to a redesigned frontispiece accompanying the biographical sketches (fig. 9–19). At least seven editions—some of them reprintings—appeared between 1833 and 1850. Eight years after the first edition, a Washington bookseller advertised in the *National Intelligencer* the arrival of a new shipment of the work, illustrated "with Portraits and many engravings, in full leather binding."[15]

For those Americans unable to afford a leatherbound volume, more popularly designed works were available. In 1848, Benson J. Lossing, an early writer of illustrated history, published *The Lives of the Presidents of the United States; Embracing a Brief History of the Principal Events of Their Respective Administrations*. New York publisher H. Phelps and Company issued the work in soft covers with patriotic decoration (plate 11). A portrait of each president and a drawing of his home accompanied each brief biography (figs. 9–20 and 9–21). The volume also included the Declaration of Independence, the Constitution, and Washington's farewell address, together with a list of current cabinet officers and a table of governmental expenditures.

Other books combined a survey of the nation's history with biographies of the presidents.[16] Accounts of presidential administrations also increasingly came to provide the basic organization of histories of the United States, both for school textbooks and for popular publications. Among them was Charles A. Goodrich's widely used schoolbook *A History of the United States of America*, first published in 1822 and repeatedly revised to become the most popular textbook in United States history prior to the Civil War.[17] John Frost's *The Picto-*

Figure 9–20. Pages from Benson J. Lossing's *Lives of the Presidents* (New York: H. Phelps and Company, 1848), with illustrations of Jefferson and Monticello. College of William and Mary.

Figure 9–21. Pages from Lossing's *Lives of the Presidents*, with illustrations of Van Buren and Lindenwald. College of William and Mary.

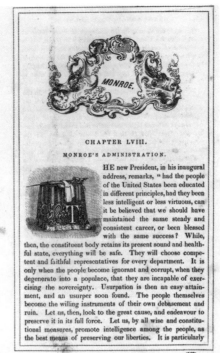

Figure 9–22. Pages from John Frost's *Pictorial History of the United States* (Philadelphia: Walker and Gillis, 1846). Ellis Library, University of Missouri–Columbia.

Figure 9–23. Advertisement for *The True Republican*, 1848. Ellis Library, University of Missouri–Columbia.

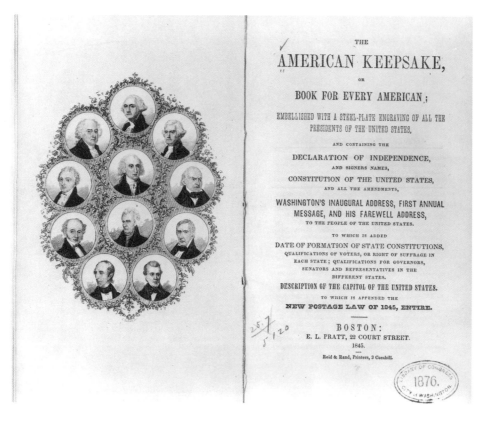

Figure 9–24. Frontispiece and title page of *The American Keepsake* (Boston: E. L. Pratt, 1845). Engraving by E. Hobart. Library of Congress.

rial History of the United States of America (1846) also offered chapters on each presidential administration introduced by a full-page portrait of the president. Each of the portraits was presented in a patriotically ornate frame with the national eagle at the top and a copy of the Constitution of the United States placed before the portrait at the bottom of the frame (fig. 9–22).[18] Frost employed the same portraits—more poorly drawn and without the elaborate frames—in his *The Presidents of the United States: From Washington to Fillmore*, published in 1852.[19]

Among the advertisements bound in a volume of Frost's *Pictorial Life of General Washington* (1848) was a full page promoting *The True Republican* as "A Book for every American!" (fig. 9–23). Containing the inaugural addresses and other messages of the presidents—along with the Declaration of Independence, the Constitution, and other documents—the work was touted as "embellished with elegant portraits of all the presidents, engraved on steel, as large as the size of the page will admit, executed by one of the best artists in Philadelphia." And the "Price only One Dollar!" The

portrait of each president accompanied his inaugural address or addresses.[20]

Similar to *The True Republican* was *The American Keepsake, or Book for Every American*, a volume offering a steel-plate engraving of all the presidents of the United States (fig. 9–24). Published in Boston, the book also contained the texts of the Declaration of Independence, the Constitution, and several major addresses by Washington, together with voter qualifications in each state and the new postage law of 1845.[21] Another work of the same type, published in New York in 1855, was entitled *The American's Own Book*. The volume combined the nation's cherished documents and major presidential addresses with biographical sketches.[22] Miniature portraits of all the presidents composed what had become a familiar frontispiece (fig. 9–25). Comparable books appeared without presidential portraits or other illustrations, but the popularity of illustrated works grew rapidly.

Spending the night at a small inn in Lebanon, Illinois, in 1842, Charles Dickens described in his *American Notes* the inn's two par-

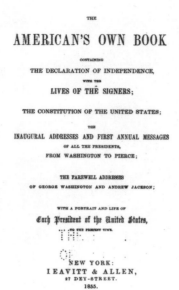

Figure 9–25. Frontispiece and title page of *The American's Own Book* (New York: Ieavitt and Allen, 1855). The portraits of Polk, Taylor, and Fillmore were added to an earlier plate of the presidents through Tyler, engraved by Oliver Pelton. Library of Congress.

lors, noting in particular that they were "decorated with coloured prints of Washington, and President Madison."[23] An American traveler may have been less likely to record such observations, for the portraits of Washington and other presidents had long been seen on the walls of public rooms and private homes. But Dickens's comments are of interest in providing evidence of the widespread popularity of colored presidential prints, which inexpensive lithography and hand coloring made widely available. Portrait prints remained the most common medium for the presentation of presidential likenesses, and the technology of lithography and methods of mass production resulted in the increasing popularization of these images.

In 1849 a columnist writing for the *Connecticut Courant* visited the lithographic establishment of Kelloggs and Comstock in Hartford to report the revolutionary changes lithography had brought to the visual arts. "Prints are now produced from drawings on stone, which possess nearly all the beauty and delicacy of the best steel and copperplate engravings," he wrote, "and at a price which brings them within the easy reach of all classes. Scarcely a cottage or hamlet can be found, however ob-

scure or isolated, but what displays upon its walls more or less specimens of this art." Visiting the pressrooms, he reported that the presses of Kelloggs and Comstock were "running off daily from 3000 to 4000 copies of various popular prints for general sale, of which over 600,000 are published annually by this firm." In the sizing room, he found efficient machinery applying sizing by rollers at the rate of twenty-five to thirty sheets per minute. In the coloring room, the columnist watched "some 25 or 30 young ladies, all intently occupied with the paint brush," and he found their work performed "with a dexterity and skill surprising to one who has never witnessed it." After coloring, the prints were pressed smooth in a powerful press and packed into boxes for marketing. "Orders are received from every portion of the United States," he noted, "and no village or hamlet in our land is without specimens from this establishment."[24]

The catalog of prints available for sale by Kelloggs and Comstock listed nearly four hundred different lithographs. "Of these prints, more than a hundred thousand copies have been sold from a single design," the *Courant* writer reported. "The portrait of 'Washington' takes the lead, and next to him stands old

Figure 9–26. *Martin Van
Buren, President of the
United States.* **Lithograph,
10½ x 10⅝ inches, by
Charles Fenderich. Printed
by Pierre S. Duval, Philadel-
phia; published by Charles
Fenderich, Washington, 1839.
National Portrait Gallery,
Smithsonian Institution.**

Rough and Ready." When this column appeared, Zachary Taylor's inauguration was still a month away, and the writer wondered how much the hundred thousand copies of Taylor lithographs sold in the previous two years had contributed to his recent election. Resigned to the acceptance of the new technology, he concluded, "This mode of electioneering no one can either gainsay or resist."[25]

Despite the extent of its list and the popularity of its prints of Washington and Taylor, the Kelloggs firm published only a partial presidential series. Several other firms, however, following the example of the Pendleton lithographs of the first five presidents, published complete sets of all the presidents. In 1839 Carusi's Music Store in Washington advertised: "Engravings, Lithographs . . . among which are the portraits of all the Presidents of the United States."[26] It is not known to which presidential prints the advertisement referred,

but the set published by George Endicott (figs. 2–30, 2–31, and 2–32) was widely obtainable. Henry Robinson was also publishing a similar series of lithographs, available both from New York and from his store on Pennsylvania Avenue in Washington. Robinson's hand-colored lithograph of John Adams (plate 18) is an example from his series in the style of Endicott's prints or the Pendleton lithographs (fig. 2–23). Although the Kelloggs of Hartford never offered a complete set of all the presidents, their artists also were influenced by the Pendleton lithographs and their imitators, as can be seen in the lithograph of John Quincy Adams (plate 19). In the style of the Pendleton lithographs, the likeness of Adams was taken from Asher Brown Durand's portrait of the sixth president (fig. 2–43). The composition of the print, which appeared after Adams's death, indicates that it was of the presidential-series genre rather than a memorial print.

Figure 9–27. *John Tyler, President of the United States.* Lithograph, 11⁵⁄16 x 10⁵⁄8 inches, by Charles Fenderich. Published by Charles Fenderich, Washington, D.C., 1841. National Portrait Gallery, Smithsonian Institution.

Not all popular portrait prints were derivatives of paintings or other engravings and lithographs. Charles Fenderich, an accomplished artist who established a "Lithographic Repository" in Washington in 1837, drew most of the portraits for his lithographs from life, including those of Presidents Van Buren (fig. 9–26), Tyler (fig. 9–27), and Polk.[27] The Van Buren print was published in 1839; Tyler's, in 1841. Both were inscribed as drawn from life, and the lithograph of Tyler was signed and dated on the stone by the artist. Little more than six weeks after Tyler became president, the *National Intelligencer* advertised:

PRESIDENT TYLER.—W. Fischer has this day received from the hands of the celebrated artist, Mr. Charles Fenderich, a striking likeness of John Tyler, President of the United States. Persons wishing to possess a copy will please apply at Stationers' Hall.[28]

In 1846 C. S. Williams of Philadelphia published a set of hand-colored lithographs, uniform in style, of the eleven presidents from Washington through Polk. The likenesses are of uneven quality, the best of them being the portraits of more recent presidents (fig. 9–28). An elaborate rectangular frame presents each oval bust portrait in a formal setting. Above the frame, the title "Portraits of the Presidents" indicates the series, and each president is identified beneath his portrait by name and order of holding office. In contrast to many popularized versions of presidential images, the Newsam series retained a reserved formality.

Figure 9–28. *Portraits of the Presidents*. Lithographs, each about 10¼ x 8⅞ inches, of Andrew Jackson, Martin Van Buren, John Tyler, and James K. Polk, from series of the presidents drawn on stone by Albert Newsam. Lithographed by Pierre S. Duval; published by C. S. Williams, Philadelphia, 1846. Harry T. Peters "America on Stone" Lithography Collection, Smithsonian Institution.

Plate 18. *John Adams: Second President of the United States*. Hand-colored lithograph, 15 x 12 inches, by Henry R. Robinson, New York and Washington, circa 1833–1842. Library of Congress.

Plate 19. *John Quincy Adams. Sixth President of the United States*. Hand-colored lithograph, 14 x 9¾ inches, by E. B. and E. C. Kellogg, New York, [1848]. Library of Congress.

Plate 20. *James K. Polk. Eleventh President of the United States.* Hand-colored lithograph, 13 x 9 inches, by Nathaniel Currier, New York, [1845]. Library of Congress.

Plate 21. *James K. Polk. Freedom's Champion.* Hand-colored lithograph, 11¹⁵⁄₁₆ x 8¹¹⁄₁₆ inches. Published by Sarony and Major, New York, 1846. National Portrait Gallery, Smithsonian Institution.

262

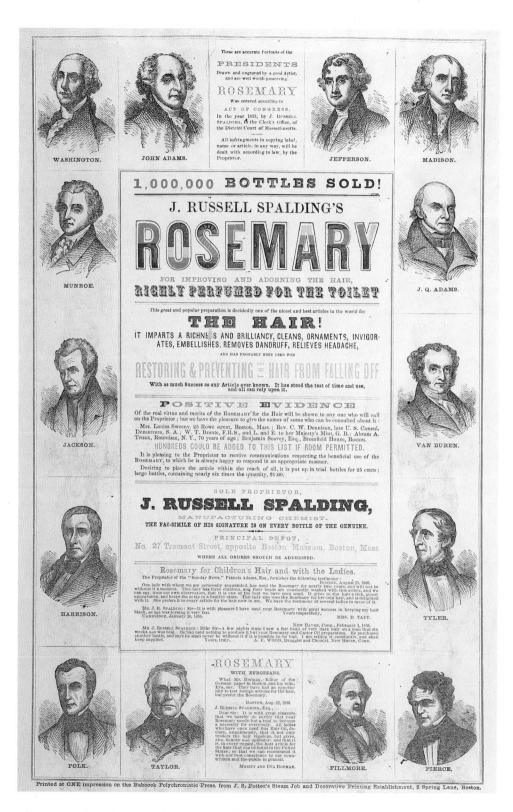

Plate 22. Advertisement for J. Russell Spalding's "Rosemary," a product for "improving and adorning the hair." The colored poster, 14½ x 8¾ inches, was "printed at ONE impression on the Babcock Polychromatic Press, from J.S. Potter's Steam Job and Decorative Printing Establishment." Boston, 1856. American Antiquarian Society.

263

Plate 23. *Portraits of the Presidents.* Advertisement for Charles C. Savage's *Illustrated Biography, or Memoirs of the Great and Good* (New York: Rufus Blanchard, 1853). Hand-colored poster, 31 x 23 inches, circa 1853. American Antiquarian Society.

Plate 24. *The Presidents of Our Great Republic.* Decorated stationery, 11³⁄₈ x 8¹³⁄₁₆ inches. Sold by Charles Magnus, New York, circa 1854–1856. The engraved surface is 6 x 8 inches, hand colored. Private collection.

Plate 25. *National Republican Chart.* Hand-colored lithograph, 43⅝ x 25¹³⁄₁₆ inches. Published by H. H. Lloyd and Company, New York, 1860. National Portrait Gallery, Smithsonian Institution.

Plate 26. *Washington and Lincoln. The Father and the Saviour of Our Country.* Hand-colored lithograph, 14⅞ x 11 inches. Published by Currier and Ives, New York, 1865. Library of Congress.

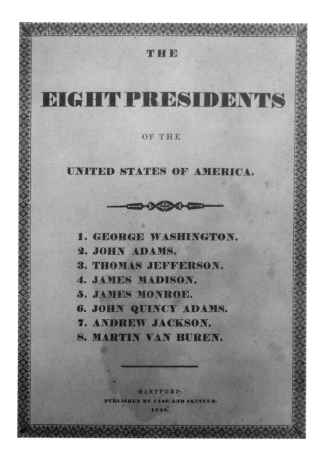

Figure 9–29. *The Eight Presidents of the United States of America.* Each portrait about 12 x 10 inches. Cover and lithographs of Presidents Washington through Van Buren by Nathaniel Currier; published by Case and Skinner, Hartford, 1840. National Portrait Gallery, Smithsonian Institution.

THOMAS JEFFERSON.

Third President of the United States.

JAMES MONROE

5th President of the United States.

JAMES MADISON

Fourth President of the United States.

JOHN QUINCY ADAMS.

6th President of the United States.

ANDREW JACKSON
7ᵗ President of the United States

MARTIN VAN BUREN.
Eighth President of the United States

The likenesses were drawn on stone by Albert Newsam and lithographed by Pierre S. Duval. Jackson's portrait was one of the more revealing in the series, having been taken from the painting by William James Hubard, which Newsam had earlier engraved (fig. 5–22). The likenesses of Van Buren, Tyler, and Polk followed the superior lithographs of Charles Fenderich.[29]

The boldest, most innovative, and most successful popularizer of presidential portraiture was Nathaniel Currier, whose style of lithography others soon copied, while his extensive publication of a variety of inexpensive prints earned him wide recognition. Currier advertised his prints as published "for the People," and they retailed for as little as fifteen to twenty-five cents.[30] An ambitious entrepreneur who had begun work as an apprentice in the Pendleton lithography shop in Boston, Currier started his own business in 1835.

Because he did not date many of his early prints, it is impossible to be precise as to when Currier began to publish presidential portraits, but a set of lithographs of the first eight presidents was available by 1840. In that year a portfolio of Nathaniel Currier's presidential lithographs, each portrait about 12 x 10 inches in size, was published by Case and Skinner in Hartford, Connecticut (fig. 9–29).[31] The lithographs were accompanied by one-page biographical sketches of each president, interleaved so that portraits and biographies faced each other. The volume was bound in a cover of heavy, pink paper with the name of each president below the title *The Eight Presidents of the United States of America*. A decorative border framed the cover.

Currier's lithographs appear to have been derived largely from the series of presidential portraits published by George Endicott. For the first five presidents, Endicott's series had been copied from the Pendleton lithographs of Stuart's series painted for John Doggett.[32] So far removed from Stuart's portraits and even Pendleton's lithographs are Currier's prints that only the form remains. Character has been lost from the portraits of most of the presidents, none left more wooden than Jefferson.

ZACHARY TAYLOR,
Twelfth President of the United States.

Figure 9–30. *Zachary Taylor, Twelfth President of the United States.* Lithograph, 13 x 9 inches, by Nathaniel Currier, New York, 1849. Library of Congress.

The style in which Stuart had painted the first five presidents as working leaders—some seated at their desks, all with papers and books at hand—was replicated in the popular lithographs. But the mass-produced prints—published for profit and to fill a market demand—were lacking in artistic quality. At the same time, their importance lies less in their contribution to the arts than in their availability to everyman—among them, those politically involved Americans who voted in the presidential election of 1840 in greater numbers than ever before.

Currier continued to add to the set and published a uniform series of individual presidential portraits through the presidency of Lincoln.[33] Currier's lithograph of Zachary Taylor (fig. 9–30) is an example of his continuation of the style popularized by the Pendleton series and its imitators. As time passed, Currier's artists provided newer and more arresting popu-

lar portraits of presidents. President Polk was the subject of several such prints. His portrait appeared in a bold rendition of the traditional style (plate 20). Polk was also pictured as a care-laden wartime president in a lithograph highly ornamented with stars and stripes and martial symbols deemed appropriate to the leader of a nation at war with Mexico (fig. 9–31).

Although America's most successful popularizer of art and portraiture, Currier had ample competition. A lithograph of Polk published by Sarony and Major in 1846 presents a highly stylized image of the president and focuses attention on the explosive Oregon issue (plate 21). On the table beside him lies a document regarding Oregon, which the president, pen in hand, has signed announcing an end to joint occupation of the territory with Great Britain. The document is clear in maintaining 54°40′ as the controversial northern boundary of the territory, but Polk subsequently agreed to the compromise at the 49th parallel. Unlike this print, Currier's lithographs eschewed controversial issues.

Currier gave new popularity to prints with the portraits of all the presidents on a single sheet and set a style for patriotic prints soon widely copied by other printmakers. The earliest example appeared in 1842 with the portraits of all the presidents through John Tyler, then in the White House (fig. 9–32).[34] Displaying traditional oval portraits, the print is formal and the embellishments subdued, though the quality of the portraits does not equal that of many earlier engraved plates. Subsequent updating of Currier's print added not only new presidential portraits but also more elaborate design and increasingly patriotic symbolism. The print of *The Presidents of the United States,* published in 1847 while Polk was in office (fig. 9–33), was more popular in character with portraits that were even less carefully done than those in the 1842 example, though still superior to the likenesses found in some of the popular prints of his competitors (see fig. 3–13).

The portraits were also weak in the Currier lithograph published in 1850 presenting the presidents from Washington to Fillmore (fig. 9–34). The print, however, is an eye-catching one, especially with the hand coloring that highlighted the flags and other patriotic em-

Figure 9–31. *James K. Polk, Eleventh President of the United States.* Lithograph, 11½ x 8⅝ inches, by Nathaniel Currier, New York, 1846. From a daguerreotype by John Plumbe, Jr. National Portrait Gallery, Smithsonian Institution.

Figure 9–32. *The Presidents of the United States*. Lithograph, 15 x 10 inches, by Nathaniel Currier, New York, 1842. The copyright copy is endorsed, "Deposited in the Clerks Office for the Southern District of New York July 30, 1842." Library of Congress.

Figure 9–33. *The Presidents of the United States.* Lithograph, 15 x 9¼ inches, by Nathaniel Currier, New York, 1847. Library of Congress.

Figure 9–34. *The Presidents of the United States. Washington 1789 to Fillmore 1850.* Lithograph, 13½ x 9 inches, by Nathaniel Currier, New York, 1850. Library of Congress.

bellishments, which the War with Mexico had widely promoted. Currier's artists sometimes added a drawing of Trumbull's painting of the signing of the Declaration of Independence to the design of presidential prints (plate 15).

By midcentury, Americans were bombarded by numerous lithographs with individual and collective presidential portraits. They could decorate the walls of their homes with presidential portraits and write letters on stationery emblazoned with presidential likenesses (figs. 4–13 through 4–16, plate 24). They were also increasingly exposed to advertisements presenting presidential images to sell products and services or to promote political parties or causes. This proliferation of presidential images makes it often impossible to draw a clear line between popularization and exploitation.

The poster *Portraits of the Presidents*, 31 x 23 inches, was certain to attract attention (plate 23). A hand-colored floral border frames individual portraits of each president through Franklin Pierce, and a brief biographical sketch appears below each portrait. In the center of the print a drawing shows Washington receiving his commission as commander-in-chief of the continental army. A viewer has to read the print at the bottom of the sheet to discover that the print was an advertisement for the *Illustrated Biography, or Memoirs of the Great and Good* by Charles C. Savage, published by Rufus Blanchard in New York. All of the portraits on the poster were taken from that work, lauded as including over 250 portraits of eminent persons "of all Nations from the period of Homer to the present time, being the most comprehensive pictorial work on Biography ever published." The publisher sought agents from every part of the United States and Canada to sell the "handsomely bound" volume priced at $2.50. It is unlikely that many Americans would have objected to this advertisement displaying presidential portraits, and it no doubt graced the wall of many a shop or office.

More exploitative advertisements may have been displayed with equal prominence, but some viewers must have been surprised to see the portraits of their presidents employed on an advertisement for "Rosemary," a product to restore and prevent hair loss and also relieve headaches (plate 22). J. Russell Spalding, who claimed that a million bottles of his "great and

popular preparation" had been sold, seemed proud to have his advertisement for "Rosemary" framed with portraits of the presidents. Describing the images as accurate portraits "drawn and engraved by a good Artist," he asserted that they were "well worth preserving." The striking poster, containing portraits of all the presidents through Pierce, appeared in color in 1856, presenting an impressive example of popular advertisement. The print was credited as "Printed at ONE impression on the Babcock Polychromatic Press, from J.S. Potter's Steam Job and Decorative Printing Establishment," Boston.

Spalding's advertisement for "Rosemary" must have been successful, for he issued a revised version of it after Buchanan became president, adding the new president's portrait (fig. 9–35). The example reproduced here was printed in black and white and had a line at the top announcing, "Circulars like this will be furnished to dealers, with their Card printed on." On this print the "card" of the pharmacy shop of Hazard and Caswell of Newport, Rhode Island, has been imprinted at the bottom and a postscript added to report that a fresh supply of "Spalding's Celebrated Rosemary" had just been received direct from the factory. One change in the design from the earlier advertisement is the bold print used to call attention to the Boston Museum as the landmark for locating Spalding's place of business opposite it.

The popularization of the presidency may seem to have reached the limits of acceptability when presidential portraits were employed to promote a product "for improving and adorning the hair." But equally blatant exploitation was also employed for political purposes. *The Dollar Weekly Times*, costing one dollar per year and published in Cincinnati, Ohio, was described by the publisher as "Devoted to Literature, Science, the Arts, Mechanics, Agriculture, Commerce, Education, Morals, etc., etc.," and the editor vowed to be "Independent in All Things, Neutral in Nothing."[35] In the 1850s the paper zealously championed the American party, popularly known as the Know Nothing party. In a column under a portrait of Washington, the editor in 1855 proclaimed the first president to be "the first Know Nothing." He also printed Washington's portrait with the American electoral ticket in the presidential

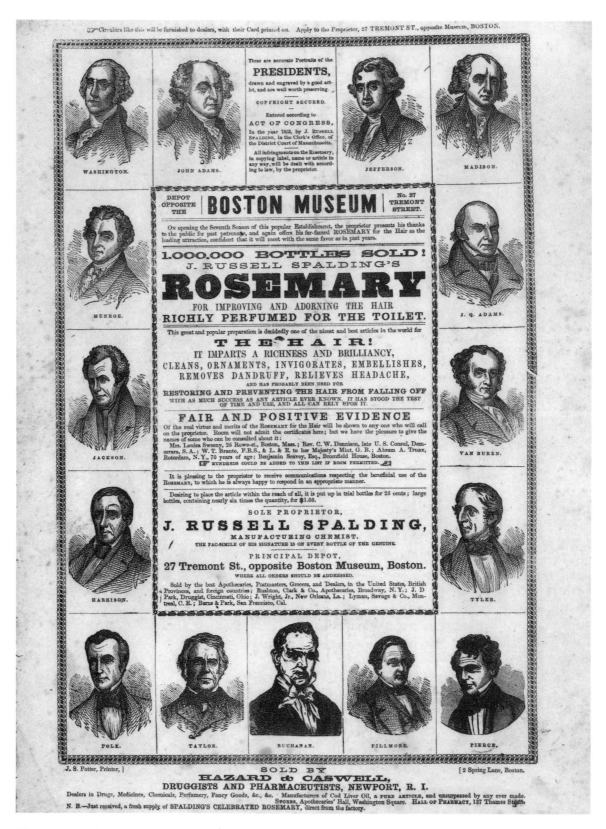

Figure 9–35. Advertisement, 14½ x 8¾ inches, for J. Russell Spalding's "Rosemary," a hair-grooming product. Printed by J. S. Potter, Boston, circa 1859. A revised version, in black and white, of plate 22. American Antiquarian Society.

Figure 9–36. Advertising Supplement, 27¾ x 21¼ inches, to the *Dollar Weekly Times*, Cincinnati, Ohio, [1855]. American Antiquarian Society.

Figure 9–37. *Lewis Cass, Democratic Candidate for 12th President.* Lithograph, 13¼ x 9½ inches, by Nathaniel Currier, New York, 1848. The print deposited for copyright is endorsed June 6, 1848. Library of Congress.

Figure 9–38. *Zachary Taylor, the People's choice for 12th President.* Lithograph, 13¼ x 9½ inches, by Nathaniel Currier, New York, 1848. The print deposited for copyright is endorsed June 23, 1848. Library of Congress.

election of 1856.[36]

Not content with associating his paper and party with the most celebrated president, the Ohio editor tried to associate all the presidents with his cause. In an advertising supplement to the *Dollar Weekly Times*, he sought literally to wrap the flag around his paper by draping the bold letters of the TIMES with stars and stripes (fig. 9–36). The borders of the full-page advertisement, published while Pierce occupied the White House, are filled with flag-draped portraits of each of the presidents, separated by advertising text promoting departments of the weekly paper.[37] In the center of the busy print, the editor proclaims the paper's defense of the American cause against "DEMAGOGUEISM! or the insidious wiles of CATHOLICISM!" Readers are requested to post the sheet "in some conspicuous place." No doubt the portraits of all the presidents prompted many supporters of Know Nothingism to do so.

It was to be expected that partisans of presidential candidates would seek to associate their candidates with the heritage of the presidency, and printmakers were ready to oblige. During the presidential campaign of 1848, Nathaniel Currier published separate prints of Lewis Cass, the Democratic party candidate (fig. 9–37), and Zachary Taylor, the Whig party candidate (fig. 9–38), both in the style that Currier's popular presidential prints had made familiar. Each nominee's portrait was framed by portraits of all the presidents in the same manner that Washington's portrait was commonly honored. In 1860 H. H. Lloyd and Company of New York published the *National Republican Chart* (plate 25), a hand-colored lithograph printed on paper measuring 48 x 29 inches, which may have been the most impressive campaign poster of that election year. Centered at the top of the print, Washington's portrait appears above the portraits of Abraham Lincoln and vice-presidential nominee Hannibal Ham-

lin, framed with split-rail fences. Portraits of all of Washington's successors in the presidential office fill the borders of the poster. A map of the United States—showing free and slave territory—occupies a prominent place on the poster, which also contains the Republican platform for 1860 and numerous quotations from Lincoln. The words of two former presidents—Washington and John Quincy Adams—speaking against slavery are also quoted. Among the miscellaneous information on the chart can be found the presidential electoral vote from 1796 through 1856 and the birth dates of all the presidents.[38]

On October 15, 1860, Grace Bedell, an eleven-year-old girl living in Westfield, New York, wrote to presidential candidate Lincoln that her father had just returned "from the fair and brought home your picture and Mr. Hamlin's. . . . I think that rail fence around your picture makes it look very pretty." The child went on to write that her father was going to vote for Lincoln and that if she were a man she would also vote for him. But the main intent of the letter was to suggest that Lincoln "would look a great deal better" if he would grow a beard. "All the ladies like whiskers," she assured Lincoln, "and they would tease their husband's to vote for you and then you would be President."[39] It is this suggestion, which Lincoln later followed, that has made Grace Bedell's letter famous, but her charming note also supplies rare information about the dissemination of popular prints. Besides the record of Grace's father buying the appealing lithograph at the Chautauqua County fair, it may be imagined that he hung it on the wall of their home when he returned. His young daughter could study not only the portrait of the presidential candidate but also the portraits of all the previous presidents of the United States. No better example can be cited of the powerful presence of the presidency in American culture.

CHAPTER X
Presidential Images in American Culture

ENGRAVINGS, lithographs, medals, and other material objects displaying presidential images provide a variety of insights into American culture. They project a sense of national identity, a pride in a growing historical record, and an active political awareness among the people. They also reveal how deeply politics permeated the everyday lives of ordinary people. Americans read newspapers filled with political news, talked politics in inns and taverns, and debated political issues in courthouses and town squares throughout the land. They also hung portrait prints of presidents on the walls of their homes, poured water and drinks from pitchers decorated with presidential portraits, drank whiskey from bottles adorned with presidential profiles, and dipped snuff from boxes decorated with a favorite president's portrait. When a president died, Americans wore mourning ribbons adorned with the departed president's portrait and purchased prints of presidential deathbed scenes.

By the mid-nineteenth century, Americans could decorate the walls of their homes with hand-colored lithographs and chromolithographs, including patriotically embellished presidential prints. They could place an illustrated volume of presidential biographies, or of presidential addresses, on the parlor table. They could subscribe to illustrated magazines whose artist-reporters recorded major events

that often involved the president. They could provide their children with quick history lessons by purchasing inexpensive prints with the portraits of all the presidents of the United States—sometimes presented as a "National Galaxy." Popular prints commonly offered more than presidential portraits, fixing in the eyes of viewers—young and old—the heritage of the Declaration of Independence, the Constitution, and the symbols of Liberty, Justice, and Union.

The sparse attention often given to the quality of the likenesses of individual portraits in many popular prints of the presidents may have resulted from lack of skills or from motives of profit. At the same time, the effect was to make some such prints less a device to reveal the likenesses of individual presidents than a scheme to display the historical record of the presidency. The presidents portrayed in popular prints—especially those prints presenting portraits of all the presidents—commonly appeared more stern and solemn than they did in the original portraits from which popular images derived. Gilbert Stuart set the style of solemnity in his portraits of Washington, but even Stuart recorded John Quincy Adams with a slight smile in the last presidential likeness he was to take (fig. 5–19). Later presidential portraits by George P. A. Healy and others rarely offered likenesses as serious and stern as they appeared in popular reproductions. More than the lack of artistic skills and haste in production may explain such transformation. Popular images seem to have reflected a public expectation that presidents be serious and somber authorities.

Popular prints offering portraits of all the presidents in a grand design on a single sheet not only celebrated the presidency but also subordinated individual presidents to the institution of the presidency, making it easier to criticize and oppose individual presidents without threatening the presidency. Though fears of executive power persisted, producing from time to time proposals to amend the Constitution to reduce presidential power, these efforts were never successful. Amid the differing strands of American political culture, the presidency emerged as the central unifying agent and the foremost symbol of the American republic.

Mass-produced prints played an important role in reinforcing public perceptions of the president as the center of the Union and its preserver. President Jackson's declaration that the Union must be preserved, widely displayed in popular prints, strengthened those associations. Like Washington's portrait, which was repeatedly republished in the 1850s, Jackson's declaration appeared on a number of prints as the threat to the Union mounted in the years before the Civil War. The increasing display of national symbols in the 1850s revealed a concern for the Union, but it did not halt a growing division, as the nation struggled to reconcile the principles of its most cherished symbols—the Declaration of Independence and the Constitution of the United States. Yet, after the breakup of the Union in 1861, the historical role of the president as defender of the Union strengthened Lincoln's efforts to restore that Union.

The iconographic record of the presidency from Washington to Lincoln indicates that the Constitution held a more important place among the icons of the republic than generally has been noted. Michael Kammen in his book on the Constitution in American culture emphasizes the sparsity of examples of iconographic evidence relating to the Constitution in the young nation.[1] While it is true that such popular works as the engraving of John Trumbull's painting of the signing of the Declaration of Independence and the early facsimiles of the text of that document gave it public attention unmatched by the Constitution, there is at the same time substantial reference to the Constitution in the popular images of the presidency.

In an early example, President John Adams was pictured holding the Constitution in his hand in an engraving by George Graham (fig. 5–3), after a painting by William Winstanley. President Madison rested his hand on the Constitution on the table beside him in the engraving by David Edwin after a painting by Thomas Sully (figs. 5–12 and 5–13). The Constitution appeared as an icon in portraits of James Monroe by both Charles Bird King (fig. 5–14) and Samuel F. B. Morse (fig. 5–17). Andrew Jackson was shown holding the document in his hand in the engraving by Francis Kearny (fig. 5–20), who had copied a print of Jefferson holding the Declaration of Independence (fig. 5–9).

In Gilbert Stuart's influential Lansdowne portrait of Washington (plate 2), the Constitution appeared in the title of one of the books beneath the table beside him. But in 1832, when John Vanderlyn codified Washington's image for the portrait commissioned to hang in the House of Representatives, he moved the Constitution to the top of the table and placed Washington's hand directly on the document (plate 3). The Constitution remained in this more central place in George P. A. Healy's full-length portraits of Fillmore and Buchanan (figs. 5–34 and 5–37). Healy followed Vanderlyn's model in both canvases by placing the hand of the president on a copy of the Constitution. In a three-quarter-length portrait of President Pierce, however, Healy imitated Stuart by putting the Constitution in the title of a book (fig. 5–36). The Constitution was firmly in Washington's hand when Charles Shober joined portraits of Washington and Lincoln in a popular lithograph celebrating the restoration of the Union in 1865 (fig. 4–19).

In Jonathan Clark's 1812 print of *The First Great Western Empire* (plate 5), the Constitution supported the Temple of Freedom. In the medal celebrating Jefferson's inauguration it was the rock on which the republic stood (fig. 6–12). The Constitution was a foundation stone of the Union in the decorated invitation to Buchanan's inaugural ball in 1857 (fig. 4–10). In John Frost's *Pictorial History of the United States of America* (1846), the Constitution appeared as the dominant icon embellishing the portrait of each of the presidents (fig. 9–22). The entire text of the Constitution was included with the portraits of all the presidents on the poster *National Galaxy* in 1844 (fig. 2–45). In the panoramic *Family Monument from the History of Our Country* (fig. 2–64), J. M. Enzing-Miller pictured Washington surrounded by the symbols of the Republic, including Liberty, Justice, the Declaration of Independence, and the flags of Union. But no icon was more central to the scene than that of the Constitution to which Washington swore allegiance. The depiction affirmed the role of the president as the agent of the Constitution and reflected the importance of both the instrument and the agent in American political culture.

From the outset of the republic, presidents of the United States were conscious of their images. Though early presidents often thought in terms more of the office than of the man, the two were never separable. Washington aspired to make the presidency convey an image of strength and dignity and introduced ceremonial practice to elevate the office. While not wishing to undermine either the strength or dignity of the position, Jefferson as president endeavoured to make the image of the head of a republic more republican in character by reducing public display, ceremonies, and rituals. When he walked to his inauguration in 1801—instead of arriving in a fancy carriage as Washington and John Adams earlier had done—he showed an awareness of the power of images. Later presidents—including Jefferson's protégé, James Monroe—acquiesced in the public thirst for pageantry, and the presidential office increasingly became the object of a widening drama. President Jackson created a popular image more controversial than he anticipated when he opened the doors of the White House to all comers at his inaugural reception in 1829. How controversial a president's image could be was abundantly displayed by the flood of presidential caricatures that appeared during Jackson's two terms.

Seeking to promote unity after the divisive War of 1812, Monroe sought to renew the place of the presidency as the center of national unity by following Washington's example of making an extended tour of the country after becoming president. By the 1850s, when the transportation revolution brought about by the development of railroads had greatly lessened the difficulties of travel, presidential tours had become an expected part of presidential duties. Covered by traveling artist-reporters and depicted in the new, popular illustrated magazines, presidential movements were revealed to the public with a fullness of pictorial representation and an immediacy of reportage that brought the institution of the presidency into the everyday consciousness of Americans as never before.

Although presidents were much sought after by portrait painters, no early president appears to have taken any measure to ensure that pleasing likenesses of himself were presented to the public. In reference to his own likeness, Jefferson spoke of the "miserable caracatures" of his portrait appearing in popular prints, and he was pleased when Jean-Antoine Houdon's image of him was used on an elegant medal celebrating his inauguration (fig. 6–12). Yet he took no steps to promote any portrait of himself. John Quincy Adams regarded his portrait by Gilbert Stuart (fig. 5–19) as the only adequate likeness, but it was uncompleted when Stuart died in 1828 and not engraved before Adams left office. Andrew Jackson was the first president to have a resident portrait painter at the White House, but his employment of Ralph E. W. Earl was designed less to ensure that suitable portraits were offered to the public than to provide employment for a favorite in-law of his late wife. President Polk recorded in his diary numerous sittings for portrait painters, but he seemed far less concerned about the images to be created than about the time taken from his busy schedule. "These sittings for artists are becoming very irksome and fatiguing," he confided after several sittings for George P. A. Healy in 1846, "and I think I will not again yield my consent to sit for any other, at all events during the Session of Congress."[2] He alleviated the pressure somewhat by sitting for two portraitists at the same time.

By 1840 the widespread use of images in presidential campaigns had demonstrated a growing awareness of the influence of visual representations in elections. Numerous pictures of William Henry Harrison with a log cabin in the background conveyed an appealing portrayal that aroused wide support. In the presidential election of 1844, a print of James K. Polk in a presidential pose offered another example of an awareness of the influence of campaign imagery (fig 5–33). The thousands of copies of lithographs with portraits of Gen. Zachary Taylor that were sold during the War with Mexico clearly played a role in his presidential nomination in 1848. By the time Lincoln ran for president in 1860, presidential candidates were in demand to sit for photographers, and Lincoln did so frequently.[3] Yet from Washington to Lincoln presidential images had as important an influence in a broad cultural sense as in a narrow partisan way. They served to represent the institution of the presidency and the American experiment in republican government. They provided assurances of legitimacy and evidence of stability; they reinforced a growing national pride and strengthened popular confidence in the growing Republic.

In the historical memory of the presidency recorded in popular prints the partisanship of the office was often ignored or forgotten, except in campaign broadsides and caricatures. When the portraits of the first four presidents—two Federalists and two Republicans—were grouped together under the same canopy in an early 1812 example of the images of all the presidents engraved on a single plate (fig. 2–18), the bitterness between the second and third presidents resulting from the election of 1800 had not yet ended. At the same time, the political continuity assumed in popular portrayals of the presidents was real, and the tradition of the repeated peaceful transfer of political power from one administration to the next and from one political party to another was an achievement worthy of celebration.

Yet the historical memory of unity and continuity in the presidency perpetuated in the images of popular prints may have blurred or hidden the weaknesses and inadequacies of the individuals who held the high office. In the decade of the 1850s the images of the presidency alone could not save the Union. Artist Enzing-Miller's picture of the history of America in his monumental engraving in 1858 (fig. 2–64) presented a historical memory of the steady progress of the United States—at the pinnacle of which stood the leadership of the presidents of the United States. The artist's picture of a line of successors to Washington that seemed to promise no end to the continuity of the leadership and progress of the Republic, however, may have presented a false sense of security in a nation whose drift toward disunion presidential leadership seemed helpless to reverse.

Under the weight of intensifying sectionalism, the strength of the presidency as a force for unity waned in the 1850s and collapsed in 1861. But in a postwar, reunited nation, the earlier traditions would be revived. Less than two years after Appomattox, John S. C. Abbott evoked a style set decades earlier when he published a new *Lives of the Presidents of the United States of America, from Washington to the Present Time*, "illustrated with portraits of all the presidents engraved on steel, pictures of their private residences, and fifteen other wood engravings of the most interesting scenes in their lives."[4]

The character and role of the presidency may have been impressed more vividly on the public mind by visual representations, images, and symbols than by the words of the Constitution or the reports of government proceedings in newspapers and government documents. In a more pervasive way than otherwise experienced, the visual images of the presidency enhanced a common political culture. In the early years of the republic the circulation of engravings and other visual arts was limited but nonetheless sufficiently widespread to promote some commonality of visual experiences. With the extraordinary broadening of visual horizons by the techniques of lithography, electrotyping, and chromolithography, and the employment of artist-reporters to record political events, Americans by the mid-nineteenth century were experiencing a view of the political world about them previously only dimly glimpsed. Those widening horizons enable us to see more distinctly the centrality of the presidency in American culture and enhance our understanding of American society in the young republic.

NOTES

NOTES TO CHAPTER I
The First President Enshrined

1. Wendy C. Wick, *George Washington an American Icon: The Eighteenth-Century Graphic Prints* (Washington, D.C., 1982), 54, 111; Charles Henry Hart, *Catalogue of the Engraved Portraits of Washington* (New York, 1904), no. 249. An advertisement in the *American Minerva and New-York Advertiser*, April 23, 1795, sought subscribers to purchase the print at five dollars each. William Kelby, comp., *Notes on American Artists, 1754–1820, Copied from Advertisements Appearing in the Newspapers of the Day* (New York, 1922), 38.

2. Christina H. Nelson, "Transfer-printed Creamware and Pearlware for the American Market," *Winterthur Portfolio* 15 (1980): 101.

3. For other examples of pottery pieces employing the same, or a similar, design see Mariam Klamkin, *American Patriotic and Political China* (New York, 1973), 62; Robert H. McCauley, *Liverpool Transfer Designs on Anglo-American Pottery* (Portland, Me., 1942), plate III.

4. For an examination of Washington as hero see Barry Schwartz, *George Washington: The Making of an American Symbol* (New York, 1987), 41–89.

5. "Probationary Odes," Ode V, "To a Truly Great Man," *National Gazette* (Philadelphia), June 22, 1793.

6. "Belisarius," in *Aurora* (Philadelphia), September 11, 1795, quoted in Donald H. Stewart, *The Opposition Press of the Federalist Period* (Albany, N.Y., 1969), 524.

7. Thomas Paine, *Letter to George Washington, President of the United States* (Baltimore, 1797), 36. The letter was dated Paris, July 30, 1796. See also Stewart, *Opposition Press*, 528.

8. For an example see Davida Tenenbaum Deutsch, "Washington Memorial Prints," *Antiques* 111 (1977): 324.

9. *Commercial Advertiser* (New York), January 7, 1800, in Rita Susswein Gottesman, *The Arts and Crafts in New York, 1800–1804: Advertisements and News Items from New York City Newspapers* (New York, 1965), 456; Schwartz, *Washington*, 91–102; Deutsch, "Washington Memorial Prints," 327.

10. The locket was advertised for sale in the *Columbian Centinel* (Boston), January 15–29, 1800. Margaret W. Brown, "Washington Funeral Gold Medals," *The Numismatist* 67 (1954): 114–22.

11. *Aurora* (Philadelphia), December 31, 1799.

12. Advertisement from *Philadelphia Gazette*, December 30, 1799, quoted in Deutsch, "Washington Memorial Prints," 328.

13. Richard J. Wolfe, *Early American Music Engraving and Printing: A History of Music Publishing in America from 1787 to 1825 with Commentary on Earlier and Later Practices* (Urbana, Ill., 1980), 234.

14. Wick, *Washington: American Icon*, 142; Deutsch, "Washington Memorial Prints," 326. Mark Edward Thistlethwaite, *The Image of George Washington: Studies in Mid-Nineteenth Century American History Painting* (New York, 1979), discusses historical paintings of Washington on his deathbed and provides illustrations of both paintings and lithographs of the 1840s and 1850s (pp. 183–88, 304–5). Nathaniel Currier published at least eight different lithographs of Washington's deathbed; the earliest dated example is from 1841. *Currier and Ives: A Catalogue Raisonné*, intro. Bernard F. Reilly, Jr., 2 vols.

(Detroit, 1984), 1:172–73.

15. *Aurora* (Philadelphia), December 21, 1799; Wick, *Washington: American Icon*, 142.

16. Quoted in Deutsch, "Washington Memorial Prints," 326, where the companion print also is reproduced.

17. *Philadelphia Gazette*, January 23, 1800, quoted in Wick, *Washington: American Icon*, 140.

18. Anita Schorsch, *Mourning Becomes America: Mourning Art in the New Nation* (Clinton, N.J., 1976), 4–6.

19. The later state is reproduced in Deutsch, "Washington Memorial Prints," 324. Hart, *Engraved Portraits of Washington*, nos. 147, 147a, indicates that the first version followed the profile by Joseph Wright, but no example with a Wright image has been found, and I have accepted the print published here as the first state. See also Katharine McCook Knox, *The Sharples: Their Portraits of George Washington and His Contemporaries* (New York, 1972), 70–79.

20. For an additional example see Nelson, "Transfer-printed Creamware," 101–2.

21. Wick, *Washington: American Icon*, 140.

22. Anita Schorsch, "A Key to the Kingdom: The Iconography of a Mourning Picture," *Winterthur Portfolio* 14 (1979): 41–42, 47, 51–54, 60.

23. *Commercial Advertiser* (New York), January 23, 1800, in Wick, *Washington: American Icon*, 147–49; Gottesman, *Arts and Crafts in New York, 1800–1804*, 48, 52–53.

24. *Temple of Reason* (New York), December 20, 1800, in Gottesman, *Arts and Crafts in New York, 1800–1804*, 51; Wick, *Washington: American Icon*, 72, 157; Deutsch, "Washington Memorial Prints," 328. The design was inspired by Robert Strange's 1786 engraving of Benjamin West's *Apotheosis of Princes Octavius and Alfred*. Phoebe Lloyd Jacobs, "John James Barralet and the Apotheosis of George Washington," *Winterthur Portfolio* 12 (1977): 130–31; Wick, *Washington: American Icon*, 157.

25. *Aurora* (Philadelphia), December 19, 1800, in Alfred Coxe Prime, ed., *The Arts and Crafts in Philadelphia, Maryland, and South Carolina, 1786–1800: Gleanings from Newspapers* ([Topsfield, Mass.], 1932), 80–81; *Aurora*, February 3, 1802, quoted in Jacobs, "Barralet and the Apotheosis of Washington," 133–34.

26. For a detailed examination of the symbolism in Barralet's work, see Jacobs, "Barralet and the Apotheosis of Washington," 115–37.

27. *Aurora* (Philadelphia), December 19, 1800, in Prime, ed., *Arts and Crafts in Philadelphia, Maryland, and South Carolina*, 80–81.

28. *Mercantile Advertiser* (New York), April 14, 1802, in Gottesman, *Arts and Crafts in New York, 1800–1804*, 51–52; Wick, *Washington: American Icon*, 166. On Barralet's symbolism see also Garry Wills, *Cincinnatus: George Washington and the Enlighten-*

ment (New York, 1984), 74, 79.

29. On the rattlesnake as symbol see Wick, *Washington: American Icon*, 13, 19, 87.

30. Ibid., 72, 166; Jacobs, "Barralet and the Apotheosis of Washington," 123–25; Deutsch, "Washington Memorial Prints," 329.

31. For other examples see Nelson, "Transfer-printed Creamware," 101; Schorsch, *Mourning Becomes America*, 30; and McCauley, *Liverpool Transfer Designs*, plate XXV.

32. Jacobs, "Barralet and the Apotheosis of Washington," 134, 134n; Margaret B. Klapthor and Howard A. Morrison, *George Washington: A Figure upon the Stage* (Washington, D.C., 1982), 228–29.

33. Harold Holzer, Gabor S. Boritt, and Mark E. Neely, Jr., *The Lincoln Image: Abraham Lincoln and the Popular Print* (New York, 1984), 199–202.

34. Samuel Miller, *A Brief Retrospect of the Eighteenth Century*, 2 vols. (New York, 1803), 2:406–7.

35. Emily E. F. Skeel, ed., *Mason Locke Weems: His Life and Ways*, 3 vols. (New York, 1929), 2:385; Mason L. Weems, *The Life of Washington*, ed. Marcus Cunliffe (Cambridge, Mass., 1962), xviii-xix.

36. Dunlap to his wife, January 1, 1806, *Diary of William Dunlap (1766–1839)*, 3 vols. (New York, 1930), 2:364.

37. Washington memorial rings and lockets were advertised in the *New-York Gazette and General Advertiser*, January 22, 1800, reprinted in Gottesman, *Arts and Crafts in New York, 1800–1804*, 95. Washington mourning rings were advertised in the *Aurora* (Philadelphia), January 13, 1800. For an example of a Washington ring, see Klapthor and Morrison, *Washington: A Figure upon the Stage*, 224. For medal and locket see fig. 1–4 above.

38. *Mercantile Advertiser*, February 24, 1800, in Gottesman, *Arts and Crafts in New York, 1800–1804*, 387–88.

39. *Commercial Advertiser* (New York), September 11, 1800, in ibid., 132–33.

40. *Commercial Advertiser* (New York), January 9, 1800.

41. Circular, American Academy of Fine Arts, New York, September 20, 1824, reprinted in William T. Whitley, *Gilbert Stuart* (Cambridge, Mass., 1932), 180.

42. Rembrandt Peale to Jefferson, January 8, 1824, Thomas Jefferson Papers, Library of Congress. See also Peale to Congressional Committee on Portrait of Washington, March 16, 1824, Lillian B. Miller, ed., "The Collected Works of Charles Willson Peale and His Family," microfiche edition (New York, 1980).

43. Whitley, *Gilbert Stuart*, 182; Irma B. Jaffe, *John Trumbull: Patriot-Artist of the American Revolution* (Boston, 1975), 156, 315.

44. The portrait, oil on canvas, 72¼ x 54¼ inches, is described and illustrated in Carol Eaton Hevner and Lillian B. Miller, *Rembrandt Peale,*

1778–1860, A Life in the Arts: An Exhibition at The Historical Society of Pennsylvania, February 22, 1985 to June 18, 1985 (Philadelphia, 1985), 66–67. Peale is quoted on p. 66.

45. *Philadelphia Museum* 1 (1824): 13–14; Whitley, *Gilbert Stuart*, 183. The portrait hangs today in the restored old Senate chamber in the United States Capitol.

46. John A. Mahey, "Lithographs by Rembrandt Peale," *Antiques* 97 (1970): 235–40.

47. Published in William H. Brown, *Portrait Gallery of Distinguished American Citizens* (Hartford, Conn., 1844).

48. Peale to Jefferson, January 8, 1824, Jefferson Papers, Library of Congress.

49. Stuart's bill of complaint presented to the Circuit Court of the United States, Eastern District of Pennsylvania, May 14, 1802, and the court's injunction, May 14, 1802, are printed in E. P. Richardson, "China Trade Portraits of Washington after Stuart," *Pennsylvania Magazine of History and Biography* 94 (1970): 96–97.

50. Stuart's oil canvas of Washington painted for Sword and a reverse oil painting on glass of it by an unknown Chinese artist are reproduced in Jean Gordon Lee, *Philadelphians and the China Trade, 1784–1844* (Philadelphia, 1984), 193.

51. John Hill Morgan and Mantle Fielding, *Life Portraits of Washington and Their Replicas* (Philadelphia, 1931), xi–xxiii, 229.

52. Avraham Yarmolinsky, *Picturesque United States of America, 1811, 1812, 1813, being a Memoir on Paul Svinin, Russian Diplomatic Officer, Artist, and Author, Containing Copious Excerpts from His Account of His Travels in America* (New York, 1930), 34.

53. *American Magazine of Useful and Entertaining Knowledge* 2 (1836): 266.

54. Ralph H. Orth and Alfred R. Ferguson, eds., *The Journals and Miscellaneous Notebooks of Ralph Waldo Emerson* (Cambridge, Mass., 1977), July 6, 1852, 13:63.

55. On Krimmel's painting see Edgar P. Richardson, *American Paintings and Related Pictures in The Henry Francis du Pont Winterthur Museum* (Charlottesville, Va., 1986), 106–7; Milo M. Naeve, *John Lewis Krimmel: An Artist in Federal America* (Newark, Del., 1987), 69–71; and William T. Oedel, "Krimmel at the Crossroads: Review Essay," *Winterthur Portfolio* 23 (1988): 273–81.

56. *Port Folio* (Philadelphia) 10 (1813): 140.

57. Maybelle Mann, *Francis William Edmonds: Mammon and Art* (New York, 1977), 125; Maybelle Mann, *Francis William Edmonds*, Exhibition Catalogue (Washington, D.C., 1975), 28–29; Thistlethwaite, *Image of Washington*, 214–15.

58. *Annals of Congress*, 6 Cong., 2 Sess. (1800–1801), 796, 799.

59. *Temple of Reason* (New York), December 20, 1800, in Gottesman, *Arts and Crafts in New York,*

1800–1804, 74.

60. William C. C. Claiborne, circular letter to his constituents, February 17, 1801; Archibald Henderson, circular letter to his constituents, February 28, 1801, in Noble E. Cunningham, Jr., ed., *Circular Letters of Congressmen to Their Constituents, 1789–1829*, 3 vols. (Chapel Hill, N.C., 1978), 1:229, 243.

61. John Fowler, circular letter to his constituents, March 6, 1801, in ibid., 266; *Annals of Congress*, 6 Cong., 2 Sess. (1800–1801), 738, 758, 856, 858, 875.

62. *Spectator* (New York), January 24, 1801, in Gottesman, *Arts and Crafts in New York, 1800–1804,* 75.

63. Kirk Savage, "The Self-made Monument: George Washington and the Fight to Erect a National Monument," *Winterthur Portfolio* 22 (1987): 225–42; Constance McLaughlin Green, *Washington*, 2 vols. (Princeton, N.J., 1962), 1:170–71, 204; 2:82.

NOTES TO CHAPTER II
The Presidency Celebrated and Enshrined

1. On Adams portraiture see Andrew Oliver, *Portraits of John and Abigail Adams* (Cambridge, Mass., 1967).

2. *Federal Gazette* (Philadelphia), February 8, 1798, in Prime, ed., *Arts and Crafts in Philadelphia, Maryland, and South Carolina*, 80. The prints were published by T. B. Freeman of Philadelphia. For an example of the Washington print see Wick, *Washington: American Icon*, 122. The Adams print is reproduced in E. McSherry Fowble, *Two Centuries of Prints in America, 1680–1880: A Selective Catalogue of the Winterthur Museum Collection* (Charlottesville, Va., 1987), 319.

3. Alfred L. Bush, *The Life Portraits of Thomas Jefferson*, rev. ed. (Charlottesville, Va., 1987), 37–44; Noble E. Cunningham, Jr., *The Image of Thomas Jefferson in the Public Eye: Portraits for the People, 1800–1809* (Charlottesville, Va., 1981), 11–69, 87–95.

4. Lyon to Carey, February 18, 1801, Lea and Febiger Collection, Historical Society of Pennsylvania.

5. Mason Locke Weems to Carey, March 4, 5, 1801, in Skeel, ed., *Weems*, 2:176, 177.

6. For details on this print see Cunningham, *Image of Jefferson*, 45–50.

7. Jefferson to Martha Jefferson Randolph, April 3, 1802, in Edwin Morris Betts and James Adam Bear, Jr., eds., *The Family Letters of Thomas Jefferson* (Columbia, Mo., 1966), 221.

8. *Independent Chronicle* (Boston), March 23, 1807; Cunningham, *Image of Jefferson*, 88–91.

9. Bush, *Life Portraits of Jefferson*, 59.

10. Examples are in Cunningham, *Image of Jefferson*, 25–29, 32–41, 83, 89, 94.

11. In this period of evolving national symbols, Minerva sometimes was employed more broadly to

symbolize America as the product of rationality and law. Joshua C. Taylor, *America as Art* (Washington, D.C., 1976), 11; E. McClung Fleming, "From Indian Princess to Greek Goddess: The American Image, 1783–1815," *Winterthur Portfolio* 3 (1967): 55–56.

12. Thomas Gimbrede to Jefferson, March 6, 1809, Jefferson Papers, Library of Congress.

13. Jefferson to Gimbrede, March 7, 1809, ibid.

14. The marks of framing can be seen today on many surviving prints. A satin print of Jefferson's first inaugural address in the American Antiquarian Society, Worcester, Mass., shows clear evidence of having once been framed.

15. Entries for June 6, 26, July 6, 13, 1805, October 12, 1807, in Daybook of John Doggett, Roxbury, Mass., 1802–1809, Henry Francis du Pont Winterthur Museum, Winterthur, Del. An example of a silk broadside of Jefferson's second inaugural address is in the American Antiquarian Society.

16. See the series begun in March 1836 in the *American Magazine of Useful and Entertaining Knowledge* 2 (1836): 265–66.

17. Oliver, *Portraits of John and Abigail Adams*, 113–15, 132, 144.

18. The version that appeared in Butler's *History* was later revised to include a portrait of John Quincy Adams in the center. An example is in the Print Room, New York Public Library.

19. *The Percy Anecdotes, Revised edition, to which is added a Valuable Collection of American Anecdotes, Original and Select*, 2 vols. (New York, 1832). The engraving was printed by R. Miller. Later editions dated 1838 and 1843 that have been examined published the same print.

20. For a discussion of this print see Chapter IV.

21. Oliver, *Portraits of John and Abigail Adams*, 31, 243.

22. Prints on paper approximately this size are at the New York Public Library and the American Antiquarian Society; the engraved surface measures 9 x 10¾ inches.

23. Noble E. Cunningham, Jr., *In Pursuit of Reason: The Life of Thomas Jefferson* (Baton Rouge, La., 1987), 329–31.

24. William D. Johnston, *History of the Library of Congress*, 2 vols. (Washington, D.C., 1904), 1:275–76.

25. John Quincy Adams, Diary, September 27, 1821, Adams Family Papers, Massachusetts Historical Society, microfilm edition, reel 35; Oliver, *Portraits of John and Abigail Adams*, 161–62.

26. *Boston Daily Advertiser*, June 20, 1822; Marvin S. Sadik, *Colonial and Federal Portraits at Bowdoin College* (Brunswick, Me., 1966), 160.

27. *Evening Gazette* (Boston), August 16, 1828.

28. Fiske Kimball, "The Life Portraits of Jefferson and Their Replicas," American Philosophical Society, *Proceedings* 88 (1944): 516; Bush, *Life Portraits of Jefferson*, 52–59.

29. Sadik, *Colonial and Federal Portraits at Bowdoin College*, 159–61, 164–66.

30. Lawrence Park, *Gilbert Stuart: An Illustrated Descriptive List of His Works*, 4 vols. (New York, 1926), 2:527–28.

31. John Doggett, Jr., to Charles Beaumont, December 28, 1837, quoted in Clarence W. Bowen, ed., *The History of the Centennial Celebration of the Inauguration of George Washington as First President of the United States* (New York, 1892), 505.

32. On the availability of Houdon's bust of Franklin in Boston for Stuart to copy at the time he painted the portrait of Jefferson see Charles Coleman Sellers, *Benjamin Franklin in Portraiture* (New Haven, Conn., 1962), 307, 311.

33. Charles Francis Adams, ed., *Memoirs of John Quincy Adams, Comprising Portions of His Diary from 1795 to 1848*, 12 vols. (Philadelphia, 1874–1877), March 3, 1828, 7:460.

34. *Evening Gazette* (Boston), August 28, 1824, in Edgar E. Brandon, ed., *Lafayette, Guest of the Nation: A Contemporary Account of the Triumphal Tour of General Lafayette through the United States in 1824–1825 as Reported by Local Newspapers*, 3 vols. (Oxford, Ohio, 1950–1958), 1:108.

35. Cobb's diary for October 1815–January 1826 is quoted in Mabel M. Swan, "The 'American Kings,'" *Antiques* 19 (1931): 279, 281.

36. *Boston Monthly Magazine* 1 (December 1825): 383–84.

37. John Doggett and Co. to the Gentlemen Directors of the Royal Glass Manufactory, May 29, 1826; to Monsieur L. Destrais, Oct. 29, 1828, John Doggett and Co. Letterbook, Winterthur Museum.

38. Adams, ed., *Dairy of John Quincy Adams*, March 3, 1828, 7:460.

39. John Doggett and Co. to Charles Humberston and Co., May 31, 1828, Doggett and Co. Letterbook, Winterthur Museum.

40. Swan, "American Kings," 281.

41. Doggett and Co. to Salmon Brown, May 8, 1829, Doggett and Co. Letterbook, Winterthur Museum.

42. Doggett and Co. to Brown (per Delta for New Orleans), June 19, 1829, ibid.

43. *Catalogue of an Exhibition of Portraits, Painted by the Late Gilbert Stuart, Esq.* [Boston, 1828], 2. Library of Congress.

44. Ibid., 7.

45. *Evening Gazette* (Boston), August 16, 1828.

46. Adams, ed., *Diary of John Quincy Adams*, 7:122, 125.

47. Andrew Oliver, *Portraits of John Quincy Adams and His Wife* (Cambridge, Mass., 1970), 80–82.

48. *Die Präsidenten Der Vereinigten Staaten Nord-America* (Leipzig), example in Metropolitan Museum of Art, New York.

49. The fabric piece of this design in the National

Museum of American History, Smithsonian Institution, is too faded for the original colors to be determined with certainty.

50. Pieces of the fabric roller-printed in blue on white and in brown on white are at the New-York Historical Society. A large piece of the fabric in blue and white is at the National Museum of American History, Smithsonian Institution. Florence M. Montgomery, *Printed Textiles: English and American Cottons and Linens, 1700–1850* (New York, 1970), 341, lists the design as printed in pink and in brown. See also Herbert R. Collins, *Threads of History: Americana Recorded on Cloth, 1775 to the Present* (Washington, D.C., 1979), 78.

51. In a letter to James Madison, April 13, 1833, Morris stated that some of the heads had already been engraved by Durand (James Madison Papers, Library of Congress, microfilm edition). But in publishing the plate, he noted, "The whole have been transferred to the steel plate by Mr. Casilear" (*New-York Mirror*, August 9, 1834). In March 1833, Casilear had written: "I am still occupied with the plate I mentioned as having begun for the 'Mirror'" (Casilear to John F. Kensett, March 21, 1833, John W. Casilear Papers, Archives of American Art, microfilm D–177). The clue to the discrepancy may be found in Morris's statement to Durand that he had informed Martin Van Buren "that you were to be the engraver (or that it was to be executed under your immediate superintendence)." Morris to Durand, August 8, 1833, Asher Brown Durand Papers, New York Public Library.

52. *New-York Mirror* 12 (1834): 41.

53. William Dunlap, *A History of the Rise and Progress of the Arts of Design in the United States*, ed. Frank W. Bayley and Charles E. Goodspeed, 3 vols. (Boston, 1918; orig. pub. 1834), 3:278.

54. Durand to John W. Casilear, October 9, 1832, Durand Papers, New York Public Library.

55. *New-York Mirror* 12 (1834): 41; Bush, *Life Portraits of Jefferson*, 77–79; Cooper quoted by Bush on p. 78.

56. Morris to Adams, September 12, 1833, Adams Family Papers, Massachusetts Historical Society, microfilm edition.

57. Adams to Morris, September 20, 1833, ibid.

58. Adams to Morris, November 6, 1833, ibid.

59. *New-York Mirror* 12 (1834): 41.

60. Morris to John Quincy Adams, September 12, 1833, Adams Family Papers, Massachusetts Historical Society, microfilm edition; *New-York Mirror* 12 (1834): 41. Harold E. Dickson in *John Wesley Jarvis, American Painter, 1780–1840: With a Checklist of His Works* (New York, 1949) did not list a portrait of Monroe by Jarvis but indicated that "there is at least a tradition that he did portray Monroe" (271n).

61. Morris to Durand, September 11, 1833, Durand Papers, New York Public Library.

62. Morris to Madison, April 13, 1833; Madison to Morris, draft, [April 1833], Madison Papers, Library of Congress, microfilm edition.

63. Morris to Durand, September 11, 1833, Durand Papers, New York Public Library.

64. Durand to Casilear, September 24, 1833, ibid.

65. Morris to Durand, August 8, 1833, ibid.

66. Morris to Durand, July 12, 1833, ibid.

67. Harman to Durand, August 5, 1833, ibid.

68. Morris to Durand, August 8, 1833, ibid.

69. *New-York Mirror* 12 (1834): 41.

70. Morris to Madison, April 13, September 19, 1833, Madison Papers, Library of Congress, microfilm edition.

71. Lillian B. Miller, *Patrons and Patriotism: The Encouragement of the Fine Arts in the United States, 1790–1860* (Chicago, 1966), 152–53.

72. Asher B. Durand to Mrs. Asher B. Durand, June 10, 1835, Durand Papers, New York Public Library.

73. James B. Longacre to Asher B. Durand, April 28, 1835, ibid. The copy may have been Robert Field's copy engraved in 1807 (fig. 2–4). In engraving Jefferson's portrait for John Sanderson's *Signers to the Declaration of Independence*, vol. 7 (1827), Longacre identified it as "from the portrait by Field after Stuart." Harry Piers, *Robert Field: Portrait Painter in Oils, Miniature and Water-Colours and Engraver* (New York, 1927), 195.

74. Reed to Durand, June 18, 1835, Durand Papers, New York Public Library. In this letter Reed wrote to Durand, who had just returned to New York from Boston: "I will not ask you to go to Brunswick now to get the Copy of Maddison as you will at least want to come home and see your family." The implication is that he would ask Durand to make the trip later.

75. John Durand, *The Life and Times of A. B. Durand* (New York, 1970; orig. pub. 1894), 110; *Catalogue of American Portraits in The New-York Historical Society*, 2 vols. (New Haven, Conn., 1974), 2:547. Reproductions of all the Stuart portraits in the set except that of Washington can be found in *Catalogue of American Portraits in The New-York Historical Society*, 1:5, 11, 386, 399; 2:514, 547.

76. Reed to Durand, March 11, 12, 1835, Durand Papers, New York Public Library.

77. Durand to Mrs. Durand, February 28, 1835, ibid. Reed requested the president to sit for Durand in a letter to Jackson, February 21, 1835. Andrew Jackson Papers, Library of Congress, microfilm edition.

78. Asher B. Durand to John Durand, March 15, 1835, Durand Papers, New York Public Library.

79. Durand to Mrs. Durand, March 17, 1835, ibid. Reed was quoted in Durand's letter.

80. Oliver, *Portraits of John Quincy Adams and His Wife*, 171, 174–75.

81. Durand to John W. Casilear, June 14, 1835, Durand Papers, New York Public Library.

82. *Catalogue of American Portraits in The New-York Historical Society*, 1:5.

83. An impression of this engraving is in the New-York Historical Society.

84. Quoted in Irving Brant, *James Madison*, 6 vols. (Indianapolis, 1941–1961), 6:521.

85. Roger A. Fischer and Edmund B. Sullivan, *American Political Ribbons and Ribbon Badges, 1825–1981* (Lincoln, Mass., 1985), 2–3, 10. For more examples than those described in this paragraph, see ibid., 49.

86. A very similar border with some of the same embellishments can be found framing the portrait of Joseph Markle in a lithograph by Albert Newsam in 1844. Wendy Wick Reaves, "Portraits for Every Parlor: Albert Newsam and American Portrait Lithography," in *American Portrait Prints: Proceedings of the Tenth Annual American Print Conference*, ed. Wendy Wick Reaves (Charlottesville, Va., 1984), 87.

87. *Evening Transcript* (Boston), May 22, 1841.

88. Currier's *Death of Washington, Dec. 14 A.D. 1799* was deposited for copyright January 12, 1841, and received by the Department of State February 4, 1841. The copyright print of *Death of Harrison, April 4 A.D. 1841* is endorsed as deposited May 10, 1841. Both prints are in the Prints and Photographs Division, Library of Congress.

89. The print is reproduced in Stanley J. Idzerda, Anne C. Loveland, and Marc H. Miller, *Lafayette, Hero of Two Worlds: The Art and Pageantry of His Farewell Tour of America, 1824–1825* (Hanover, N.H., 1989), 57.

90. Currier's *Death of Genl. Z. Taylor, 12th President of the United States* was deposited for copyright July 18, 1850. This copy is in the Prints and Photographs Division, Library of Congress.

91. For other examples of Taylor memorial ribbons see Fischer and Sullivan, *American Political Ribbons*, 93–95.

92. An example of Currier's print is in the Prints and Photographs Division, Library of Congress. The verse on the ribbon mourning Jackson declared: "His fair renown shall never fade away, / Nor shall the Mention of his name decay. / Though to the Dust his mortal past we give, / His Fame in Triumph o'er the Grave shall live."

93. Mary Healy Bigot, *Life of George P. A. Healy, Followed by a Selection of His Letters* [Chicago, 1913], 24–25.

94. Dickson, *John Wesley Jarvis*, 214–15, 354; John W. Ward, *Andrew Jackson: Symbol for an Age* (New York, 1955), xi-xii.

95. Quoted in Paul C. Nagel, *Descent from Glory: Four Generations of the John Adams Family* (New York, 1983), 197.

96. The two death-scene lithographs and the daguerreotype by Hass are published in Oliver, *Portraits of John Quincy Adams and His Wife*, 283, 304–5. The mourning ribbon (fig. 2–62) lauded: "In his

public character / He was of untiring industry and unbending integrity. / In his private character / He was generous and of exceeding good nature. / He loved his Country with a sincerity / Which seemed to distinguish him from all mankind. / His fame is so blended within the hearts of his Countrymen / that it will live when all the frail monuments of art / shall have crumbled into dust." No deathbed print or mourning ribbon for Polk has been located.

97. No painting of the work has been located. Although this engraving was signed J. M. Enzing-Miller, the artist is listed as Enzing-Müller in most reference works and as Johann Michael Enzing Müller in the American Art-Union Exhibition Record. Mary B. Cowdrey, *American Academy of Fine Arts and American Art-Union, 1816–1852*, 2 vols. (New York, 1953), 2:263.

98. Copyright Record Books: District Courts, 1790–1870, 181:46, microfilm, Library of Congress. The engraving was reissued in 1874 and again in 1893 under the title *Historical Monument of Our Country*. Impressions of both are in the Prints and Photographs Division, Library of Congress.

99. Odell Shepard, *The Lore of the Unicorn* (London, 1930), 241–43.

NOTES TO CHAPTER III
The Presidency and the Declaration of Independence

1. Gardner to Jefferson, February 13, 1813, Jefferson Papers, Library of Congress.

2. Jefferson to Gardner, February 19, 1813, ibid.

3. Benjamin Owen Tyler, *A Candid Statement of Facts, in Answer to an Unwarranted Denunciation of My Publication of the Declaration of American Independence, Made by Mr. John Binns, Editor of the Democratic Press, in His Paper of the 9th and 18th of April, 1818* (Washington, D.C., 1818), 35–36.

4. Binns's proposal, March 1816, in *Democratic Press* (Philadelphia), June 8, 1816. Binns sent a copy of his proposal to Jefferson in June 1816. Jefferson Papers, Library of Congress.

5. *Port Folio* (Philadelphia), 4th ser., 1 (May 1816): 449.

6. *Democratic Press* (Philadelphia), April 9, 18, 1819.

7. Tyler, *A Candid Statement*, 5–7, 35–36; *Aurora* (Philadelphia), April 13, 1818; photographic copy of Tyler's print in Prints and Photographs Division, Library of Congress. Tyler's print is reproduced in John Bidwell, "American History in Image and Text," American Antiquarian Society, *Proceedings* 98 (1988): 251. Bidwell also provides an annotated list of broadside editions of the Declaration of Independence on pp. 285–302.

8. *Democratic Press* (Philadelphia), November 16, 1819; *Niles' Weekly Register* (Baltimore) 17 (Novem-

ber 20, 1819): 192.

9. *Port Folio* (Philadelphia), 4th ser., 7 (1819): 79; *Democratic Press* (Philadelphia), December 4, 1818, January 22, 1819.

10. *Democratic Press* (Philadelphia), November 16, 1819; John Binns, *Recollections of the Life of John Binns . . . Written by Himself* (Philadelphia, 1854), 234–36.

11. Reprinted in *Democratic Press* (Philadelphia), November 19 and 16, 1819.

12. Tyler, *A Candid Statement*, 9–10.

13. Reprinted in *Democratic Press* (Philadelphia), November 29, 1819.

14. Sean Wilentz, *Chants Democratic: New York City and the Rise of the American Working Class, 1788–1850* (New York, 1984), 43.

15. An earlier state of this plate is identical except for a medallion containing a view of the United States Capitol in the place of the portrait of Zachary Taylor, indicating publication during President Polk's administration. An example is in the William J. Campbell Collection, American Philosophical Society, Philadelphia.

16. Jaffe, *John Trumbull*, 236–45; Oliver, *Portraits of John and Abigail Adams*, 62–63; Julian P. Boyd, ed., *The Papers of Thomas Jefferson*, 20 vols. (Princeton, N.J., 1950–1982), 10:xxvii, 179; Cunningham, *In Pursuit of Reason: The Life of Thomas Jefferson*, 102.

17. *National Intelligencer* (Washington, D.C.), November 19, 20, 1838.

18. A wide distribution of this print is indicated by the copy of the print at the New-York Historical Society, which has printed at the bottom the names and addresses of the firms of Rufus Blanchard, Cincinnati, Ohio, and D. Needham, Buffalo, N.Y.

19. A similar lithograph published by E. B. and E. C. Kellogg, Hartford, Conn., can be found at the American Antiquarian Society.

20. A similarly large but less elaborate lithograph of the presidents through Polk and the Declaration of Independence, by F. Michelin, published by J. H. Colton, New York, 1846, is in the Prints and Photographs Division, Library of Congress.

NOTES TO CHAPTER IV
The Presidency and the Union

1. Wick, *Washington: American Icon*, 35–36, 101; Wendy J. Shadwell, *American Printmaking: The First 150 Years* (Washington, D.C., 1969), 43–44.

2. Hart, *Engraved Portraits of Washington*, listed only five states of the print (pp. 354–57), but recent scholarship has identified six. Shadwell, *American Printmaking*, 43–44; Wick, *Washington: American Icon*, 101.

3. Jefferson to John Adams, November 25, 1816, in Lester Cappon, ed., *The Adams-Jefferson Letters: The Complete Correspondence Between Thomas Jefferson and Abigail and John Adams*, 2 vols. (Chapel

Hill, N.C., 1959), 2:498.

4. Oliver, *Portraits of John and Abigail Adams*, 31, 243.

5. Klapthor and Morrison, *Washington: A Figure upon the Stage*, 191; Neil MacNeil, *The President's Medal, 1789–1977* (New York, 1977), 14; Alpheus H. Hart, *Washington Historical Buttons* (Hightstown, N.J., 1949), 21–23, 53.

6. For other ceramic pieces with President Jefferson's portrait framed by ribbons or wreaths of states see Cunningham, *Image of Jefferson*, 98–102. On pottery designs see Alan Smith, *The Illustrated Guide to Liverpool and Herculaneum Pottery, 1796–1840* (New York, 1970).

7. All copies seen—two in the Rare Book Room of the Library of Congress and the one reproduced here from the Henry Francis du Pont Winterthur Museum—are of the eighth edition.

8. Robert V. Remini, *Andrew Jackson*, 3 vols. (New York, 1977–1984), 2:234–35; John C. Fitzpatrick, ed., *The Autobiography of Martin Van Buren*, American Historical Association, *Annual Report for 1918*, 2 vols. (Washington, D.C., 1920), 2:415.

9. James D. Richardson, ed., *A Compilation of the Messages and Papers of the Presidents, 1789–1897*, 10 vols. (Washington, D.C., 1900), 3:294.

10. An example of a letter, dated April 6, 1858, on a black and white decorated sheet with President Pierce's portrait in the center of the design (similar to fig. 4–13) is in the Salisbury Family Papers, American Antiquarian Society.

11. This edition was printed for Lange and Kronfeld, 201 William Street, New York. In 1889 for the centennial of Washington's inauguration, the firm of Charles Magnus revived the design with Washington's portrait in the center and Lincoln at the top, publishing an expanded version with portraits of all the presidents through Benjamin Harrison added. An example of the print is in the Manuscripts Department, Duke University Library.

12. Both sides of the Lincoln example are reproduced in James W. Milgram, *Abraham Lincoln Illustrated Envelopes and Letter Paper, 1860–1865* (Northbrook, Ill., 1984), 107.

13. The extract was edited, but the omissions do not alter the meaning. Full text is in John C. Fitzpatrick, ed., *The Writings of George Washington*, 39 vols. (Washington, D.C., 1931–1944), 35:217–18.

14. The depository copy is in the Prints and Photographs Division, Library of Congress.

15. Joshua Taylor offers a somewhat different interpretation of this print in *America as Art*, 27.

16. On the development of chromolithography in the United States see Peter C. Marzio, *The Democratic Art: Pictures for a 19th Century America, Chromolithography, 1840–1900* (Boston, 1979).

17. Holzer, Boritt, and Neely, *The Lincoln Image*, 192–94; see also Harold Holzer, "Lincoln and Washington: The Printmakers Blessed Their

Union," *Register of the Kentucky Historical Society* 75 (1977): 204–13.

18. A similar, but larger, print by Charles Shober with the same title and legend was also published in 1865. An example is in the Prints and Photographs Division, Library of Congress.

NOTES TO CHAPTER V
The Presidential Stance

1. Marianna Jenkins, *The State Portrait: Its Origin and Evolution*, Archaeological Institute of America and College Art Association of America, *Monographs on Archaeology and Fine Arts*, no. 3 (n.p., 1947), 1, 9–10, 25–26; Charles Merrill Mount, *Gilbert Stuart: A Biography* (New York, 1964), 205.

2. Wick, *Washington: American Icon*, 40–41, 106–7.

3. Oliver, *Portraits of John and Abigail Adams*, 92–93, 248.

4. The publisher, David Kennedy of Philadelphia, also published a similarly inscribed print of *His Excellency George Washington, Lieut. Genl. of the Armies*, which is reproduced in Wick, *Washington: American Icon*, 129.

5. Henry Adams to Charles Francis Adams, Jr., April 22, 1893, in J. C. Levenson, Ernest Samuels, Charles Vandersee, and Viola Hopkins Winner, eds., *The Letters of Henry Adams*, 6 vols. (Cambridge, Mass., 1982–1988), 4:97–98.

6. Adams to J. B. Binon, February 7, 1819, quoted in Oliver, *Portraits of John and Abigail Adams*, 1–2.

7. Mount, *Stuart*, 204–11; Eleanor Pearson DeLorme, "Gilbert Stuart: Portrait of an Artist," *Winterthur Portfolio* 14 (1979): 353–54.

8. Bervic's engraving would have been available to Stuart in Philadelphia, for in 1791 Jean Baptiste Ternant, the French minister to the United States, presented copies of the print to President Washington and to Secretary of State Jefferson from the twenty prints he brought with him from Paris. Thomas Jefferson Memorial Foundation, *Report of the Curator 1981*, 15.

9. Rigaud's portrait of Louis XIV is reproduced in Jenkins, *State Portrait*, fig. 56.

10. "Furnishing Plan for the Second Floor of Congress Hall," report prepared by the staff of Independence Hall Historical Park, October 1963, part C. United States Senate Historical Office.

11. Wills, *Cincinnatus*, 171–72, 227–28; Lillian B. Miller, "The American Revolution as Image and Symbol in American Art," in *1776*, ed. John Browning and Richard Morton (Toronto and Sarasota, 1976), 82–83; Mount, *Stuart*, 208; Schwartz, *Washington*, 53–54.

12. *Commercial Advertiser* (New York), June 27, 1800, in Gottesman, *Arts and Crafts in New York, 1800–1804*, 50–51.

13. *New-York Gazette and General Advertiser*, June 26, 1800, in ibid., 49–50; *Aurora* (Philadelphia), June 12, July 2, 1800; *Independent Chronicle* (Boston), June 23, 1800. Stuart's reference to a "Mount Vernon" portrait is confusing. No portrait of Washington was taken by Stuart at Mount Vernon, and none by him hung there before or at the time Stuart published this notice. Stuart may have been referring to what later became known as the "Athenaeum" likeness, but this has not been determined.

14. Dunlap, *History of the Rise and Progress of the Arts of Design*, ed. Bayley and Goodspeed, 1:232.

15. Hart, *Engraved Portraits of Washington*, no. 297.

16. Gustavus A. Eisen, *Portraits of Washington*, 3 vols. (New York, 1932), 1:83–85, 233; Morgan and Fielding, *Life Portraits of Washington and Their Replicas*, 265–69. Stuart used the same pose in a similar portrait of Washington painted for Peter Jay Munro, now in the New York Public Library.

17. Bush, *Life Portraits of Jefferson*, 37–44; Cunningham, *Image of Jefferson*, 11–12, 23–53, 87–88.

18. *Aurora* (Philadelphia), September 8, 1800.

19. Ibid., February 23, 1801.

20. Ibid., September 8, December 17, 1800, February 23, 26, 28, April 7, 15, May 2, 6, 1801; *Epitome of the Times* (Norfolk), June 5, 1801.

21. For Tiebout's bust engraving of Jefferson see fig. 2–1. Edwin's bust engraving is reproduced in Cunningham, *Image of Jefferson*, 22, 44.

22. *Aurora* (Philadelphia), March 1, 1809.

23. Ibid.

24. Theodore Bolton, "The Life Portraits of James Madison," *William and Mary Quarterly*, 3d ser., 8 (1951): 32.

25. Oliver, *Portraits of John Quincy Adams and His Wife*, 7–8.

26. Sully to Durand, March 21, 1825, Charles Henry Hart Autograph Collection, Archives of American Art, Smithsonian Institution.

27. Sully to Durand, [April] 4, 1825, Robert Graham Collection, ibid. The letter is dated March 4, 1825, but it clearly was written after Sully's letter to Durand dated March 21, 1825.

28. Sully to Durand, June 8, 1825, Asher B. Durand Papers, New York Public Library, microfilm in Archives of American Art, Smithsonian Institution.

29. Morse to his mother, November 28, December 17, 1819, Edward L. Morse, ed., *Samuel F. B. Morse, His Letters and Journals*, 2 vols. (Boston, 1914), 1:226–27. See also Anna Wells Rutledge, *Catalogue of Paintings and Sculpture in the Council Chamber, City Hall, Charleston, South Carolina* (Charleston, 1943), 23–24.

30. Paul J. Staiti and Gary A. Reynolds, *Samuel F. B. Morse* (New York, 1982), 38.

31. Oliver, *Portraits of John Quincy Adams and His Wife*, 8–11, 77–78.

32. *Boston Patriot and Mercantile Advertiser*, Au-

gust 4, 1830; Oliver, *Portraits of John Quincy Adams and His Wife*, 127–33.

33. Remini, *Jackson*, 1:380–81.

34. David Tatham, "John Henry Bufford: American Lithographer," American Antiquarian Society, *Proceedings* 86 (1976): 67–68.

35. Bates to Earl, March 14, 1832, William S. Pendleton to Earl, March 14, 1832, Ralph E. W. Earl Papers, American Antiquarian Society.

36. Earl to Pendleton, March 22, 1832, ibid.

37. Bates to Earl, March 28, 1832; Pendleton to Earl, March 30, 1832, ibid.

38. Bates to Earl, May 18, [1832], ibid.

39. Earl to Bates, May 16, June 2, 16, 1832, ibid.

40. Bates to Earl, August 31, 1832, ibid.

41. Letter by unidentified author, Washington, February 11, 1837, published in *Boston Statesman*, February 25, 1837, reprinted in *Nashville Union*, April 11, 1837. Transcription in Catalogue of American Portraits, National Portrait Gallery, Smithsonian Institution.

42. Ibid. The small canvas, 23 x 16 inches, is at the Hermitage.

43. *National Gazette* (Philadelphia), November 8, 1830.

44. Reaves, "Portraits for Every Parlor," in *American Portrait Prints*, ed. Reaves, 91–93, 123–24; Katharine Martinez, "Portrait Prints by John Sartain," ibid., 151–52; *National Gazette* (Philadelphia), November 8, 1830.

45. *Register of Debates in Congress*, 22 Cong., 1 Sess. (February 14, 16, 1832), 1809–10, 1824–27. About the same time, Congress commissioned Horatio Greenough to execute a marble, full-length, pedestrian statue of Washington, copying the head of Houdon's Washington. Ibid., 1809, 1829–30. See also Lillian B. Miller, "John Vanderlyn and the Business of Art," *New York History* 32 (January 1951): 33–34; Kenneth C. Lindsay, *The Works of John Vanderlyn: From Tammany to the Capitol, A Loan Exhibition October 11 to November 9, 1970* (Binghamton, N.Y., [1970]), 133.

46. Verplanck to Washington Allston, February 21, 1832, Jared B. Flagg, *The Life and Letters of Washington Allston* (New York, 1892), 253.

47. Henry Inman to A. Clark, December 24, 1838, Harriet Sartain Collection, Historical Society of Pennsylvania, microfilm in Archives of American Art, Smithsonian Institution; John Sartain, *Reminiscences of a Very Old Man* (New York, 1899), 233, quoted in Martinez, "Portrait Prints by John Sartain," in *American Portrait Prints*, ed. Reaves, 143. See also Ann Katharine Martinez, "The Life and Career of John Sartain (1808–1897): A Nineteenth Century Philadelphia Printmaker" (Ph.D. diss., George Washington University, 1986), 20.

48. Milton Kaplan, "Heads of States," *Winterthur Portfolio* 6 (1970): 135–36.

49. John Sartain Papers, Historical Society of Pennsylvania, Archives of American Art, microfilm reel P–27, 467–69, 476, Smithsonian Institution.

50. Lambdin's portrait was exhibited in Philadelphia at the Artists' Fund Society exhibitions in 1842 and 1843 and was listed as owned by W. H. Morgan, the publisher of Sartain's engraving in 1842. Anna Wells Rutledge, ed., *Cumulative Record of Exhibition Catalogues: The Pennsylvania Academy of the Fine Arts, 1807–1870; The Society of Artists, 1800–1814; The Artists' Fund Society. 1835–1845* (Philadelphia, 1955), 120.

51. Kaplan, "Heads of States," 136, 138. Jackson's portrait was identified as painted by Dennis M. Carter, but that portrait is not known today.

52. To meet the popular demand for prints of President Lincoln, engravers put Lincoln's head on the bodies of earlier statesmen as well as presidents. Ibid., 137, 139–40.

53. Bigot, *Life of George P. A. Healy*, 22, 24–25; George P. A. Healy, *Reminiscences of a Portrait Painter* (New York, 1970; orig. pub. 1894), 138–62; Oliver, *Portraits of John Quincy Adams and His Wife*, 250–68; Catalog of American Portraits, National Portrait Gallery.

54. *Statutes at Large and Treaties of the United States of America* 11 (Boston, 1859): 227–28.

55. [James Alfred Pearce], chairman of joint committee on the Library of Congress, to Howell Cobb, secretary of the Treasury, January 30, 1858. Letterbook of Librarian of Congress, January 5, 1857–October 3, 1859, p. 311, Library of Congress Archives, Series D, Manuscripts Division, Library of Congress. Fillmore's portrait is not identified in the requisition for payment, but this identification is supported by information in the files of the Catalog of American Portraits, National Portrait Gallery.

56. Letterbook of Librarian of Congress, January 5, 1857–October 3, 1859, pp. 373–76, 469–70, 475–76, 478–79, 481–82, 492–93, 495–96, 614, 628, 632–33, 637, 641, 682, 815–16, 829–30.

57. Adams's portrait is reproduced in Oliver, *Portraits of John Quincy Adams and His Wife*, 263.

58. Letterbook of Librarian of Congress, January 5, 1857–October 3, 1859, pp. 374, 476, 628, 682.

59. Healy to Buchanan, December 15, 1859, December 25, 1860, July 30, 1861, James Buchanan Papers, Historical Society of Pennsylvania, microfilm in Archives of American Art, Smithsonian Institution.

NOTES TO CHAPTER VI
Heads of State

1. *Annals of Congress*, 2 Cong., 1 Sess. (January 12, 1792), 69–72.

2. Ibid. (March 24, 1792), 483–85.

3. William S. Baker, *Medallic Portraits of Washington* (Philadelphia, 1885), 11–12, 20–21.

4. Madison to Henry Lee, March 28, 1792, in William T. Hutchinson, William M. E. Rachal, Robert A. Rutland, et al., eds., *The Papers of James Madison* (Chicago and Charlottesville, Va., 1962–), 14:269–70; see also 14:262.

5. *Gazette of the United States* (New York), March 6, 1790.

6. Ibid.

7. Malcolm Storer, "The Manly Washington Medal," Massachusetts Historical Society, *Proceedings* 52 (1919): 5–7; Baker, *Medallic Portraits of Washington*, 43.

8. Jefferson to Martha Jefferson Randolph, June 27, 1790, in Boyd, ed., *Papers of Jefferson*, 16:577–78; Wick, *Washington: American Icon*, 101–2; Monroe H. Fabian, *Joseph Wright: American Artist, 1756–1793* (Washington, D.C., 1985), 126–27.

9. Advertisement reproduced in R. W. Julian, *Medals of the United States Mint: The First Century, 1792–1892*, ed. N. Neil Harris (El Cajon, Calif., 1977), 76.

10. Ibid.

11. *Poulson's American Daily Advertiser* (Philadelphia), November 26, 1807, cited in ibid. The medal appears to have been later copied by Thomas Halliday, a celebrated die engraver in Birmingham, England.

12. Jefferson to William Carmichael and William Short, June 30, 1793, in *The Works of Thomas Jefferson*, Federal Edition, ed. Paul L. Ford, 12 vols. (New York, 1904), 7:432–33.

13. The first Indian peace medal of Washington's presidency was dated 1789 and did not carry the president's picture. A female in the garb of Minerva, meant to represent America, presents a peace pipe. The other Washington medals, carrying the dates 1792 to 1795, have scenes similar to the 1792 medal, with a drawing of Washington. Francis Paul Prucha, *Indian Peace Medals in American History* (Lincoln, Nebr., 1976; orig. pub. 1971), 73–76. Prucha published reproductions of nine Washington medals. Ibid., 75–87.

14. Cunningham, *Image of Jefferson*, 73–77.

15. Prucha, *Indian Peace Medals*, 100–117. Joseph F. Loubat, *The Medallic History of the United States of America, 1776–1876*, 2 vols. (New York, 1878), 1:369; 2:plate 66.

16. Thomas L. McKenney to Samuel Moore, September 17, October 13, 1825, quoted in Prucha, *Indian Peace Medals*, 102.

17. Ibid., 105.

18. Adams, ed., *Diary of John Quincy Adams*, January 26, 1828, 7:414.

19. Julian, *Medals of the United States Mint*, ed. Harris, 31.

20. Prucha, *Indian Peace Medals*, 135–38; Oliver, *Portraits of John and Abigail Adams*, 219–20.

21. *Aurora* (Philadelphia), February 20, 1802. The advertisement was dated February 17.

22. Jefferson to Martha Jefferson Randolph, April 3, 1802, in Betts and Bear, eds., *Family Letters of Jefferson*, 221; Martha Jefferson Randolph to Jefferson, April 16, 1802, in ibid., 222; Samuel L. Mitchill to his wife, March 3, April 1, 1802, Samuel Latham Mitchill Papers, Museum of the City of New York.

23. *Aurora* (Philadelphia), February 20, 1802.

24. Cunningham, *Image of Jefferson*, 71–73.

25. Prucha, *Indian Peace Medals*, 95–98.

26. John Quincy Adams, Diary, May 30, 1825, Adams Family Papers, Massachusetts Historical Society, microfilm edition, reel 36.

27. John Quincy Adams, Diary, December 22, 1826, November 27, 1833, ibid., reels 40 and 42.

28. Charles Francis Adams to George W. Ware, Jr., September 13, 1876, quoted in Oliver, *Portraits of John Quincy Adams and His Wife*, 122–23.

29. Michael Kammen, "From Liberty to Prosperity: Reflections upon the Role of Revolutionary Iconography in National Tradition," American Antiquarian Society, *Proceedings* 86 (1976): 263–67; Michael Kammen, *A Season of Youth: The American Revolution and the Historical Imagination* (New York, 1978), 96–99.

30. John Quincy Adams, Diary, November 14, 1825, Adams Family Papers, Massachusetts Historical Society, microfilm edition, reel 38.

31. A medal, "James Madison President of the U. S. from 1809 to 1817," signed by Furst was struck at some unknown time. The dies for a medal by Furst of "James Monroe President of the U. S. A. A.D. 1817" also survive, but no medals from it are known to exist. Julian, *Medals of the United States Mint*, ed. Harris, 78, 79.

32. Ibid., 103.

33. Ibid., 81; MacNeil, *The President's Medal*, 22–24.

34. In Tyler's case the date used was that of William Henry Harrison's death.

35. The process was explained in a letter of Director of the Mint Robert T. Patterson to Secretary of War John C. Spencer, November 2, 1841, quoted in Prucha, *Indian Peace Medals*, 107–8.

36. Ibid., 108–9; Julian, *Medals of the United States Mint*, ed. Harris, 83.

37. Milo M. Quaife, ed., *The Diary of James K. Polk during His Presidency, 1845 to 1849*, 4 vols. (Chicago, 1910), February 12, 13, 16, 1846, 1:222, 225, 227.

38. Georgia Stamm Chamberlain, *Studies on John Gadsby Chapman: American Artist, 1808–1889* (n.p., [1963]), 30, 35.

39. Prucha, *Indian Peace Medals*, 110.

40. Julian, *Medals of the United States Mint*, ed. Harris, 84.

41. Ibid., 84–85; MacNeil, *The President's Medal*, 24. The Zachary Taylor inaugural medal is illustrated in both of these works.

42. James Ross Snowden, *A Description of the Medals of Washington; of National and Miscellaneous*

Medals; and of Other Objects of Interest in the Museum of the Mint (Philadelphia, 1861), 2–3, 41, and plate XIII.

43. The "Evacuation of Boston" medal is illustrated in Boyd, ed., *Papers of Jefferson*, 26:following p. 52.

44. The Washington medal was the only one in the series to be signed G. H. Lovett on the obverse and G.H.L. on the reverse. The John Adams and Jefferson medals were signed G.H.L. on both sides. The Madison and John Quincy Adams medals were signed G.H.L. only on the obverse.

45. Alfred H. Satterlee, *An Arrangement of Medals and Tokens, Struck in Honor of the Presidents of the United States, and of the Presidential Candidates, from the Administration of John Adams to that of Abraham Lincoln, Inclusive* (New York, 1862), 5–12, 17, 22, 27, 29, 44, 49, 52, 57, 63.

NOTES TO CHAPTER VII
Presidents Caricatured

1. John Armstrong, Jr., to Horatio Gates, April 7, 1789, Horatio Gates Papers, New-York Historical Society; C. Edward Skeen, *John Armstrong, Jr., 1758–1842: A Biography* (Syracuse, N.Y., 1981), 31.

2. James Morton Smith, *Freedom's Fetters: The Alien and Sedition Laws and American Civil Liberties* (Ithaca, N.Y., 1956), 192.

3. [William Cobbett], *The Political Censor, or Monthly Review of the Most Interesting Political Occurrences*, 3d ed. (Philadelphia, 1796), 43 and frontispiece; Raymond Walters, Jr., *Albert Gallatin: Jeffersonian Financier and Diplomat* (New York, 1957), 100, 114. The caricature is reproduced in Bernard Faÿ, *The Two Franklins: Fathers of American Democracy* (Boston, 1933), following p. 296.

4. Robert Troup to Rufus King, June 10, 1798, in Charles R. King, ed., *The Life and Correspondence of Rufus King*, 6 vols. (New York, 1894–1900), 2:345.

5. See Frank Weitenkampf, *Political Caricature in the United States in Separately Published Cartoons* (New York, 1953), 11–46. Presidential caricature is briefly surveyed in Thomas C. Blaisdell, Jr., Peter Selz, et al., *The American Presidency in Political Cartoon: 1776–1976* (Berkeley, 1976).

6. The passage was taken from *Hamlet* 3.4, but some lines were omitted from the extract.

7. The print is untitled, unsigned, and undated, but on the only known copy there is penned above the panel depicting Jefferson and Madison: "An old Philosopher teaching his mad Son economical Projects," The Free Library of Philadelphia. For detailed transcriptions from the print see Weitenkampf, *Political Caricature in the United States*, 15–16.

8. For additional examples of Jefferson in caricature see Cunningham, *Image of Jefferson*, 111–22.

9. Lorraine Welling Lanmon, "American Caricature in the English Tradition: The Personal and Political Satires of William Charles," *Winterthur Portfolio* 11 (1976): 1, 15–33, 45–50.

10. For some examples of British caricatures of Madison see Robert A. Rutland, *James Madison and the Search for Nationhood* (Washington, D.C., 1981), 121, 146.

11. The print is described and reproduced in Remini, *Jackson*, 2:122 and following p. 256.

12. Nancy R. Davison, "Andrew Jackson in Cartoon and Caricature," in *American Printmaking before 1876: Fact, Fiction, and Fantasy* (Washington, D.C., 1975), 20.

13. Merton M. Sealts, Jr., ed., *The Journals and Miscellaneous Notebooks of Ralph Waldo Emerson* (Cambridge, Mass., 1965), May 10, 1838, 5:496.

14. Davison, "Jackson in Cartoon and Caricature," 23.

15. Remini, *Jackson*, 2:186–87. Amos Kendall was appointed by Jackson to the vacated post in the Treasury Department.

16. David Tatham, "D. C. Johnston's Satiric Views of Art in Boston, 1825–1850," *Art and Commerce: American Prints of the Nineteenth Century* (Charlottesville, Va., 1978), 19–21. Johnston signed the *Exhibition of Cabinet Pictures* "Snooks," one of several pseudonyms he used, more for fun than to hide his identity. Ibid., 19.

17. Adams, ed., *Diary of John Quincy Adams*, April 25, 1831, 8:359–60.

18. On E. W. Clay see Nancy R. Davison, "E. W. Clay and the American Political Caricature Business," in *Prints and Printmakers of New York State, 1825–1940*, ed. David Tatham (Syracuse, N.Y., 1986), 91–110.

19. Adams, ed., *Diary of John Quincy Adams*, April 25, 1831, 8:360.

20. For the same election Akin also provided a series of twelve woodcuts for an anonymous anti-Jackson leaflet entitled *The House That Jonathan Built, Or Political Primer for 1832*. Maureen O'Brien Quimby, "The Political Art of James Akin," *Winterthur Portfolio* 7 (1972): 70–77, 101–3.

21. *United States Telegraph Extra* (Washington, D.C.), October 8, 1832.

22. Remini, *Jackson*, 3:151–60; Leonard D. White, *The Jacksonians: A Study in Administrative History, 1819–1861* (New York, 1954), 23–44; Merrill D. Peterson, *The Great Triumvirate: Webster, Clay, and Calhoun* (New York, 1987), 244.

23. Ward, *Jackson: Symbol for an Age*, 115–22.

24. Quoted in [Russell Jarvis], *A Biographical Notice of Com. Jesse D. Elliott* (Philadelphia, 1835), 318–19.

25. *Niles' Weekly Register* (Baltimore) 46 (May 17, 1834): 189.

26. Quoted in ibid. 46 (July 12, 1834): 329.

27. John M. Werner, "New Light on the 'Man in

the Claret Colored Coat,'" *Journal of the Early Republic* 5 (1985): 95–98.

28. Blaisdell, Selz, et al., *American Presidency in Political Cartoons*, 68–69; Weitenkampf, *Political Caricature in the United States*, 48, 63; Peter C. Welsh, "Henry R. Robinson: Printmaker to the Whig Party," *New York History* 53 (1972):27, 39–40.

29. The other figures in the drawing are Francis Preston Blair (seated), editor of the *Washington Globe*, and Nathaniel P. Tallmadge, Democratic United States senator from New York, who refused to follow the administration in financial matters and often was aligned with the Whigs in New York. Blair is urging Van Buren to slip another weight in his pocket, while Tallmadge is saying that he never thought that Van Buren would have ventured to try his weight with Clay.

30. Weitenkampf, *Political Caricature in the United States*, 73–85. Similar patterns prevailed throughout the 1840s and the 1850s.

31. Blaisdell, Selz, et al., *American Presidency in Political Cartoons*, 76.

32. The "Cuba Proclamation" in Fillmore's hand refers to his presidential proclamation of April 25, 1851, against southern annexationists participating in the filibustering expeditions of Gen. Narcisco Lopez, a leader of Spanish refugees in the United States, who sought to lead an uprising in Cuba against Spanish rule.

33. See also William Murrell, *A History of American Graphic Humor*, 2 vols. (New York, 1933–1938), 1:225, 228.

NOTES TO CHAPTER VIII
The Drama of the Presidency

1. Edgar P. Richardson, Brooke Hindle, and Lillian B. Miller, *Charles Willson Peale and His World* (New York, 1982), 91–94.

2. *Columbian Magazine* 3 (1789): 282–83.

3. Ibid., 288–90; W. W. Abbot and Dorothy Twohig, eds., *The Papers of George Washington*, Presidential Series (Charlottesville, Va., 1987), 2:108–9. On Washington's journey to New York see also Bowen, ed., *Centennial Celebration of the Inauguration of Washington*, 21–26.

4. *Currier and Ives: A Catalogue Raisonné*, numbers 7075–78. Examples are in the Prints and Photographs Division, Library of Congress. The copy reproduced here is endorsed as deposited for copyright September 13, 1845. Prints and Photographs Division, Library of Congress.

5. *Gazette of the United States* (New York), May 2, 1789.

6. An engraving titled "View of the Federal Edifice in New York" was published in the August 1789 issue of the *Columbian Magazine*, preceding p. 473.

7. Quoted in Thomas E. V. Smith, *The City of New York in the Year of Washington's Inauguration, 1789* (Riverside, Conn., 1972; orig. pub. 1889), 232.

8. *Gazette of the United States* (New York), May 2, 1789.

9. Shadwell, *American Printmaking*, 43.

10. Noble E. Cunningham, Jr., *The Process of Government under Jefferson* (Princeton, N.J., 1978), 10, 25–26, 41–45.

11. *Daily Advertiser* (New York), March 4, 1801, in Gottesman, *Arts and Crafts in New York, 1800–1804*, 459; Noble E. Cunningham, Jr., *The Jeffersonian Republicans in Power: Party Operations, 1801–1809* (Chapel Hill, N.C., 1963), 285.

12. *Ladies Magazine and Literary Gazette* 5 (1832): 116; see also Margaret Bayard Smith to Jane Bayard Kirkpatrick, March 11, 1829, in Gaillard Hunt, ed., *The First Forty Years of Washington Society in the Family Letters of Margaret Bayard Smith* (New York, 1965; orig. pub. 1906), 290–98.

13. Adams, ed., *Diary of John Quincy Adams*, March 4, 1841, 10:439–40.

14. *Sun* (Baltimore), March 5, 1841.

15. Alice Lee Parker and Milton Kaplan, *Charles Fenderich, Lithographer of American Statesmen: A Catalog of His Work* (Washington, D.C., 1959), 60.

16. Allan Nevins, ed., *The Diary of Philip Hone, 1828–1851* (New York, 1936), March 4, 1841, 530.

17. Oscar George Theodore Sonneck, *A Bibliography of Early Secular American Music*, revised and enlarged by William Treat Upton (Washington, D.C., 1945), 341–44, 449–54.

18. "Adams March," printed and sold at P. A. von Hagen & Co., Boston, is listed in ibid., 5.

19. Ibid., 341–43.

20. Abigail Adams to Mary Cranch, April 26, 1798, in Stewart Mitchell, ed., *New Letters of Abigail Adams, 1788–1801* (Boston, 1947), 164–65.

21. *Porcupine's Gazette*, April 27, 1798, reprinted in Sonneck and Upton, *Bibliography of Early Secular American Music*, 171.

22. Vera Brodsky Lawrence, *Music for Patriots, Politicians, and Presidents: Harmonies and Discords of the First Hundred Years* (New York, 1975), 143–45. Adams's portrait was probably copied from an engraving by H. H. Houston. See fig. 5–2 above.

23. Wick, *Washington: American Icon*, 125–27. Several different Washington portraits were pasted on other copies of the music. Wick published another example on p. 126. See also Harry Dichter and Elliott Shapiro, *Early American Sheet Music: Its Lure and Its Lore, 1768–1889* (New York, 1941), 21–22.

24. Nancy R. Davison, "The Grand Triumphal Quick-Step; or Sheet Music Covers in America," in *Prints in and of America to 1850*, ed. John D. Morse (Charlottesville, Va., 1970), 257–58; Wolfe, *Early American Music Engraving and Printing*, 231–39.

25. *Aurora* (Philadelphia), January 24, 1801; Richard J. Wolfe, *Secular Music in America, 1801–1825: A Bibliography* (New York, 1964), 267.

26. *American Citizen* (New York), February 26, 1801; *Daily Advertiser* (New York), March 11, 1801.

27. Margaret Bayard Smith to Susan B. Smith, March [4–5], 1809, in Hunt, ed., *First Forty Years of Washington Society*, 61.

28. Madison marches are listed in Wolfe, *Secular Music in America*, 549, 566, 650, 626, 650. Another example is illustrated in Rutland, *Madison and the Search for Nationhood*, 135.

29. Louis Dubois to Madison, March 5, 1809, in Robert A. Rutland et al., eds. *The Papers of James Madison*, Presidential Series (Charlottesville, Va., 1984–), 1:19.

30. *New York Evening Post*, July 2, 1817. The march composed by Peter Gilles, Sr., is listed in Wolfe, *Secular Music in America*, 315. For other Monroe marches see Lawrence, *Music for Patriots, Politicians, and Presidents*, 224–25.

31. Wayne Craven, "Asher B. Durand's Career as an Engraver," *American Art Journal* 3 (1971): 49–50.

32. The same scene of the Capitol (lithograph by Edward Weber and Co., Baltimore) appeared in 1849 on the cover of *President Taylor's Grand Inauguration March*, composed by Albert Holland, published by G. Willig, Jr., Baltimore. No portrait of President Taylor was included. Copy in Music Division, Library of Congress.

33. The copy in the Music Division, Library of Congress, has no stamp.

34. See David Tatham, "The Pendleton-Moore Shop: Lithographic Artists in Boston, 1825–1840," *Old-Time New England* 62 (1971): 31, 44–45.

35. *Illustrated London News* 6 (April 19, 1845): 243–44.

36. Adams, ed., *Diary of John Quincy Adams*, March 4, 1845, 12:178–79.

37. *Illustrated London News* 6 (April 19, 1845): 244. On *The Discovery Group*, which today is in storage, see Charles E. Fairman, *Arts and Artists of the Capitol of the United States of America* (Washington, D.C., 1927), 108–9.

38. *Illustrated London News* 6 (April 19, 1845): 244.

39. Polk's journey, by steamboat to Wheeling, by carriage to Cumberland, Md., and by train to Washington, is described in Charles G. Sellers, *James K. Polk, Continentalist, 1843–1846* (Princeton, 1966), 189–92.

40. *National Intelligencer* (Washington, D.C.), March 5, 1845.

41. *Illustrated London News* 6 (April 19, 1845): 243–44.

42. Ibid., 244.

43. The maker of the fan has not been identified. The fan has been said to have been carried by Mrs. Polk at her husband's inaugural ball, but no documentation of this has been located.

44. Both sides of the fan are illustrated in Amy Donovan "Change Presidents and Waltz," in *Every Four Years* (Washington, D.C., 1980), 142–43. The fan is inaccurately described in that work as made of silk and ivory.

45. *Congressional Globe*, 28 Cong., 2 Sess., March 4, 1845, 14:398–400; 31 Cong., special session of Senate, March 5, 1849, appendix, 20:326–27; *National Intelligencer* (Washington, D.C.), March 5, 1849.

46. *National Intelligencer* (Washington, D.C.), March 6, 1849.

47. *Gleason's Pictorial Drawing Room Companion* 1 (July 26, 1851): 61; (August 2, 1851): 69.

48. Ibid. (August 2, 1851): 72; (July 26, 1851): 61.

49. Ibid. (August 2, 1851): 72–73.

50. Ibid. (November 15, 1851): 305, 308–9.

51. Excerpt from *Lake Champlain Beacon* in ibid. (July 26, 1851): 61.

52. Excerpt from *Belknap Gazette* in ibid.

53. *Gleason's Pictorial Drawing Room Companion* 4 (March 26, 1853): 200. Full-page portraits of President Pierce and Vice-President William R. King were published in the issue of March 14, 1853.

54. *National Intelligencer* (Washington, D.C.), March 5, 1853. According to that report, the two members of the arrangement committee were Jesse D. Bright and Hannibal Hamlin.

55. Ibid.

56. *Frank Leslie's Illustrated Newspaper* 3 (March 7, 1857): 211.

57. Ibid. (March 14, 1857): 217.

58. Ibid., 220, 221, 228.

59. Ibid., 224, 225, 228, 229, 232.

60. Ibid. (March 21, 1857): 239.

61. Ibid., 239, 241.

62. *Harper's Weekly* 1 (March 14, 1857): 168.

NOTES TO CHAPTER IX
The Presidency Popularized and Exploited

1. *Aurora* (Philadelphia), November 19, 1804. See also Cunningham, *Image of Jefferson*, 127; Morgan and Fielding, *Life Portraits of Washington and Their Replicas*, 363.

2. For medals see Chapter VI; for earthenware pieces, see figs. 1–2, 1–3, 1–10, 1–15, 4–4, 4–5, 4–6.

3. The American Bank Note Company of New York offered sample sheets with the portraits of all the presidents from Washington through Lincoln. A sheet of presidential portraits from Washington through Jackson is the William J. Campbell Collection, American Philosophical Society. A sheet with portraits of Van Buren through Lincoln is in the New-York Historical Society.

4. *Antiques* 41 (1942): 322; Robert G. Stewart, *A Nineteenth-Century Gallery of Distinguished Americans* (Washington, D.C., 1969), 13; James B. Longacre and James Herring, eds., *The National Portrait Gallery of Distinguished Americans*, 4 vols. (Philadelphia, 1834–1839), 1:180.

5. Cunningham, *Image of Jefferson*, 79–84.

6. George S. and Helen McKearin, *American Glass* (New York, 1941), 458–59, 516–17.

7. Ibid., 459, 520–23. For presidential images on flasks see also Helen and George S. McKearin, *Two Hundred Years of American Blown Glass* (New York, 1950); and Helen McKearin, *The Story of American Historical Flasks* (Corning, N.Y., 1953).

8. The print was adapted from a plate employed in earlier publications. See figs. 2–14 and 2–15 above.

9. *Argus* (Albany), September 16, 1846, excerpt in "Critical Notices of the Statesman's Manual," bound with vol. 1 of Edwin Williams, *Statesman's Manual: Presidents' Messages, Inaugural, Annual and Special, from 1789 to 1846*, 2 vols. (New York, 1847).

10. *American Review* 4 (December 1846): 650.

11. Edwin Williams, *The Statesman's Manual: The Addresses and Messages of the Presidents of the United States, Inaugural, Annual and Special, from 1789 to 1849*, 4 vols. (New York, 1849). In the edition of 1853, the portrait of the incumbent president, Millard Fillmore, appeared as the frontispiece of vol. 4 (Edwin Williams, *The Statesman's Manual: Containing the Presidents' Messages, Inaugural, Annual and Special, from 1789 to 1851*, 4 vols. [New York, 1853]).

12. *American Review* 10 (August 1849): 219. The same engravings were also published in Edwin Williams, *The Presidents of the United States and Their Memoirs and Administrations* (New York, 1849).

13. Advertisement bound in vol. 1 of Williams, *Statesman's Manual* (1847).

14. Robert W. Lincoln, *Lives of the Presidents of the United States; with Biographical Notices of the Signers of the Declaration of Independence; Sketches of the Most Remarkable Events in the History of the Country, from Its Discovery to the Present Time; and a General View of Its Present Condition. Embellished with a Portrait of Each of the Presidents and Forty-Five Engravings* (New York, 1833).

15. *National Intelligencer* (Washington, D.C.), March 22, 24, 1841.

16. An example is *American History and Biography, Containing an Epitome of American History from the Earliest Period to the Present Time, the Biographies of the Signers of the Declaration of Independence, and the Biographies of Each of the Presidents* (New York, 1838). An engraving of Washington was published as the frontispiece, and a small copperplate engraving of each of his successors preceded each presidential biographical sketch.

17. Agnew O. Roorbach, *The Development of the Social Studies in American Secondary Education before 1861* (Philadelphia, 1937), 113–14. Many editions of Goodrich's work contained small engraved portraits of the presidents. An example is Charles A. Goodrich, *A History of the United States of America*, 3d ed. (Hartford, 1823).

18. John Frost, *The Pictorial History of the United States of America, from the Discovery by the Northmen in the Tenth Century to the Present Time*, 4 vols. (Philadelphia, 1846), vols. 3 and 4. A later edition of Frost's work titled *Pictorial History of America, from the Earliest Times to the Close of the Mexican War* (Philadelphia, 1856), reprinted and continued the same style of presidential portraits.

19. John Frost, *The Presidents of the United States: From Washington to Fillmore. Comprising Their Personal and Political History* (Boston, 1852).

20. Jonathan French, *The True Republican: Containing the Inaugural Addresses, Together with the First Annual Addresses and Messages of All the Presidents of the United States, from 1789 to 1845; Together with Their Farewell Addresses, and Illustrated with the Portrait of Each of the Presidents. To Which is Annexed the Declaration of Independence and Constitution of the United States, with the Amendments and Signers' Names. Also, the Constitutions of Many of the Most Important States in the Union* (Philadelphia, 1846).

21. *The American Keepsake, or Book for Every American; Embellished with a Steel-Plate Engraving of All the Presidents of the United States* (Boston, 1845).

22. *The American's Own Book Containing the Declaration of Independence, with the Lives of the Signers; the Constitution of the United States; the Inaugural Addresses and First Annual Messages of all the Presidents, from Washington to Pierce; the Farewell Addresses of George Washington and Andrew Jackson; with a Portrait and Life of Each President of the United States, to the Present Time* (New York, 1855).

23. Charles Dickens, *American Notes*, introduction and notes by Andrew Lang (London and New York, 1898), 217–18.

24. "Notes by a Man about Town," number 11, in *Supplement to the Courant* (Hartford), February 3, 1849.

25. Ibid. See also Frances Phipps, "Connecticut's Printmakers: The Kelloggs of Hartford," *Connecticut Antiquarian* 21 (1969): 19–26.

26. *National Intelligencer* (Washington, D.C.), March 6, 1839.

27. Parker and Kaplan, *Charles Fenderich*, 5–7, 49, 53, 54.

28. The advertisement was dated May 19, [1841], *National Intelligencer* (Washington, D.C.), May 21, 1841.

29. The portraits of the first five presidents in Newsam's series followed Gilbert Stuart's well-known images. The lithograph of John Quincy Adams was poor, and the source not recognizable (Oliver, *Portraits of John Quincy Adams and His Wife*, 276). Harrison's portrait, taken from a daguerreotype by Southworth and Hawes, is illustrated in *National Portrait Gallery: Permanent Collection Illustrated Checklist* (Washington, D.C., 1987), 128.

30. Harry T. Peters, *Currier and Ives: Printmakers*

to the American People, 2 vols. (New York, 1929–1931), 1:44; advertisement reproduced in Harry T. Peters, *Currier and Ives: Printmakers to the American People* (Garden City, N.Y., 1942), plate 5.

31. On the print of John Adams reproduced here the line "Pub. by N. Currier. Lith. 2 Spruce St. cor. Nassau. N.Y." is clearly visible. On the other prints in the portfolio only faint remnants of the same impression remain, but enough to indicate that all the lithographs in the portfolio originally were impressed with the same publisher's line.

32. See figs. 2–22 through 2–26 and 2–30 through 2–32 above.

33. Peters, *Currier and Ives* (1929–1931), 1:145–46, plates 134–37.

34. *Currier and Ives: A Catalogue Raisonné*, 544, 993.

35. *Dollar Weekly Times* (Cincinnati), December 2, 1852.

36. Ibid., March 8, 1855, August 28, 1856.

37. An advertisement containing some of the same material in this supplement was published in the *Dollar Weekly Times* (Cincinnati), November 8, 1855, suggesting 1855 as the likely date of the supplement.

38. H. H. Lloyd and Company published at least three variations of this print. A print titled *Political Chart* reproduced portraits of all earlier presidents in the borders and presented portraits of all the presidential candidates in 1860 in the center of the design. Another print, appearing after Lincoln's election, omitted portraits of previous presidents and added members of Lincoln's cabinet and several military figures. The prints are reproduced in Harold Holzer, "An All-Purpose Campaign Poster," *Lincoln Herald* 84 (1982): 42–45.

39. Grace Bedell to Lincoln, October 15, 1860, in Roy P. Basler, ed., *The Collected Works of Abraham Lincoln*, 9 vols. (New Brunswick, N.J., 1953), 4:130. Lincoln's prompt reply, October 19, 1860, is on 4:129.

NOTES TO CHAPTER X
Presidential Images in American Culture

1. Michael Kammen, *A Machine that Would Go of Itself: The Constitution in American Culture* (New York, 1986), 90–92.

2. Quaife, ed., *Diary of James K. Polk*, March 16, 1846, 1:290. See also entries for March 20, April 1, 6, 1846, 1:303, 315, 318–19.

3. As president, Lincoln continued to be the frequent object of photographers' lenses. The most extensive publication of Lincoln photographs, including all of the 120 photographs known at the time of publication, is Frederick Hill Meserve and Carl Sandburg, *The Photographs of Abraham Lincoln* (New York, 1944).

4. Published by B. B. Russell and Company, Boston, 1867.

NOTE ON SOURCES

$\mathcal{T}$HE VISUAL documents upon which this work is based are widely scattered. The most important collections of engraved prints and lithographs are in the Prints and Photographs Division of the Library of Congress. Other major collections are at the American Antiquarian Society, National Portrait Gallery of the Smithsonian Institution, New-York Historical Society, New York Public Library, American Philosophical Society, Historical Society of Pennsylvania, and Henry Francis du Pont Winterthur Museum. There are also valuable examples at the Boston Museum of Fine Arts, Metropolitan Museum of Art, and Houghton Library, Harvard University.

Major collections of medals, ceramics, and other items of material culture are in the National Museum of American History of the Smithsonian Institution, Henry Francis du Pont Winterthur Museum, American Numismatic Society, Corning Museum of Glass, and the DeWitt Collection, Hartford University. The most extensive collections of sheet music examined for the period are in the Music Division of the Library of Congress and at the American Antiquarian Society. The Catalog of American Portraits in the National Portrait Gallery, Smithsonian Institution, is an invaluable resource for the study of popular derivatives as well as portraiture.

Because engraving was slow and costly, early American magazines were sparsely illustrated. Important exceptions employed in this book are the *Columbian Magazine, or Monthly Miscellany* (Philadelphia, 1789); *Literary Magazine, and American Register* (Philadelphia, 1804); and *New-York Mirror, or a Weekly Gazette of Literature and the Fine Arts* (New York, 1834). The visual revolution in publishing in the 1840s and 1850s produced by advancing technology brought the advent of highly illustrated magazines, of which the most useful have been *Gleason's Pictorial Drawing Room Companion* (Boston, 1851–1854); *Frank Leslie's Illustrated Newspaper* (New York, 1855–1861); and *Harper's Weekly* (New York, 1857).

The most valuable manuscript sources employed were the Asher Brown Durand Papers, New York Public Library; Ralph E. W. Earl Papers, American Antiquarian Society; Adams Family Papers, microfilm edition, Massachusetts Historical Society; John Doggett Daybook and John Doggett and Company Letterbook, Henry Francis du Pont Winterthur Museum; Papers of Thomas Jefferson, Papers of James Madison, and Letterbook of Librarian of Congress, Library of Congress; "The Collected Works of Charles Willson Peale and His Family," microfiche edition, edited by Lillian B. Miller (New York, 1980); and Archives of American Art, microfilm, Smithsonian Institution.

Other useful primary sources include

Charles Francis Adams, ed., *Memoirs of John Quincy Adams, Comprising Portions of His Diary from 1795 to 1848*, 12 vols. (Philadelphia, 1884–1877); Milo Milton Quaife, ed., *The Diary of James K. Polk during His Presidency, 1845 to 1849*, 4 vols. (Chicago, 1910); *Diary of William Dunlap (1766–1839)*, 3 vols. (New York, 1930); William Dunlap, *A History of the Rise and Progress of the Arts of Design in the United States*, edited by Frank W. Bayley and Charles E. Goodspeed, 3 vols. (Boston, 1918; orig. pub. 1834); Edward L. Morse, ed., *Samuel F. B. Morse, His Letters and Journals*, 2 vols. (Boston, 1914); Edwin Morris Betts and James Adam Bear, Jr., eds., *The Family Letters of Thomas Jefferson* (Columbia, Mo., 1966); and Gaillard Hunt, ed., *The First Forty Years of Washington Society in the Family Letters of Margaret Bayard Smith* (New York, 1965; orig. pub. 1906).

The image of George Washington has received more attention than that of any other early president. For this study the most useful work has been Wendy C. Wick, *George Washington an American Icon: The Eighteenth-Century Graphic Prints* (Washington, D.C., 1982). Basic resources for the study of Washington include Charles Henry Hart, *Catalogue of the Engraved Portraits of Washington* (New York, 1904); Gustavus A. Eisen, *Portraits of Washington*, 3 vols. (New York, 1932); John Hill Morgan and Mantle Fielding, *Life Portraits of Washington and Their Replicas* (Philadelphia, 1931). Important works treating broader aspects of Washington's image are Marcus Cunliffe, *George Washington: Man and Monument* (Boston, 1958); Mark Edward Thistlethwaite, *The Image of George Washington: Studies in Mid-Nineteenth Century American History Painting* (New York, 1979); Garry Wills, *Cincinnatus: George Washington and the Enlightenment* (New York, 1984); and Barry Schwartz, *George Washington: The Making of an American Symbol* (New York, 1987).

For Washington's successors, works on presidential portraiture, prints, and iconography include Andrew Oliver, *Portraits of John and Abigail Adams* (Cambridge, Mass., 1967) and *Portraits of John Quincy Adams and His Wife* (Cambridge, Mass., 1970); Noble E. Cunningham, Jr., *The Image of Thomas Jefferson in the Public Eye: Portraits for the People, 1800–1809* (Charlottesville, Va., 1981); Alfred L. Bush, *The Life Portraits of Thomas Jefferson*, rev. ed. (Charlottesville, Va., 1987); Theodore Bolton, "The Life Portraits of James Madison," *William and Mary Quarterly*, 3d ser., 8 (1951): 25–47; and Harold Holzer, Gabor S. Boritt, and Mark E. Neely, Jr., *The Lincoln Image: Abraham Lincoln and the Popular Print* (New York, 1984).

Among studies of artists important to presidential portraiture and derivative images are William T. Whitley, *Gilbert Stuart* (Cambridge, Mass., 1932); Charles Merrill Mount, *Gilbert Stuart: A Biography* (New York, 1964); Richard McLanathan, *Gilbert Stuart* (New York, 1986); Lawrence Park, *Gilbert Stuart: An Illustrated List of His Works*, 4 vols. (New York, 1926); Edgar P. Richardson, Brooke Hindle, and Lillian B. Miller, *Charles Willson Peale and His World* (New York, 1982); Monroe H. Fabian, *Joseph Wright: American Artist, 1756–1793* (Washington, D.C., 1985); John Durand, *The Life and Times of A. B. Durand* (New York, 1970; orig. pub. 1894); Wayne Carven, "Asher B. Durand's Career as an Engraver," *American Art Journal* 3 (1971): 39–57; Paul J. Staiti and Gary A. Reynolds, *Samuel F. B. Morse* (New York, 1982); Alice Lee Parker and Milton Kaplan, *Charles Fenderich, Lithographer of American Statesmen: A Catalog of His Work* (Washington, D.C., 1959); Ann Katharine Martinez, "The Life and Career of John Sartain (1808–1897): A Nineteenth Century Philadelphia Printmaker" (Ph.D. diss., George Washington University, 1986); and Georgia Stamm Chamberlain, *Studies on John Gadsby Chapman: American Artist, 1808–1899* (n.p., [1963]).

Among relevant works of broader scope are Joshua C. Taylor, *America as Art* (Washington, D.C., 1976); Lillian B. Miller, *Patrons and Patriotism: The Encouragement of the Fine Arts in the United States, 1790–1860* (Chicago, 1966); Peter C. Marzio, *The Democratic Art: Pictures for a 19th Century America, Chromolithography, 1840–1900* (Boston, 1979); Michael Kammen, *A Season of Youth: The American Revolution and the Historical Imagination* (New York, 1978) and *A Machine that Would Go of Itself: The Constitution in American Culture* (New York, 1986); and Brandon B. Fortune, "Portraits of Virtue and Genius: Pantheons of Worthies and Public Portraiture in the Early Republic, 1780–1820" (Ph.D. diss., University of North Carolina, Chapel Hill, 1987).

Particularly helpful in studying prints are *Currier and Ives: A Catalogue Raisonné*, introduction by Bernard F. Reilly, Jr., 2 vols. (Detroit, 1984); Harry T. Peters, *Currier and Ives: Printmakers to the American People*, 2 vols. (New York, 1929–1931) and *America on Stone: The Other Printmakers to the American People* (New York, 1931); E. McSherry Fowble, *Two Centuries of Prints in America, 1680–1880: A Selective Catalogue of the Winterthur Museum Collection* (Charlottesville, Va., 1987); and *National Portrait Permanent Collection Illustrated Checklist* (Washington, D.C., 1987).

Scholarly articles pertinent to the study of early American prints include Davida Tenenbaum Deutsch, "Washington Memorial Prints," *Antiques* 111 (1977): 324–31; Phoebe Lloyd Jacobs, "John James Barralet and the Apotheosis of George Washington," *Winterthur Portfolio* 12 (1977): 115–37; Anita Schorsch, "A Key to the Kingdom: The Iconography of a Mourning Picture," *Winterthur Portfolio* 14 (1979): 41–72; Wendy Wick Reaves, "Portraits for Every Parlor: Albert Newsam and American Portrait Lithography," and Katharine Martinez, "Portrait Prints by John Sartain," in *American Portrait Prints: Proceedings of the Tenth Annual American Print Conference*, ed. Wendy Wick Reaves (Charlottesville, Va., 1984), 83–134, 135–93; David Tatham, "The Pendleton-Moore Shop: Lithographic Artists in Boston, 1825–1840," *Old-Time New England* 62 (1971): 29–46, and "John Henry Bufford: American Lithographer," American Antiquarian Society, *Proceedings* 86 (1976): 47–73; Frances Phipps, "Connecticut's Printmakers: The Kelloggs of Hartford," *Connecticut Antiquarian* 21 (1969): 19–26; Milton Kaplan, "Heads of States," *Winterthur Portfolio* 6 (1970): 135–50; and Marcus Cunliffe, *The Double Images of Lincoln and Washington* (Gettysburg, Pa., 1988).

The most useful specialized studies relating to medallic art are James Ross Snowden, *A Description of the Medals of Washington; of National and Miscellaneous Medals; and of Other Objects of Interest in the Museum of the Mint* (Philadelphia, 1861); Alfred H. Satterlee, *An Arrangement of Medals and Tokens, Struck in Honor of the Presidents of the United States, and of the Presidential Candidates, from the Administration of John Adams to that of Abraham Lincoln, Inclusive* (New York, 1862); Joseph F. Loubat, *The Medallic History of the United States of America, 1776–1876*, 2 vols. (New York, 1878); William S. Baker, *Medallic Portraits of Washington* (Philadelphia, 1885); R. W. Julian, *Medals of the United States Mint: The First Century, 1792–1892*, ed. N. Neil Harris (El Cajon, Calif., 1977); and Neil MacNeil, *The President's Medal, 1789–1977* (New York, 1977). Indispensable is Francis Paul Prucha, *Indian Peace Medals in American History* (Lincoln, Nebr., 1976; orig. pub. 1971).

The principal works on caricatures are Frank Weitenkampf, *Political Caricature in the United States in Separately Published Cartoons* (New York, 1953); Thomas C. Blaisdell, Jr., Peter Selz, et al., *The American Presidency in Political Cartoon: 1776–1976* (Berkeley, 1976); Maureen O'Brien Quimby, "The Political Art of James Akin," *Winterthur Portfolio* 7 (1972): 59–108; Lorraine Welling Lanmon, "American Caricature in the English Tradition: The Personal and Political Satires of William Charles," *Winterthur Portfolio* 11 (1976): 1–51; Nancy R. Davison, "Andrew Jackson in Cartoon and Caricature," *American Printmaking before 1876: Fact, Fiction, and Fantasy* (Washington, D.C., 1975), and "E. W. Clay and the American Political Caricature Business," in *Prints and Printmakers of New York State, 1825–1840*, ed. David Tatham (Syracuse, N.Y., 1986), 91–110; Peter C. Welsh, "Henry R. Robinson: Printmaker to the Whig Party," *New York History* 53 (1972): 25–53; and David Tatham, "D. C. Johnston's Satiric Views of Art in Boston, 1825–1850," in *Art and Commerce: American Prints of the Nineteenth Century* (Charlottesville, Va., 1978), 9–24. A general work is William Murrell, *A History of American Graphic Humor*, 2 vols. (New York, 1933–1938).

For items of material culture the most useful works have been Robert H. McCauley, *Liverpool Transfer Designs on Anglo-American Pottery* (Portland, Me., 1942); Alan Smith, *The Illustrated Guide to Liverpool Herculaneum Pottery, 1796–1840* (New York, 1970); Christina H. Nelson, "Transfer-printed Creamware and Pearlware for the American Market," *Winterthur Portfolio* 15 (1980): 93–115; Margaret B. Klapthor and Howard A. Morrison, *George Washington: A Figure upon the Stage* (Washington, D.C., 1982); Florence M. Montgomery, *Printed Textiles: English and American Cottons* and Linens, 1700–1850 (New York, 1970); Herbert R. Collins, *Threads of History: Americana Recorded on Cloth, 1775 to the Present* (Washington, D.C., 1979); Roger A. Fischer and Edmund B. Sullivan, *American Political Ribbons and Ribbon Badges, 1825–1981* (Lincoln, Mass., 1985); Helen and George S. McKearin, *Two Hundred Years of American Blown Glass* (New York, 1950); Helen McKearin, *The Story of American Historical Flasks* (Corning, N.Y., 1953); Alfred Coxe Prime, ed., *The Arts and Crafts in Philadelphia, Maryland, and South Carolina, 1786–1800: Gleanings from Newspapers* ([Topsfield, Mass.], 1932); and Rita Susswein Gottesman, *The Arts and Crafts in New York, 1800–1804: Advertisements and News Items from New York City Newspapers* (New York, 1965).

Important aids to studying early patriotic music and illustrated sheet music are Oscar George Theodore Sonneck, *A Bibliography of Early Secular American Music*, revised and enlarged by William Treat Upton (Washington, D.C., 1945); Richard J. Wolfe, *Secular Music in America, 1801–1825: A Bibliography* (New York, 1964) and *Early American Music Engraving and Printing: A History of Music Publishing in America from 1787 to 1825 with Commentary on Earlier and Later Practices* (Urbana, Ill., 1980); and Nancy R. Davison, "The Grand Triumphal Quick-Step: or Sheet Music Covers in America," in *Prints in and of America to 1850*, ed. John D. Morse (Charlottesville, Va., 1970), 257–85.

A useful reference work is Ruth S. Freitag, comp., *Presidential Inaugurations: A Selected List of References*, 3d ed. (Washington, D.C., 1969). Works published too late to be employed in this study, but important for future scholarship, include James G. Barber, *Old Hickory: A Life Sketch of Andrew Jackson* (Washington and Nashville, 1990), the catalog of a major exhibition of Jackson's portraits at the National Portrait Gallery and the Tennessee State Musuem; and Bernard F. Reilly, Jr., *American Political Prints, 1766–1876: A Catalog of the Collections in the Library of Congress* (Boston, 1991).

ACKNOWLEDGMENTS

IN MY research for this book I have benefited from the knowledge and helpfulness of scholars who are curators of major collections of prints and other visual sources. Among those who have been of continuing help throughout the course of my work, I particularly want to thank Wendy Wick Reaves, Curator of Prints, National Portrait Gallery, Smithsonian Institution; Wendy Shadwell, Curator of Prints, New-York Historical Society; and Georgia B. Barnhill, Curator of Graphic Arts, American Antiquarian Society. At the National Portrait Gallery Robert Stewart, Linda Thrift, and Bridget McAloon were also most helpful. At the National Museum of American History, Smithsonian Institution—which has the most diverse collections of materials related to this study—I am grateful for the valuable assistance of William L. Bird, Jr., Margaret Klapthor, and Keith Melder of the Division of Political History; R. Le-Gette Burris of the National Numismatics Collection; Suzanne Myers and Regina Blaszczyk of the Ceramics and Glass Division; Herbert Collins and James Bruns of the Philatelic Division; and Ann Serio of the Division of Domestic Life. At the Library of Congress Bernard Reilly, Curator of Popular and Graphic Arts, Maja Felaco of the Prints and Photographs Division, and David Wigdor, Assistant Chief of the Manuscripts Division, have been especially helpful. Senate Historian Richard Baker, Cynthia Miller, Assistant Historian of the House of Representatives, and James R. Ketchum, Curator of the United States Senate Commission on Art and Antiquities, have all aided in various aspects of my study. At Monticello Daniel P. Jordan, Director, and Susan R. Stein, Curator, have been generously helpful. Among others to whom I am indebted for their contributions to my efforts are Alberta Brandt, Henry Francis du Pont Winterthur Museum; Margaret Cook, Swem Library of the College of William and Mary; Anne Edwards and Margaret Howell, Ellis Library of the University of Missouri–Columbia; John A. Garraty, Columbia University; Meg Grasselli, National Gallery of Art; Lynda Heffley, Art and History Commission, Charleston, South Carolina; Elizabeth Carroll-Horrocks, American Philosophical Society; Charles Jarvis, Dickinson College; James W. Milgram, Chicago, Illinois; Colonel Merl M. Moore, Jr., Falls Church, Virginia; Alan M. Stahl, Curator of Medals, American Numismatic Society; Edmund B. Sullivan, Curator, Museum of American Political Life, University of Hartford; and Louis L. Tucker, Director, Massachusetts Historical Society.

The resources of many institutions have been made available to me in utilizing the diverse sources employed in writing this book. I am indebted to the following institutions and to members of their staffs who aided my research: Abby Aldrich Rockefeller Folk Art Center; American Antiquarian Society; American Numismatic Society; American Philosophical Society; Boston Public Library; Buffalo and Erie County Historical Society; College of William and Mary; Connecticut State Library; Corcoran Gallery of Art; Cornell University Library; Corning Museum of Glass; Fogg Art Museum, Harvard University; Free Library of Philadelphia; Henry E. Huntington Library and Art Gallery; Henry Francis du Pont Winterthur Museum; Historical Society of Pennsylvania; Houghton Library, Harvard University; John Carter Brown Library; Library Company of Philadelphia; Library of Congress; Massachusetts Historical Society; Mead Art Museum, Amherst College; Metropolitan Museum of Art; Museum of Fine Arts, Boston; Museum of the City of New York; National Gallery of Art, National Museum of American Art, National Museum of American History, National Portrait Gallery, Smithsonian Institution; New-York Historical Society; New York Public Library; Pennsylvania Academy of the Fine Arts; Philadelphia Museum of Art; Princeton University Library; State Historical Society of Missouri; Tennessee State Library and Archives; Thomas Jefferson Memorial Foundation, Monticello; University of Hartford; University of Missouri–Columbia; University of Virginia; Virginia Historical Society; Virginia State Library; The White House; Yale University Art Gallery.

To my wife, Dana, I am indebted for her careful note-taking on several research trips and for her continuing interest in the project. For the support of my scholarship, I am grateful for research and travel grants received from the Weldon Spring Research Fund of the University of Missouri and the Research Council of the Graduate School of the University of Missouri–Columbia. The publication of this book has benefited greatly from the exceptional editorial talents of Jane Lago, managing editor, and Beverly Jarrett, director and editor-in-chief, of the University of Missouri Press.

INDEX